Boys of the Battleship
North Carolina

Boys of the Battleship
North Carolina

★★★★★★★★★★★★★★★★

Cindy Horrell Ramsey

JOHN F.
BLAIR
PUBLISHER WINSTON-SALEM, NORTH CAROLINA

Published by John F. Blair, Publisher

*The paper in this book meets the guidelines
for permanence and durability of the Committee on
Production Guidelines for Book Longevity
of the Council on Library Resources.*

COVER PHOTOGRAPHS COURTESY OF BATTLESHIP *NORTH CAROLINA* COLLECTION
DESIGN BY DEBRA LONG HAMPTON

Library of Congress Cataloging-in-Publication Data
Ramsey, Cindy Horrell.
  Boys of the battleship North Carolina / by Cindy Horrell Ramsey.
      p.   cm.
  Includes bibliographical references and index.
  ISBN-13: 978-0-89587-339-2 (alk. paper)
  ISBN-10: 0-89587-339-7
  1. North Carolina (Battleship : BB-55)—History. 2. North Carolina (Battleship : BB-55)—Biography. 3. World War, 1939–1945—Naval operations, American. 4. World War, 1939–1945—Campaigns—Pacific Area. 5. United States. Navy—Biography. I. Title.
VA65.N63R36 2007
940.54'5973—dc22   2006102127

And in loving memory of
Paul Anthony Wieser
September 17, 1920–December 12, 2006
No one loved the Showboat more.

★★★★★★★★★★★★★★★★

This book is dedicated to all the "boys"
who served aboard the battleship USS *North Carolina*
and to my father, Roy Barefoot Horrell, who served
faithfully in the 95th Infantry of the
United States Army during World War II.
We owe our lives and our freedom to them all.

Contents

Preface

Boys of the Battleship North Carolina is not a definitive history of the World War II battleship, nor was it ever meant to be. It is a story set in the 1940s, seen through the eyes of young sailors and based on the tender memories of white-haired men who loved their ship then and still do, who treasured their country then and still do, who were patriotic and proud and remain so to this day. It is a story of boys running away from hardship or journeying toward adventure or filled with such a desire to serve their country that they never paused to consider what that commitment meant. It is a story of boys who matured into men by manning a massive floating fortress, taking her through every major battle in the Pacific, and bringing her home as one of the most decorated American battleships in World War II.

But *Boys of the Battleship North Carolina* is not a history book, although history is revisited; it is not a technical accounting of naval warfare, although the ship's technology was cutting edge; it is not a military manual, although life in the Navy is the driving force. It is a human story, a story of life and death, of love and loss, of fighting and frivolity. *Boys of the Battleship North Carolina* is not a story of captains or admirals, but of the boys who served under those officers with one common thread that tied them all together—the ship known as the "Showboat."

When personal recollections could be verified, they were, using official records from the National Archives, naval manuals, and documents from the ship's archives, including pictures, war diaries, deck logs, and action reports. But when personal stories could not be proven, no great measures were taken to discredit those memories, for they are sacred, seen again through misty eyes, told and retold with aging voices, held as treasure in the hearts of generations, too valuable to be tarnished by an exhaustive search for fact.

More than 7,000 officers and enlisted men served aboard the *North Carolina* during her service, and only a few of the boys come alive on the pages to follow. But the goal of this narrative is to allow those few to represent the whole, to become all the boys who gave up so much of their youth as they crossed the gangplank from being civilians to becoming sailors, as they walked onto the teak decks of the BB55 and into history as a vital part of the Showboat's legacy.

Sailors know the difference between a fairy tale and a sea story. A fairy tale begins, "Once upon a time." A sea story starts simply, "Now, this is no bullshit."

Boys of the Battleship North Carolina is a sea story.

COURTESY OF WALTER ASHE

Boys of the Battleship
North Carolina

Thanks to the dedication of thousands of North Carolinians, including countless schoolchildren who carried change to school, the battleship North Carolina *was saved from becoming scrap. She rests in a cove of the Cape Fear River at Eagle Island in Wilmington, North Carolina, where she serves as a memorial to all North Carolinians killed in World War II.*

CHAPTER ONE

Migration

★★★★★★★★★★★★★★

"I fell in love with her when I saw her. I'm talking about the ship, not my wife. I don't know. There was just something about it to see that huge thing sitting in the Navy yard. It was love at first sight, really."
Jackson Belford, former crew member

They migrate here each spring. Flock to the Southeast. Alight in the middle of memory. The lady who draws them waits patiently for their annual return. Though a quarter-million others are awed by her each year, she truly comes alive when her boys arrive home. But their numbers are diminishing. All too soon, they will be extinct.

The USS *North Carolina* rests in a cove of the Northeast Cape Fear River in Wilmington, North Carolina. To the Navy, she is designated BB55, a bureaucrats' shorthand that carries a certain poetic symmetry and fits neatly on hats. Each year around her birthday, her crew members embrace her as they reunite with old friends. Even in their 80s and 90s, some men are still agile, can tour the entire ship, show their children, grandchildren, great-grandchildren where they slept, where they ate, how the guns fired, where they were when the torpedo struck. They mount the stairs with ease, younger blood seeming to pulse through their veins. Others come with oxygen tanks, wheelchairs, walking sticks, crutches.

Each year, an increasing number are noticeably missing.

A few still wear their uniforms—crisp white bell-bottom pants, white jumper tops, black kerchief ties, and white Dixie Cup hats; or jeans and chambray shirts; or dress blues with white braid edging the collar. They wear their ribbons and medals with pride. Many more are dressed in street clothes, their ball caps or polo shirts stitched with bold gold letters proclaiming their status as BB55 former crew members. Reaching the top of the gangway, many stop, turn, salute the flag, ask a phantom officer, "Permission to come aboard, sir?"

06 April 2001

Herb Weyrauch travels from Minnesota for the reunion celebrating the 60th birthday of the USS *North Carolina*. Joining him from all across the country for the adventure are four of his five children—sons Skip, Ted, and Jere and daughter CarolAnne. It is the first time any of the children have seen the ship and the first time their father has returned to her decks since departing in 1943.

"There she is, Dad! There she is!" son Jere says as the family drives across the Cape Fear Memorial Bridge and spies the battleship off to the right towering over the swampy shore of Eagle Island. Their father is moved by the sight of the Showboat.

"So what brought you to tears the first time you saw her since the war?" asks Jere a few minutes later. "Fond memories?"

"Yeah," is all that Herb can say.

"Good times or all of it, sort of a package?" Jere asks his dad.

"She was home for 28 months," he answers.

"Is it a source of pride?"

"Yep."

Herb Weyrauch, 2001
Courtesy of Drewimage

The family discusses the new camouflage paint job, geometric slashes of various shades of gray, darker than Herb remembers when he was on board. The ship wore several different styles during the war. In the visitor center, Herb's grown children are elated when they find their father in a group photo of the crew on the ship's fantail.

"That's him! We found him, we found him!" CarolAnne exclaims.

They spend the day touring the ship with their father.

The next afternoon, Herb makes himself comfortable in a red leather straight-back chair inside a makeshift studio aboard the ship, where oral histories are being taped. He is tall and still slender, physically fit for a man in his 80s. His silky white hair is an elegant contrast to the bright blue backdrop, which matches his shirt and highlights his eyes twinkling behind large silver-rimmed glasses. He smiles readily and laughs often, unsure if he can divulge secrets about codes and ciphers even though decades have passed since war's end. His voice breaks at times, especially when he talks about his wife.

United States Naval Academy products like Herb were prohibited from getting married for two years after graduation. The Pearl Harbor attack changed many things. In the spring of 1942, academy graduates were told the marriage ban had been lifted.

"I called Anne up and said, 'I can get married, do you want to get married?'" Herb remembers with a smile. "She said, 'Sure.' She didn't question it, even though it was April Fool's Day!"

Everyone laughs. But as Herb continues talking about those happy memories so far in the past but near to his heart, recent tragic events overtake his emotions.

"She's gone," he says. He hesitates, bows his head, and brings the fingers of his right hand up to his lips. "I'm sorry."

They were married 56 years before she died.

★★★★★★★★★★★★★★★★

Robert Fennelly and his wife, Juanita, travel 13 hours from Welaka, Florida, for the crew reunion. The 60th anniversary is not their first visit, nor will it be their last. They are still newlyweds when they attend the 2001 reunion, married about three years. Bob credits Juanita's love and compassion for helping him open up the recesses of his memory and talk about the war. He hadn't spoken of his experiences for more than 50 years.

"You build a wall around yourself, you know?" he says when an especially sad memory brings him near tears. "You don't let people get near you. But you have to."

He no longer tries to hide his tears when he journeys back to his youth and the six years he spent growing up aboard the *North Carolina*. He is not ashamed of the goose bumps that raise the hair on his arms.

Bob and Juanita Fennelly, 2001
COURTESY OF DREWIMAGE

He is not afraid to be proud either.

"We thought we were the best ship in the Navy," he says. "And we were." And the pride goes even deeper than that. "We thought Fifth Division was the best division on the ship. Still do." He smiles.

The crew ate, slept, worked, played, and fought by divisions—assigned locations on the ship that determined their duties.

Bob wears a ball cap from 10 years earlier. Black with gold braid, it was unmistakably made specifically for the crew. A large decal on the front of the cap says, "U.S.S. NORTH CAROLINA," arched across the top of a gold-stitched replica of the ship. Underneath the ship's likeness, "50th Anniversary" sits atop the years—"1941 ★ ★ ★ 1991." The bill has the same gold letters and even more identification and proclamations, including the designation "Former Crew Member."

His attire is typical of these men—their caps and shirts and jackets with the BB55 insignia. They are so proud of the years they served, the contribution they made to history, still awed by the beauty and bulk of the ship that they—mere boys at the time—took into war and brought safely home.

"I was 17," Bob says, "Seventeen. Amazing." The interview chair becomes a time machine, transporting him back 60 years and bringing him forward one memory at a time. He speaks softly, barely audibly at times, moving to the front of his chair as he recalls the past. He is of average build with a narrow white mustache tickling his upper lip. He wears large-lensed glasses with narrow tortoiseshell frames. In his ear is a hearing aid.

"I was crazy. Waited until recently to get mine," he says, pointing to his ear. "None of us can hear. All that noise from the guns."

★★★★★★★★★★★★★★★

As crew members walk the teak decks, line the bow rail, and reminisce with old shipmates, they are transported back more than six decades to a time when many of them stood there for the very first time.

11 July 1942

The USS *North Carolina* steamed into Pearl Harbor. She was a magnificent ship—the first in a new class of battleships, simultaneously monstrous and fast. She was two and a half football fields long and so wide she could barely pass through the Panama Canal. At any given time, 2,339 sailors manned the ship—a total of more than 7,000 during the six years she served—most of them young and new to the Navy, eager to serve their country, but having no idea what lay ahead.

As they entered Pearl Harbor, standing at attention in dress whites along the bow rails, they saw the devastation scanty news reports had not revealed—huge battleships sunk, smaller destroyers demolished, oil slicks blanketing the water. Some of them were sure they saw body parts floating amidst the debris.

In port, seasoned sailors worked at cleaning up the harbor and repairing damaged vessels to make them seaworthy again. As the mast of the *North Carolina* appeared above the island trees, word spread quickly through the harbor. Small skiffs skimming across the oily water slowed as the sailors stared. Sparks from the welders' torches ceased as the men lifted their masks to get a better view. Sailors hurried from below deck to see what was causing all the commotion. Civilians lined the shores. A great cheer rose from the islands, drifting up to the puzzled sailors aboard the *North Carolina*. *Why are they cheering for us? We haven't done anything.* But it was the promise of what they could do, would do, that brought cheers. They felt humbled, proud, scared, determined.

13 June 1940

The triumphant entry into Pearl Harbor in July 1942 was prefaced by years of preparation that had begun long before the massive ship first floated. Among the more than 57,000 people gathered in the Brooklyn Navy Yard the day she was launched was a small eight-year-old boy, Herbert B. Turkington. His parents had traveled with him there to see the first battleship built in the United States in more than 18 years and to witness the first launching of a battleship in that shipyard since 1919. Although the national and worldwide significance of the event may have been lost on the boy, the immediate sights and sounds of that sunny summer afternoon were not. As he stood on the dock about midway along the ship's seemingly interminable length, the gray bulk of her hull rose out of the slipway and towered above his head like a skyscraper on a New York City street.

Officers, sailors, and Marines gathered in their dress uniforms of dark blue or khaki or white. The cobblestone streets within the Navy yard gates bustled with gentlemen in suits, while ladies in fancy dresses, matching hats, and white gloves created a kaleidoscope of color. Red, white, and blue bunting billowed all along the walkways, provoking a sense of Americanism that even young Herbert could feel as he listened to the patriotic music played by the Navy band.

What he couldn't have known or understood was the great sense of pride that many of the spectators felt as they studied every detail of the ship's construction. For it was their husbands, brothers, fathers, sons who had created her beginning on October 27, 1937, when the keel was laid and the ship began to take shape.

While the *North Carolina* was being built, several other ships were also under construction. The civilian employment in the Brooklyn Navy Yard rose from about 4,000 to a peak of 87,000, and an annex was built across the Hudson River in Bayonne, New Jersey. A Navy ferry system connected the two, but all work on the *North Carolina* was performed in Brooklyn.

While the event was certainly reason to rejoice and would be followed by extravagant parties with free-flowing refreshments, bounteous feasts, and lavish libations, the moments leading up to the launch were filled with apparent reflection and deep thought. The throng of thousands was so quiet, in fact, that each blow of the workmen's enormous sledgehammers reverberated throughout the gathering as they began to dislodge the scaffolding cradling the ship above the bed of greased ways that would glide her into the water. Herbert watched muscles bulge on the arms of the worker nearest to him as the man gripped the wooden handle, lifted the heavy hammer, brought it up over his right shoulder, and swung it down against the support wedge in one seemingly effortless motion. Then, when only a few of the supports were left in place, all the men stopped.

Everyone stood in silent attention as the national anthem filled the air. The officers and sailors, Marines and civilian men removed their hats and saluted the flag; the child raised his small right hand to his eyebrow. He glanced around at the workers standing ready at the remaining supports with sledgehammers resting against their left legs, right hands planted firmly across their hearts. In their dark blue shipyard attire, they stood no less tall and straight than the men in military uniform.

Herbert's father swung him up onto his shoulders, but from his position so far down along the starboard side of the ship, Herbert could not see the ceremony taking place at the bow, so he spent that time visually investigating the wooden framework and wondering how in the world that great big boat would get to the water. Underneath the ship, metal tracks—wider than his daddy was tall—were covered in thick yellowish orange grease. They extended farther than Herbert could see in both directions. He could hear people talking into a microphone, but he was so interested in the grease that he didn't pay much attention to what they were saying. He understood something important was about to happen, however, when he heard shattering glass and a woman's voice say loudly and clearly, "I christen thee the United States Ship *North Carolina*." The band struck up the exciting strains of "Anchors Aweigh."

Immediately and in unison, the workers raised their huge hammers and knocked out the remaining supports. The ship settled down onto the greased ways and began to descend into the water, slowly at first, then picking up speed. Herbert was sure he saw smoke. The huge cheer from the crowd and the foghorns from ships in Wallabout Basin and along the East River created a cacophony of celebration. The child watched in awe as the bulbous bow of the ship passed him. His small head tilted backwards, his eyes followed the bulge up to the top, where two huge holes with lines running through them looked like eyes staring back at him. Sailors and shipyard workers stood at the rail. Down below, handkerchiefs

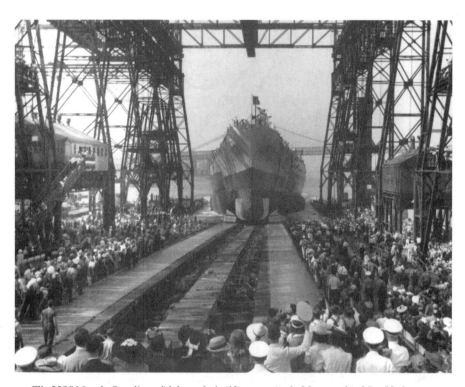

The USS North Carolina *slid down the building ways in the Navy yard in New York on June 13, 1940, to the cheers and jubilation of military, civilians, and shipyard workers.*
COURTESY OF BATTLESHIP *NORTH CAROLINA* COLLECTION

As soon as the launching celebration subsided, the North Carolina *was returned to her berth and the scaffolding reappeared as workers labored furiously to prepare the ship for commissioning. Shipyard workers erected the superstructure and installed gun mounts as part of that process. (The warning at the top of this photo exemplifies the strict regulations governing photographs during and after the war. These photos are now part of the public domain and those restrictions no longer apply.)*
COURTESY OF BATTLESHIP NORTH CAROLINA COLLECTION

fluttered like doves' wings in the hands of admiring women. The spectators waved, the sailors and workers waved, so Herbert waved, too.

When the ship had settled into the water and the tugs began to maneuver her into a slip where she would be completed, the little boy's father lifted him off his shoulders and placed him on one of the timbers that had supported the ship but now lay flat on the cement. His mother raised the camera, and Herbert smiled. The adventure would become a treasured memory tucked away in his heart, easily recalled even into old age—that day he witnessed the launching of a legend.

★★★★★★★★★★★★★★★

Few of the spectators realized that the launching was an engineering feat accomplished not just in those moments, but actually begun at three the previous morning and continued in calculated steps that followed a detailed and meticulously timed procedure. On the ground, 10 officers and 645 civilians of various trades participated, while five officers, a hundred enlisted men, and 133 civilian tradesmen worked simultaneously aboard the ship.

Even after she was launched, much more work needed to be done before the *North Carolina* would be ready for service. The main hull was the only completed component. Tugs maneuvered the ship to Pier C, Berth 2, Navy Yard, New York, where construction would continue in the stage called "fitting out." Internal and external structures would be completed, machinery installed, the superstructure erected, and firepower added. Most of that work could be done while the ship was afloat, but she would have to be dry-docked for the propellers to be installed. In dry dock, the ship rested on blocks as the water was pumped out from under her, leaving workspace underneath. Estimates projected more than a year to commissioning, and even then she would not be ready for battle.

The pre-commissioning crew—the first of the more than 2,000 crew and officers who would call her home—began arriving in New York in March 1941. They included Herb Weyrauch, Joseph Smits, Walter Ashe, Lincoln Hector, and Charlie Rosell. While Weyrauch was fresh out of the naval academy, the others had some naval experience under their belts.

★★★★★★★★★★★★★★★★

As a child, Weyrauch had been interested in radio, receiving his amateur radio license in 1932 when he was 13 years old and a freshman in high school. Reading about the rafting adventures of Huckleberry Finn and the seafaring tale of *Moby Dick* gave him wanderlust, and he daydreamed of outfitting a sailboat to circumnavigate the globe. In his junior and senior years of high school, he became continually more restless until one day his undirected energy landed him in the principal's office.

"I'm disappointed to see you here," Principal Roland Keist said to him. "Aren't you the boy who delivers my daily paper?"

"Yes, sir," Weyrauch answered.

"We need to redirect some of this energy now that you are

Herb Weyrauch, 1941
COURTESY OF HERB WEYRAUCH

getting older and should be maturing," the principal said. "What long-range plans have you made?"

"I'm going to travel around the world," Weyrauch responded. "In my own boat."

"I see," Mr. Keist said as he sat in contemplation of how best to continue the conversation with the boy. "There may be a better way."

"What would that be, sir?"

"The Navy could provide valuable seagoing experience," Mr. Keist offered.

"The Navy?"

"Well, yes. But you might want to think about setting your sights higher than being a seaman. You're an intelligent boy, Weyrauch, from a good family. If you work hard from here on out, you might be able to attend the naval academy and go in as an officer."

"Thank you, sir."

Weyrauch thought a lot about what his principal had said. At home, he discussed the possibilities with his family. His uncle Hugo Weyrauch was especially supportive. Being politically active and a staunch supporter of his district's representative, he contacted Congressman Leo Allen of the Thirteenth District of Illinois to make his nephew's interest known. The congressman encouraged young Weyrauch to study hard and take tougher classes in school to prepare himself.

"The entrance examinations are quite competitive," he explained.

To enhance his prospects, Weyrauch's parents encouraged him to attend at least one year of college, which he did at Cornell College in Mount Vernon, Iowa. Weyrauch participated in football and wrestling while at Cornell College, building his strength, endurance, and physical maturity. Not wanting to work so hard and then be disqualified by flat feet, he set a daily routine of picking up marbles with his toes.

Weyrauch never took the entrance exams, as Congressman Allen appointed him to the academy without that requirement. He passed the rigorous physical exam and on July 9, 1938, took the oath of office as a midshipman in the United States Navy. He was set to graduate in June 1941, but his was the first academy class whose graduation was accelerated due to growing hostilities in the European theater. He graduated on February 7, 1941, and was assigned to the *North Carolina*, along with 10 of his classmates.

★★★★★★★★★★★★★★★★

When Joseph Smits was small, his father deserted him and his mother, left them stranded in Texas. She made her way back to her mother's home and filed for divorce in Chicago, where they lived with Smitty's grandma. Two years later, his dad came looking for him and took him away from his grandmother while his mother wasn't home. He never saw them again.

Smitty's dad moved him to Milwaukee, but he was a traveling salesman and left the boy with one relative or another. Being a bit too rebellious for anyone to manage, Smitty found himself in boarding school on an Indian reservation in Oneida, Wisconsin, until his father remarried four years later and they moved to Minnesota. Smitty and his step-mom, just 11 years older than he was, were at odds from day one, but his father was on the road and they were stuck with each other. Later, a baby brother arrived, and Smitty's new position as babysitter further deepened his misery.

As an adolescent in Duluth, Smitty became an entrepreneur of

Joseph "Smitty" Smits
COURTESY OF JOE SMITS

sorts. He and his buddies picked up coal that fell off the trains, put it in a gunnysack, and sold it house to house for 25 cents a bag. But it was scarce and filling the bags was tedious, so they decided to improve the process, hopping the coal cars and tossing basketball-sized chunks of anthracite coal over the side until the railroad cops ran them off. The chunks shattered into small pieces as they hit the ground, so the boys had no trouble filling their sacks with an abundance of coal to sell.

Smitty hated school and was miserable at home. In September 1939, when he was in the 11th grade, he joined the United States Naval Reserve and was assigned to the USS *Paducah*, an old World War I gunboat tied up in Duluth for use by the reserves. He wore his first set of blues with pride as he attended three meetings on the *Paducah*. That was all it took for the Navy to snare Smitty. In December 1939, he enlisted in the regular Navy and was sent to boot camp at Great Lakes, Illinois. He was thereafter called by his surname, Smits, and his pay was $21 per month.

Apprentice seamen were automatically promoted on time served, but that usually happened after being assigned to a ship, not in boot camp. What Smits didn't know was that his time in the reserves counted toward that promotion, so while he was in boot camp, he was promoted to seaman second class. His chief ragged him about the promotion.

"Hey, Smits," he said. "How did a little old puke like you get a promotion? You sure ain't nothing outstanding."

Smits stood all of five foot six and weighed 120 pounds soaking wet. The ragging didn't bother him much, though, especially when he put $15 extra in his pocket the next payday.

After completing boot camp, Smits was assigned to the USS *Colorado*, another ship of World War I vintage. He spent day in and day out for more than two months chipping paint and repainting while the ship was docked in San Pedro, California. When the *Colorado* set sail for Hawaii, Smits became so seasick that he thought he was going to die. He went to sick bay, where the pharmacist's mates only laughed at him.

"Go away. When you get your sea legs, you'll be okay," one told him.

So Smits found a place to hide on deck and lay there for three days before he began to feel human again. When he was finally able to stay upright without emptying his insides all over the place, he reported for duty. His superior officer wanted to know where he'd been, and Smits suffered the consequences of his seasickness. Every dirty job that needed to be assigned landed in his lap all the way to Hawaii.

★★★★★★★★★★★★★★★★

Walter Ashe also led a tumultuous childhood. His mother and father divorced when he was small, and he moved from Florida to California. Although he had two older sisters, he and his mother lived alone. At night when she was out, little Walter curled up on the steps leading up to the apartment and slept in the stairwell waiting for her return, too scared to stay in the apartment by himself. When he did remain inside, the frightened boy turned on every light and tried to sleep, always with a butcher knife at arm's reach.

He entered Long Beach Military Academy when he was seven, but his internal rage erupted when one of the kids made him mad, and Walter stabbed him with a steel-nubbed pen. He left the academy, and he and his mother moved to another part of Los Angeles, where they lived in a one-room apartment with a pull-down bed that he shared with her. The kids in the apartment complex played in the streets of the neighborhood—games like marbles, hide-and-seek, and kick the can. Even though money was scarce, Walter went to the Saturday matinees with his friends. One day, his mother gave him a special outfit she had purchased for him to wear to the movies. He said no, but she persisted.

"But all the kids will laugh at me," Walter said, pleading with his mother not to make him wear the new clothes.

"Only because they're jealous," she answered, insisting that he get dressed.

Reluctantly, Walter put on the white shirt, short white trousers, white socks, and white shoes. He snuck into the movie after it started and left before the end.

He and his mother moved often. Going from one school to another, Walter fought all the time. He attended at least two more

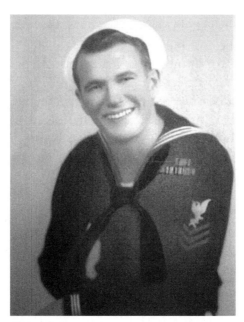

Walter Ashe
COURTESY OF WALTER ASHE

military schools and several different public schools and spent a year at the forest rangers' school. His mother became increasingly ill, entered a nursing home, and died when Walter was just a teenager. Through the mother of a friend, he learned of a couple looking for a boy to adopt—Mr. and Mrs. Taylor, who insisted that he call them Mom and Dad. They lived in Monterey Park and had chickens, ducks, turkeys, pigeons, rabbits, and a German shepherd. But Walter was not accustomed to the discipline and supervision of Mr. Taylor. Eventually, he was asked to leave.

Walter had spent most of his time in school drawing cartoons. His sister Virginia saw promise, so she enrolled him in art school and paid for his training. She had a friend who knew an executive at Walt Disney Studios. Through that friend, they made an arrangement that if Walter completed art school, he would be offered a job. But Walter didn't finish. He and a friend started talking about the Navy. They read all the brochures and pictured themselves riding in rickshaws in China, being served by geisha girls in Japan, and enjoying the swaying palm trees and hula hips in Hawaii. Walter loved art, but drawing in school was more like work than pleasure. And he knew the cost burdened his sister. So at 18, he and his new cohort decided to join the Navy. Walter was accepted, but his friend was not—he had flat feet.

Walter, who became known in the Navy by his surname, Ashe, did spend time in Shanghai, where he met many of those beautiful girls while on duty with the Asiatic Fleet before being transferred to the *North Carolina*.

★★★★★★★★★★★★★★★★

Lincoln Hector became part of the Asiatic Fleet as well. Although his parents divorced when he was a year old, Lincoln had a stable and close family life in Santa Maria, California. His mother, her two brothers, and their father created a happy childhood. His uncles taught him how to shoot a Winchester .22 and later to drink beer. But money was tight, and he decided his best course of action at 17 was to join the Navy. At least he would have a place to sleep, food to eat, and some money coming in every month. He started at $21.00 a month, but then the government cut everyone's pay to

Lincoln Hector
COURTESY OF LINCOLN HECTOR

$17.50 per month for six months. Even the Navy was struggling financially.

Lincoln joined the Navy in 1936 and served in the Asiatic Fleet through 1940. By the time he was transferred to the *North Carolina* in March 1941, he was considered an old man by most of the new crew. Lincoln Hector was 21.

Charlie Rosell
COURTESY OF CHARLIE ROSELL

Charlie Rosell was only 16 when he joined the Navy in 1939. He just wanted to get out of Arkansas, and the Navy offered him that clichéd chance to see the world. Following four months of boot camp in San Diego, Rosell had just begun his 10-day leave when Germany invaded Poland. President Roosevelt declared a national emergency, and all leaves were canceled. Rosell was assigned to the USS *Zane*, where he would stay until the spring of 1941.

On March 10, he became part of the pre-commissioning detail of the *North Carolina* and was assigned to the number-two fireroom. The ship was powered by four steam turbines. Each turbine was located in a separate engine room/fireroom with two boilers in each. Steam lines and exhaust lines and fire lines and fuel lines and flushing lines and stripping lines and gauges and wheels and valves filled the spaces. The boys in the firerooms were required to know every little detail of their work area so well that if the ship were damaged and power lost to the lights, they could do their jobs in the dark. If they failed, the ship would be dead in the water. For nearly a month prior to the ship's commissioning, they drilled constantly when they were not eating or sleeping. While other members of the pre-commissioning crew were helping construct and supply the ship, the boys in the boiler rooms were burning images of their workspace into their young brains. Months later, they would be thankful for the rigorous training.

CHAPTER TWO

Joining Up

"The whole state of North Carolina can feel real pride in this colossal battleship. Its very power is fascinating. It commands our respect and it will help us command respect of the world. It speaks a language even a dictator can understand."

North Carolina governor Clyde Roark Hoey
at BB55 launching ceremonies, June 13, 1940

01 March 1941

Walter Ashe snuggled deeper into the covers at Mother Taylor's California home. *Boy, this bed sure beats those bunks aboard ship*, he thought, thankful for a place to call home and not wanting the night to end. He slowly opened his eyes. Even though darkness enveloped him beneath the covers, he could feel his escapades from the night before pounding in his temples. He inched the covers down little by little until he saw the sun through the slits in the blinds.

Startled to full consciousness by the realization that the sun was already up, Ashe jumped to his feet. He tugged on the dark blue pants he had thrown on the floor the night before, hopping around on one foot, then the other. His eyes searched the room for socks and shoes as he fastened all those hellacious buttons. He yelled goodbye to Mother Taylor and pulled his shirt over his head, sticking his arms through the sleeves just in time to grab the doorknob, open the door, and slam it behind him. He took the steps two at a time and sprinted across the yard to the car.

The tires spun in the sand as he backed out of the driveway. He slammed the gearshift into drive, jerked the steering wheel around sharply, and sped through the streets of Los Angeles. He ignored the lights and barely saw the stop signs, racing through town toward the port in San Pedro where he had left the USS *Bridge* to go on one night of liberty. He had been transferred off the *Mississippi* at Pearl Harbor and had caught the *Bridge* back to the States before moving on to his next assignment. He whipped the car into the parking lot, jumped out, and ran toward the ship. Long before he reached the docks, he knew he had a problem. The ship was not there.

Oh, my god, what am I going to do? he thought. Everything he owned was in his sea bag on that ship—his uniforms, his diaries, his cartoons, his records, his orders. His orders were to report to the Brooklyn Navy Yard for assignment to the USS *North Carolina*. Ashe had built a reputation for getting into tight spots, but he wondered how in hell he was going to get himself out of this one. He walked dejectedly down the docks toward where the ship had been. There, leaning against one of the posts, was his sea bag with the envelope containing his orders lying on top. He looked straight up, let a small smile spread across his lips, picked up his orders and his sea bag, and strutted up the dock toward his car.

The train ride from California to New York was long but uneventful, taking Ashe right into the city, where he caught a subway to the Brooklyn Navy Yard. When he entered the gates of the Navy yard and walked toward where his new ship was being built, he didn't really know what to expect. This was his fourth ship since joining the Navy in 1935, and he had spent time in exotic places like Shanghai. But he wasn't prepared for what he saw. The *North Carolina*, although still being built, appeared sleek and streamlined and huge. He was startled by his own reaction to the unfinished ship—she was beautiful.

★★★★★★★★★★★★★★★★

When Herb Weyrauch first saw the BB55, he didn't think she was a very impressive sight. Scaffolding surrounded her, and hoses and pipes draped off her sides. Cranes and other machinery sat on the docks while shipyard workers busied themselves getting her ready for her crew. As part of the pre-commissioning detail, Weyrauch went aboard the ship occasionally, but he didn't spend as much time there as he might have liked. He spent his days inside a vault in the shipyard. It was about six feet square, just large enough for himself and his partner, Norman Wynkoop, to get their work done. Each morning after sleeping in their own private stateroom aboard the receiving ship *Seattle*, Weyrauch and Wynkoop walked to the vault, waited for the time lock to open, then closed themselves in the confined space behind the heavy door for the duration of their workday. The walls and door of the vault were so thick that a radio would not even play inside it, so they worked in silence.

Weyrauch and Wynkoop, under the direction of Lieutenant Commander Seth A. Shepard, were charged with the duty of preparing the ship's complement of registered publications—the classified manuals and codes and ciphers that would enable the ship to communicate. Basic policies and procedures for combat operations had to be prepared and updated in published texts. The paperwork and changes that needed to be made came from the District Naval Headquarters in lower Manhattan.

The two young ensigns had to account for every single piece of paper they touched—every page and every item on the page. Anything that was replaced and discarded must be burned in the incinerator in the shipyard. Weyrauch and Wynkoop were required to count every piece, log it on a form, take it to the incinerator together, then both sign off on a formal document saying that each piece had been destroyed.

Every night, the young officers locked the safe containing their

Crewmembers help shipyard workers load supplies during the fitting out stage of construction.

day's work. They returned the next morning to wait for the time lock to let them back in. Their work requirements during those first few weeks immediately instilled a strong sense of duty and responsibility in them, and they learned to be excellent secret keepers.

After a long day's work, they enjoyed dining in the wardroom with senior officers. Weyrauch reveled in the status his rank afforded and enjoyed lavish parties in Manhattan, including a gala affair at the Barbizon Plaza on the south end of Central Park. The young naval officers were invited to make the party a success, and as far as Weyrauch was concerned, they succeeded.

★★★★★★★★★★★★★★★★

In Pearl Harbor, Joseph Smits had been transferred to the cruiser *New Orleans*, where he started out on the deck crew, transferred to mess cook, and then spent a couple of years in the fireroom. When he reported to New York for duty on the *North Carolina* in March 1941, Smits felt sure that his experience in the fireroom would place him in the same job there. That was what he wanted, but as most of the enlisted men quickly learned, their wants rarely had any bearing on their assignments.

Smits was first assigned to the electrical division, but that didn't last long. The ship was still under construction, and Smits was ordered to sweep up one of the compartments containing a huge switchboard. As he was busily sweeping up the construction debris, a large cable lay in his way. It extended across the room and ran under the switchboard. Smits bent down and lifted the cable so he could sweep under it. He saw a bright white flash and felt himself flying across the room. Then everything went black. Smits had been knocked unconscious by the force of the cable coming in contact with switches on the board. He was not the only thing knocked out, however. His mistake had shorted out all power to the ship and to half of the shipyard. As he surveyed his body after he regained consciousness, Smits was amazed to find he had suffered no injuries other than a burned hand. When he asked to be transferred to the fireroom the next day, his request was immediately granted.

MORNING ROUTINE IN THE BUTCHER SHOP.

Lincoln Hector was the first man in charge of the butcher shop on the ship. In the weeks leading up to commissioning, he stayed busy placing orders for supplies, including meat and other items that would fill the iceboxes. A week before the ship was to be commissioned, Hector and the other butchers, bakers, cooks, and scullery hands moved on board. The *North Carolina* was the pride of the United States Navy, and the crew would eat well. Hector chopped the huge slabs of meat to prepare them for the cooks. Before commissioning, the crew was still relatively small, but it would continue to increase. When the ship was fully manned, chopping enough meat for nearly 2,500 mouths to eat three times a day would be a full-time job.

★★★★★★★★★★★★★★★★

Ships join the Navy just like sailors do. The pre-commissioning crew worked feverishly for weeks and the shipyard workers labored for years to get the ship ready to become an official member of the United States fleet.

During that time before the *North Carolina* was ready for her crew, Ashe lived on an old German cruiser, the *Camden*, ate on the

Seattle, and worked in the main supply building in the Navy yard typing invoices and ordering supplies. As storekeeper third class, Ashe was in charge of the storerooms—the warehouse where all the excess materials for every division of the ship would be kept so that when the *North Carolina* was at sea, a continuous supply of materials would be available to replace those that were used. He had to catalog materials and keep them neatly arranged and organized so access was quick and efficient.

That was no small task. The ship had its own barbershop, laundry, post office, store, butcher shop, bakery, dentist office, doctor's office, pharmacy, hospital, jail, chapel, soda fountain, ice-cream shop, print shop, photographer's darkroom, cobbler shop, carpentry shop, machinist shop, tailor shop, and restaurants in the form of galleys and mess halls. And there were radio rooms and switchboards and telephone circuits, as well as an entirely different world in officers' country.

Ashe liked being in the storeroom. It made him feel important. When he was on the USS *Asheville,* he had spent most of his time in the engine room as a fire tender. Working in the belly of the ship, he felt invisible, like no one even knew he existed. But then he was transferred to the storeroom. Shipmates had to ask him for what they needed. Everybody knew his name. He had the keys.

09 April 1941

In a ceremony of great pomp and splendor, the *North Carolina* was commissioned five months ahead of schedule. President Franklin D. Roosevelt was unable to attend the ceremonies but sent a telegram message instead: "It is with extreme regret that I find myself unable to be present at the exercises attending the commissioning of the Battleship *North Carolina.* It has been eighteen long years since the last great ship of the line, the USS *West Virginia,* joined the United States fleet. To the officers and men of this new and great man-o'-war I extend cordial greetings and all good wishes for a happy cruise, a happy ship. Throughout her service may the *North Carolina* be a symbol of progress through strength

Officers and crew of the North Carolina *gathered on the ship's fantail on April 9, 1941, for the highly celebrated commissioning of America's newest, biggest, fastest battleship.*
COURTESY OF BATTLESHIP NORTH CAROLINA COLLECTION

and a tangible evidence of American readiness for its own defense. I know she will help to protect this country faithfully in traditional Navy fashion."

Early that morning, the initial crew of 82 officers and 1,108 enlisted men began to board the ship. They carried their sea bags of belongings into their newly assigned living quarters and chose a bunk and a locker. For many of them, it would be their home for several years. For some of them, it would be the last home they ever had.

"We are foreshadowing with this ship the greatest Navy the world has ever seen," said Secretary of the Navy Frank Knox during his commissioning speech.

Newspapers across the country proclaimed the *North Carolina* the world's mightiest ship. Every combination of words that could emphasize the power, size, and strength of the ship was used and reused in headlines that said, "New battleship a symbol of might," "Our big stick gets bigger," "Here, Uncle Sam, is a big ship for you," "New super dreadnought joins the Navy." She was described as "the deadliest queen of the sea," "the world's toughest warship," "king of the heavyweights," and the "most formidable" ship in the Navy.

But the great dreadnought was not yet ready for battle, so the Pier C scaffolding reappeared and the work lines and hoses once again draped from the ship to the dock. The shipyard workers and a much larger crew were back at work preparing for the day the ship would steam out of New York Harbor under her own power for the first time.

★★★★★★★★★★★★★★★★

Being from a little town in northern Illinois, Weyrauch quickly became infatuated with New York City. He and one of his former classmates often went on liberty together, riding the subway to their favorite watering hole in Greenwich Village, Nick's. Weyrauch strutted the streets of New York dressed in his dark blue uniform and white officer's hat, proud of what he had accomplished and enjoying the attention showered on the *North Carolina* crew. The men, fast becoming celebrities because of the ship's status, soon became accustomed to being accosted by newspaper reporters and photographers. All that attention might have gone to his head just a bit, but one union shipyard worker quickly brought him back to earth.

Ensign Weyrauch mounted the gangway leading from the dock to the ship and headed toward the wardroom for a scheduled meeting with his commanding officer. After he passed one of the five-inch gun mounts, he saw a shipyard worker leaning back against an unpainted bulkhead. He was wearing blue overalls and a lightweight jacket, obviously enjoying the warm sunshine, his eyes closed, head tilted back against the steel. Weyrauch stopped abruptly. He took in the scene before he spoke. All around them, riveting tools popped and hammers pounded, and he could not imagine how this man could just lie there with his tools spread out beside him, seemingly oblivious to the work that needed to be done. Weyrauch was infuriated by what he considered the man's laziness. He stiffened his body and spoke loudly with an officer's authority.

"What in the hell do you think you're doing? Why aren't you working?" Weyrauch demanded. "Don't you know we're getting ready for a war? Don't you have a job to do?"

Startled, the man opened his eyes and looked up at the young officer towering over him with disdain.

"Answer me," Weyrauch ordered.

The worker appeared to be embarrassed. "Well," he explained, "I am a caulker. I caulk metal seams, and I can't caulk seams until somebody else makes the seams for me to caulk."

"I'm sure there's plenty of other work to be done," Weyrauch responded, a little less haughtily.

"Well, yes there is, but not for me," the man replied. "I have one job to do, and I can't do anything else. Trade restrictions. Ask my supervisor if you don't believe me."

Weyrauch, thoroughly embarrassed, realized immediately that he had overstepped his bounds. He learned two valuable lessons that day. First, should he have any questions about a Navy yard worker, his place was not to address him personally but to take the issue up with the worker's supervisor. Second, the language he had spit out and the attitude he had displayed were not befitting an officer in the United States Navy. He made a mental note to apply the positive affirmation principles he had been taught at the academy and to remember the lessons he learned that afternoon in the shipyard.

The ship was like a small town with 21 distinct neighborhoods, called divisions, for enlisted men. Her city blocks went 10 levels up and five down. Her main deck, covered in teak for insulation purposes and better absorption of shrapnel from bullets or bombs, was just over 728 feet long, and her width, or beam, spanned more than 108 feet. More of the battleship sat below the water than was visible above the surface.

Most of the guns would be installed on the main deck, although some of the antiaircraft guns would be found as high as the third level of the superstructure, the part of the ship that towered above the main deck in 10 levels. A large officers' wardroom, officers' living quarters, a few enlisted sailors' berthing quarters, ammunition storage areas, and a few maintenance and repair shops were located in the interior spaces of the main-deck level of the superstructure. But most enlisted men's living quarters were located below the main deck on the second and third decks below the water line, while the senior officers, the captain, and the admiral maintained quarters in the superstructure. Operational controls were located in the upper levels; the added height aided visibility. Computerized control rooms called "directors" located on those upper decks contained the radar equipment, controls, and crew to aim and fire some of the guns below, while the big cannons were actually fired from a location deep within the ship.

As crew came aboard, each man was assigned to a specific division, which determined his duties. Sailors would live, sleep, eat, work, and play with others from their division. Few would ever socialize with or even meet those from other divisions, just like residents in different neighborhoods often don't. But the arrangement differed from a land-based town in one very distinct way that no sailor ever forgot. Even though they didn't know each other, their lives depended on one another, depended on each one doing his job and doing it well.

This photo of the North Carolina *leaving the Brooklyn Navy Yard for the first time during shakedown was taken by 16-year-old Stephen Hustvedt from the roof of the Towers Hotel in Brooklyn. Stephen is the son of the ship's first commanding officer, Captain Olaf M. Hustvedt.*
COURTESY OF BATTLESHIP NORTH CAROLINA COLLECTION

CHAPTER THREE

Shakedown

★★★★★★★★★★★★★★★★★★★

"We are making history here today, for it is significant and memorable that the very first service of Christian fellowship and Divine Worship to be held in the North Carolina *happens on Easter Sunday morning. By our presence here today, we are pledging ourselves to do our part to make the* North Carolina *a good ship, a happy ship, and a home."*
Church-service program, 13 April 1941

The first church service on the ship was held Sunday, April 13, 1941, at 1000 hours. The program not only proclaimed the historical significance of the day but also introduced the ship's creed to the crew.

North Carolina Creed

1. I BELIEVE in the American way of life and in the United States Navy that gives me opportunity to prove my patriotism.

2. I BELIEVE it is a high privilege to serve in this great, new ship—and I pledge myself to strive to be worthy.

3. I BELIEVE in the home from which I came, and in the strength that comes from frequent family communications.

4. I BELIEVE in clean speech, and I will do my part to keep this ship free from profanity and vulgarity.

5. I BELIEVE in doing my job, in keeping a clean record and a clear conscience, and in saying my prayers.

6. I BELIEVE in being a shipmate, by holding up my end of the load and by doing to others as I would have others do to me.

7. I BELIEVE in the joy of living and the inner satisfaction that comes from working hard and playing hard.

20 April 1941

In the *Sunday Mirror*, above a photograph of the ship's company aboard the *North Carolina* during the commissioning ceremonies, the word *achieved* heralded the accomplishments of thousands of people. The lengthy cutline underneath read,

Early in April, the U.S. Navy commissioned its deadliest battleship, the *North Carolina*. It was the first new battleship built for the Navy in 18 years. It was also a perfect symbol of Uncle Sam at work. The 35,000-ton dreadnaught, bristling with nine 16-inch guns, was commissioned six months ahead of schedule at the Brooklyn Navy Yard. For months, 20,000 workmen, representing 17 different crafts and trades, had been busy in and around the ship, without any fanfare, and more important, without any labor difficulties. These workers are not Navy enlisted men. They are civilians employed by the yard, or working for private contractors. About 1,000 of them are from the WPA. All of them are well paid and they know it. The *North Carolina* is a symbol of what industry can do when there is no strife, of what has been done and can be done for our Army, Navy and our merchant ships—the men and steel that will make America impregnable.

5 May 1940

After Paul Wieser graduated from high school, he wasn't really sure what he wanted to do with his life. His high-school gang, the Batch, spent a lot of time hanging out at the skating rink and going to the candy store. He'd run into his neighbor, Jean, every now and

Paul Wieser
COURTESY OF BATTLESHIP *NORTH CAROLINA* COLLECTION

then, but they weren't really dating, or at least weren't supposed to be. His parents had let him know in no uncertain terms that they didn't think dating was the proper thing to do, and although he and Jean snuck around a bit to be together, Paul was a pretty strait-laced kid. He didn't drink, didn't curse, didn't smoke. His gang just enjoyed innocent fun.

Paul had liked taking printing classes in high school. The school was equipped with type and presses, and he loved helping publish the football programs. He heard about this guy looking for help who lived not too far from his own home. Paul found him and was impressed with his print set-up. They discussed what Paul would be doing—printing as well as delivery—and Paul thought that would be an interesting job, so he accepted. When he went home that night, excited to tell his family that he had found a job, his older brother quickly told him, "You're not going back there again!" The printer was making forms for illegal race betting, his brother told him, so Paul's first job was a washout before it even began.

He then moved on to a company that made envelopes and other paper products. The only job opening was in the box department, but Paul accepted it. His duty was to run the machine that cut and creased the cardboard so the women farther down the assembly line could fold it into boxes. Paul did not adjust the machine—his immediate supervisor did that—but when the boxes did not fit to-gether well, when the corners did not match, the women fussed at Paul. After two weeks of disgruntled women, Paul had enough.

He took his two-weeks' pay, went to the dentist, and had his teeth fixed. He then informed his mother and father that he was going to join the Navy. He started out at the recruiting station near his home in Newark. The final paperwork and physicals would be done in New York, so he went home that night with some of his papers in hand.

That evening after dinner, he sat down next to his father and handed him the papers to read. After perusing the forms, Paul's father looked up at him.

"You see this six years right here, son?" his father asked. "That's a long time."

"I know," he replied. "But I want to do it."

His father did not try to discourage him anymore.

18 February 1941

Paul's home in New Jersey was only 16 miles from New York City, and the train ran right through his town. When it arrived at Pennsylvania Station, Paul had only a short walk to the Naval Recruiting Station. A large group of boys joined Paul in line as they completed paperwork and preliminary physicals to be accepted into the service. When the medic told him to open his mouth, Paul was glad he had spent that money on his teeth.

"Go get some lunch and come back this afternoon," the boys were told. So Paul joined a group of the guys for their last hour of civilian life.

After lunch, they were sworn in and became property of the United States Navy. About six that evening, the new recruits marched to the dock, where an excursion ship took them to boot camp in Newport, Rhode Island. The overnight trip was an eye-opening experience for the sheltered and innocent Paul Wieser. Some of the passengers were drinking and gambling and getting louder by the minute. Female passengers also boarded the boat, and from his compartment, Paul could hear creaking and groaning. Arrival at boot camp did nothing to assuage his anxiety. As the boys entered the building where they would undergo their physicals, they received a cardboard box.

"Put your clothes in here, and set the box up against the wall," the officer told them.

Paul lost his identity as a civilian as the clothes went into the box and a large mercurochrome number 33 was painted on his chest. He became known as Wieser.

His possessions consisted of a hammock and the following items, which, except for his mattress, he would learn to pack into his newly acquired sea bag:

2 cook aprons	1 pair leggings
1 white woven belt	1 mattress
1 pair blankets	2 mattress covers
1 blacking outfit	1 neckerchief
1 whisk broom	1 overcoat
1 scrub brush	1 pair overshoes
1 toothbrush	1 pillow
1 hairbrush	1 pillow cover
1 watch cap	1 sewing kit
3 cloth stops	2 chambray shirts
1 hair comb	2 pair shoes
2 heavy drawers	1 pair gymnasium shoes
4 light drawers	4 pair cotton socks
2 dungaree pants	2 pair woolen socks
1 pair woolen gloves	1 outfit toilet articles
12 handkerchiefs	2 towels
3 white Dixie Cup hats	2 blue trousers
1 jackknife	4 white trousers
1 jumper, dress blue	1 bathing trunks
2 jumpers, undress blue	2 heavy undershirts
3 jumpers, undress white	4 light undershirts
1 jersey	

During the first few weeks of boot camp, the new recruits were confined to "D" barracks. They called it "detention" because they were not allowed to leave the grounds or congregate with any of the other recruits. During those few weeks, the boys received all their shots and were given a gradual introduction into Navy life. But it was tough, and as the weeks of reveille, marching, and training progressed, Wieser found himself hearing his father's words over and over again.

"You see this six years right here, son? That's a long time."

17 April–19 May 1941

Dock trials were conducted on the *North Carolina*'s engines individually and in various combinations. Joseph Smits and Charlie Rosell, in their respective firerooms, were ready. They were experienced from their duty on other ships and had trained so much on the BB55 in the previous weeks that they felt confident they could do their jobs with their eyes closed, or almost. During the dock trials, the boys performed all the duties necessary to light the oil-burning boilers that heated the water and pumped steam to the engines. When the turbines increased RPMs, the steam pressure would go down, and the boys in the firerooms would open more burners in the boiler to make more fire to bring the steam pressure back up to 600 pounds. Watching the gauges was one of their most important jobs. The pressure must not vary more than a pound or two in either direction. If the steam pressure became too great, a safety valve would pop, sending a column of steam straight up through the stack into the air. It could be seen from miles away. During wartime, that giveaway could risk the ships and crews in an entire task force.

During the engine tests, the tug *Britannia* kept a line taut on the ship to restrain her, so to some degree, the tests were like being under way without actually moving—like pressing the gas pedal and brake on a car at the same time.

During the months of April and May, large numbers of crew members arrived at the ship. Supplies continued to be loaded and fuel pumped into the tanks. The ship received 3,585 barrels of fuel on April 23 and 299,502 gallons on May 4. On May 19, fueling was completed from Standard Oil barges—19,231 barrels of oil and 3,023 barrels of diesel fuel. But filling the tanks with fuel was just one of a multitude of tasks that needed to be accomplished in preparation for the first time the ship would steam under her own power.

29 April 1941

When Wieser's name appeared on the list of boys at boot camp who were being sent on assignment, he and the others loaded onto a canvas-covered truck for the next leg of their adventure into the world of Navy life. After the truck traveled through the gates, Wieser could see the large buildings of the officer-training war college diminishing in the distance. He was not sorry to see them disappear.

The truck rolled along the roads of Rhode Island, down the coast, and into New York, where it stopped in the Brooklyn Navy Yard. As the boys disembarked from the truck, Wieser could immediately see the battleship *North Carolina*. Scaffolding encircled her, and hoses draped off her sides and onto the dock. He thought to himself, *We're not going anywhere in that thing.* He shifted the weight of his sea bag on his back. Wrapped around it was the hammock that he had not used in the barracks.

The large group of new BB55 crew members marched up the gangway onto the fantail of the ship amidst shipfitters and lines and hoses and machines. Officers divided the new sailors into groups and led them down to various compartments, where they were told to grab a mattress and choose a bunk. Their papers were processed, and each was assigned to a particular division aboard the ship. Wieser wanted to be assigned to the print shop, but he was selected for Fifth Division, the deck division. He chose a living compartment right off the main passageway. It was small, bunks stacked only three high instead of the normal five, and he selected the center one. The error of his choosing soon became apparent to him—the passageway was a mass of activity throughout the day and night. As soon as the opportunity arose, he moved to another compartment, one so close to his battle station in mount seven of the five-inch guns that all he had to do was step outside his compartment and he was next to the mount.

Con Edison, which provided electricity for New York City, was located close to the Brooklyn Navy Yard. Soot from the plant rained down on the ship, giving new seamen in the deck division plenty of busywork. Every day, they would sweep the decks and clean the equipment, removing normal soil and all the black mist deposited from the four large stacks of the plant.

Maintaining the teak deck was just one of the jobs allotted to the deck crew. To give the teak a polished appearance, the boys used holystones—circular pieces of cement about eight inches in diameter and three inches thick with a hole in the center. By placing a wooden mop-length handle through the hole, the boys could use circular motions to clean the grime off the wood. They stood shoulder to shoulder in a long line so they missed no area of the deck. One sailor would be on sand detail, dumping buckets of sand onto the deck as an abrasive, and another would use the water hose to moisten the sand, then wash the deck clean after the others had thoroughly scrubbed it. When one area was clean, the entire line detail would move to another position. Fortunately for the men entrusted with holystoning, each division was responsible for only a portion of the deck. If officers of the deck ever thought their boys didn't have enough to do, they would send them topside after a rain to dry the teak.

Wieser learned to sew as he covered the lifelines with heavy canvas, wrapping and stitching. The sewing needle was large and the canvas tough, so he used a palm thimble—a leather fingerless glove that fit over his sewing hand with a metal area nestled just below the valley of the thumb and forefinger, dimpled to catch the end of the needle, giving more leverage to push the needle through. Short stitches were required. Any seaman who tried to finish faster by elongating his stitches was sure to be reprimanded. A series of three parallel lifelines ran the entire perimeter of the ship, so quite a few short stitches were needed, giving the deck crew adequate work to fill their days.

Clean soot, sew canvas.

But much more work needed to be done before the *North Carolina* could begin sea trials and become a fighting member of the United States fleet. Painting was a never-ending task. After the shipbuilders prepared some areas with paint, the new BB55 crew members put on the finishing touches. Living compartments had to be prepared, painted, and cleaned daily.

Fifth Division was also in charge of the smaller boats that were aboard ship on the starboard side. Sixth Division held the same jobs as Fifth, but on the port, or left, side of the ship. The ship owned 14 boats of varying sizes, seven on each side, and the deck crew was responsible for maintaining them. While the ship was being completed, the deck crew had to gather materials and create the skids to hold the boats, which were kept on the boat deck, one up from the main deck. The boys fine-tuned the method of stacking the boats, nestling them inside each other from largest on the bottom to smallest on the top. The boats were raised, lowered, and maneuvered by a boat crane several decks up the superstructure, and keeping that crane clean and in good working order was also the responsibility of the deck crew. The rigging for moving the boats varied from boat to boat, so crew members had to learn how to make the riggings and remember which boat used which rigging.

19 May 1941

The ship was ready for her first trial run under her own power. One hundred fifty mostly civilian yard workers, engineers, and other technicians had come aboard the previous day in anticipation of the event. At 0515, the ship got under way, assisted by 10 tugs and accompanied by two destroyers for protection against submarine attack and four Coast Guard cutters, two as minesweepers and two as escorts.

One more hurdle must be crossed before the BB55 could leave the harbor. The ship was equipped with CXAM-1 radar, which required an antenna that towered above any other structure on the ship. The bedspring antenna was attached to the top of a mast built with a pivot designed especially for the *North Carolina*. The antenna was perched so high that the mast had to be cranked down for the ship to pass under the Brooklyn Bridge. Once past the bridge, it was cranked back up.

The BB55 arrived in Delaware Bay at 2013 hours and dropped anchor for the night. Early the next morning, at 0454, she headed back to New York.

Daily outings tested the ship's machinery while many of those who built her were aboard to detect any problems. When their work was completed each day, the sailors loved liberty in New York.

4 July 1941

Walter Ashe locked the storeroom office and headed toward his

The CXAM-1 *air-search radar antenna was placed atop the foremast of the ship. The antenna, which became known as the "bedspring," extended so high above the deck that the foremaast had to be lowered for the ship to pass under the Brooklyn Bridge.*
COURTESY OF BATTLESHIP *NORTH CAROLINA* COLLECTION

living quarters. He was ready to celebrate his freedom, his independence, his right to go out and get drunk. He stripped off his dirty uniform and stuffed it into his laundry bag, grabbed a towel, and headed to the showers. As usual, a long line was waiting.

"Hey, Korba," he said to his buddy. "Where you want to go tonight?"

They tossed around some ideas and decided the two most important things were drinks and food, in that order. They'd start with the closest bar and go from there.

When he finished in the shower, Ashe put on his white bell-bottom pants, slipped on his black socks and shoes, pulled his white jumper over his head, and tied the black silk neckerchief so it hung just right, the knot up higher than regulation. It looked better that way. He ran his comb through his thick red hair and set his Dixie Cup hat flat on his head to pass inspection. Once he cleared the gangway, he would tilt it far enough back to let his locks show and just enough to the side to give it a bit of attitude. New York streets were calling.

By the time Ashe and his buddy reached the 72nd Street Diner, they had imbibed enough to alter their forward motion. They climbed on the barstools and ordered some food. While he ate, Ashe kept eyeing the donuts stacked in a pyramid on a plate next to the register. When he finished eating, he helped himself to one of the donuts and ran out the door, even though he had money in his pocket. Korba was a little slower with a bit more stagger and couldn't keep up. From a block or so down the street, Ashe looked over his shoulder and saw his friend being pummeled by the big Greek cook from the diner. He ran back to help.

Ashe swung and hit air. He adjusted his aim and landed one blow, then another. But the cook was big and strong and sober, so neither Ashe nor Korba nor a combination of the two was doing much damage. As the two staggering sailors swung and spun, a crowd began to gather on the sidewalk to watch the fight. The wail of police sirens became louder and louder. The cook pelted the boys, one blow landing just below Ashe's left eye, ripping his face open and sending blood gushing. That ended the fight.

Ashe held his handkerchief to his head as he and Korba ran down the street away from the approaching sirens. The sailors jumped onto the subway in their blood-spattered uniforms and noticed the other passengers moving a little farther away, sending disapproving glances in their direction.

When they arrived back at the ship, Ashe went to the yard dispensary for treatment. But his injuries were too severe, and medics transferred him to the United States Naval Hospital in Brooklyn to be patched up and stitched. He had taken quite a beating, requiring a hospital stay of 14 days.

Lester Tucker
COURTESY OF BATTLESHIP *NORTH CAROLINA* COLLECTION

22 May 1941

Lester Tucker boarded the BB55 as one of her new crew members. When he had heard back in 1939 that the Navy had real butter, he decided to join. He watched his mother each week soften their lump of uncolored margarine and mix in that little packet of powder that would color it to look like butter—or at least it was supposed to look like it. It certainly didn't taste like butter.

Tucker was born in Texas and grew up in California. Just before joining the Navy, he served a short stint in the Civilian Conservation Corps, where recruiters bombarded the boys with films and pictures of beautiful battleships. Lester wanted butter and wanted to go to aviation school, so he joined the Navy. He received his basic training at the United States Naval Training Station in San Diego. But instead of aviation school, he was sent to hospital corps school and spent his first duty at the Pearl Harbor Naval Hospital.

His desire to become an aviator continued to grow, and when

the opportunity came to at least work toward that goal, Tucker voluntarily left the hospital corps and became a seaman second class aboard the USS *Memphis*. He still wasn't in aviation, but at least he was on a ship. When he joined the *North Carolina*, her airplanes were not yet aboard, but he knew they would come soon, and he hoped to finally join the aviation division.

05 June 1941

During shakedown—the time between commissioning and putting the ship into service—the crew ate well. A typical breakfast included fresh fruit, cereal, fried ham steaks, bacon or sausage, gravy, fried potatoes, pastries, eggs, milk, coffee, and butter. Lunch—dinner on the bill of fare—usually included soup followed by veal, fish, ham, or turkey complemented by green vegetables, salads, potatoes, pies, bread, butter, and coffee. Supper started with grilled porkchops or roast beef or fried oysters or stuffed peppers with several sides of vegetables, bread, butter, jams, and coffee.

In the first of what would be many typical loading exercises to keep enough food aboard for general mess, deck hands loaded 20,000 pounds of potatoes, 700 pounds of celery, 1,100 pounds of cantaloupe, 400 pounds of radishes, 409 pounds of flounder, 400 pounds of scallops, 2,552 pounds of oranges, 1,540 pounds of string beans, 1,500 pounds of cauliflower, 968 pounds of lettuce, 2,200 pounds of sweet potatoes, 1,360 pounds of tomatoes, 2,000 pounds of cabbage, and 1,024 pounds of luncheon meat.

★★★★★★★★★★★★★★★★

When the day's work was complete and the crew could leave on liberty, George Conlon stood at his locker and looked into the small mirror hanging inside the door. Running a comb through his thick, curly black hair, he thought about Goergina Maria; just the musical lilt of her name made him smile. Being a New York native, Conlon spent his liberty in his hometown while the ship was in the Brooklyn Navy Yard. He dressed in his tailor-mades—the white bell-bottom pants with buttoned fly, the tight-fitting jumper that

North Carolina *sailors carried crates of needed supplies aboard ship in preparation for what lay ahead.*

hugged his five-foot-10-inch, 170-pound frame and drew approving glances from the young New York girls who were smitten by just the sight of sailors around town. Impending war sent a heightened urgency through the already electrified city, and the sailors were celebrities even before they left port.

Conlon felt lucky. He could visit his family and friends even on day passes from the ship. Many of the other boys in his division were from states all across the country, states he had only heard about in school. But he was learning more about those faraway places when he sat around in the aviation workshop with Tucker and the other boys and swapped stories. Some of his shipmates made it home on weekend passes if they didn't live too far away, but some couldn't go home at all. Yes, Conlon felt lucky.

Goergina was a telephone operator from New York, and the guys in the division knew Conlon was seeing her. How could they not know? He talked about her all the time. They liked to pick on Conlon, josh him a little bit every time he went on liberty. George and Goergina—just their names provided fodder for slapstick silliness from the boys. But they all liked Conlon; he was a pleasant guy to be around, and they were glad to see him happy. But some might have been just a bit envious every time he left the ship on liberty.

Conlon made sure he had his liberty pass in his pocket and walked across the teak deck. At the head of the gangplank, he stopped to receive permission to leave the ship. His heart pounded as he walked the paved roads of the Brooklyn Navy Yard to the huge iron gates guarded by Marines, received permission to exit, and went to meet Goergina.

★★★★★★★★★★★★★★★★

The first half of 1941 saw Nazi aggression escalate in the European theater. In March, President Roosevelt signed the Lend-Lease Act, giving him the power to offer equipment through selling, lending, or other types of exchange to any country that needed help defending itself against the Axis powers. In April, Yugoslavia and Greece surrendered to the Nazis. May saw heavy German bombing in London, and the *Bismarck* sank the British ship *Hood*. In June, the United States froze German and Italian assets, Germany attacked the Soviet Union, and the Nazis began mass murders. In July, the United States froze Japanese assets and suspended relations with Japan.

During the months of July and August, shipyard workers continued to tweak the *North Carolina*, working with a sense of urgency, going along on trial runs and repairing any problems found when they returned to the shipyard. The ship steamed in and out of the Brooklyn Navy Yard so often that it commanded enormous attention from the public and the news media. Articles marveling at her size and beauty appeared regularly in New York newspapers and beyond, but one journalist reportedly said the ship was a $70 million waste of taxpayers' money and was nothing but a "Show Boat," referring to the popular Broadway musical. Down in the Philadelphia Navy Yard where the BB55's sister ship, the *Washington*, BB56, was built and entered trials, resentment grew because the *North Carolina* garnered all the attention.

Crew members relished the notoriety, especially when they took liberty in the city, but they were also serious about their duty, continuously learning their jobs, scrubbing the deck, cleaning the equipment, memorizing the parts of their assigned guns— discovering how many men it took to man the gun, how each one's job was so closely intertwined with the others' that they had to become like a fine-tuned machine themselves, the gears of their motions slipping seamlessly into place.

On August 24, the BB55 made full-power runs at 27 knots, faster by several knots than any other American battleship had ever run. The next day, the ship welcomed a large group of additional engineers, yard workmen, and naval personnel aboard for the next round of tests. That day in speed trials, the ship reached 28 knots, or over 30 miles per hour, off Cape May, New Jersey.

26 August 1941

The *North Carolina* returned to Gravesend Bay at the lower end of New York Harbor and took aboard a large contingent of observers for what would be the next, and possibly most exciting, part of those early trials: gunnery. Among that group of watchful eyes, numerous news correspondents anxiously anticipated the fireworks, already contemplating leads for their reports to the people of the United States. Just what kind of firepower did the ship have? Would she pass her tests? How would the enlisted men handle the most technologically advanced ship in the United States Navy? Their questions were soon answered, but writing the leads did not come easy.

Despite the care and precision taken in designing the ship and her armaments, no one knew for sure what would happen when the main battery of nine 16-inch guns exploded with their mighty firepower, so precautions were taken. While the ship was anchored in Gravesend Bay, crew members manned all 14 of her boats and motor launches and steered them back to the Brooklyn Navy Yard for fear the concussions would rip them apart. After the BB55 steamed down the channel and out of the harbor, her three OS2U Kingfisher aircraft, which had recently been brought aboard, were catapulted into the sky and flew to the naval air station in Norfolk, Virginia, for safekeeping.

★★★★★★★★★★★★★★★

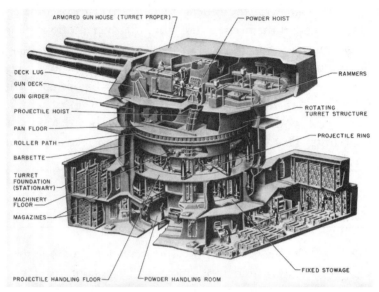

ARMORED GUN HOUSE (TURRET PROPER)

POWDER HOIST

DECK LUG

GUN DECK

GUN GIRDER

PROJECTILE HOIST

PAN FLOOR

ROLLER PATH

BARBETTE

TURRET FOUNDATION (STATIONARY)

MACHINERY FLOOR

MAGAZINES

RAMMERS

ROTATING TURRET STRUCTURE

PROJECTILE RING

FIXED STOWAGE

PROJECTILE HANDLING FLOOR

POWDER HANDLING ROOM

The 16-inch gun mounts, known as turrets, occupied five levels of the ship. Three turrets were constructed on the North Carolina, *two on the bow and one behind the superstructure, each with three big cannons. More than 150 men were required to keep each turret working properly and the guns firing. Built to go head to head with the guns of other battleships at sea, the 16s became the major weapon for island bombardment. Diagram originally from* Naval Ordnance and Gunnery, NAVPERS *16116-B, September 1950.*

Courtesy of Battleship North Carolina Collection

The 16-inch guns were the main battery of weaponry aboard the *North Carolina* class of battleships. Sixteen was the measurement of the gun bore—the hole through which the projectile traveled. The barrels themselves were 61 feet, four inches long and protruded from massive circular structures that could rotate from side to side. These gun houses, located on the main deck, topped off five other levels extending all the way to the bottom of the ship that created the entire gun turret. Those levels contained the gunpowder, the projectiles, and the communications circuits. Each gun house held three guns, and the *North Carolina* had three turrets—two on the forward part of the ship and one at the back—for a total of nine monstrous cannons. Each individual gun could fire a round every 30 seconds, but that feat could be accomplished only by a total of three officers and 177 enlisted men distributed throughout the six levels of each turret—or a total of 540 men.

The guns were developed for two different kinds of engagement and fired two types of projectiles—a 2,700-pound armor-piercing one for fighting with enemy ships and a 1,900-pound high-capacity projectile for bombarding buildings, airfields, and other targets on land. Each projectile was fired with a blast of 540 pounds of gunpowder contained in six 90-pound powder bags that smelled like ether. The armor-piercing shells could travel 21 miles at 1,568 miles per hour, while the bombardment shells traveled 23 miles at 1,797 miles per hour—the equivalent of shooting two compact cars per gun every minute all the way across the state of Delaware.

The 540 men stationed inside the 16-inch gun turrets represented nearly one-quarter of the full complement of crew. But when everything was working as it should, the guns were actually fired from the main battery plotting room, three decks below the main deck, using an analog computer, radar, and a large control switchboard.

★★★★★★★★★★★★★★★★

The guests aboard the *North Carolina* stuffed cotton in their ears and huddled out of the way of the crew preparing to make history. At general quarters manning their assigned battle stations, most of the crew could not witness the sight firsthand but could hear and feel its effects. Each time they felt the ship shudder with a successful salvo, they were grateful, for deep in their minds they could not shake the fear of what could happen if something went wrong and even one turret full of gunpowder exploded.

At 1600 hours, the ship began the firing tests of the 16-inch cannons, individually at first, each one sending up a mighty roar as it belched fire and steel into the air. Combinations of cannons fired, sending shudders through the ship, shaking dust loose to sift down through the air vents.

The tests of the big guns continued for two days with no mishaps and no damage to the ship.

28 August 1941

Paul Wieser had been manning his battle station inside mount seven for the five-inch guns during the previous days' testing of the 16s. The five-inch gun crews could do nothing during those tests but stay inside the gun mount and listen to the roar outside. But their turn had arrived.

The five-inch guns were called the "secondary battery." They could also be used for shore bombardments, but they were the first defense against attacking aircraft. Each five-inch gun—five being the diameter of the bore—could fire a 55-pound projectile up to eight miles. Fifteen pounds of powder housed inside a 12-pound brass casing provided the charge. Each mount contained two guns. The gun crew for each gun included a powder man, a projectile man, a hotcase man, and a gun captain. Also inside the mount were a mount captain, a site-setter with a periscope, a pointer, who monitored the up-and-down motions of the guns, and a trainer, who tracked the back-and-forth motions.

These guns were located on both sides of the ship inside completely enclosed mounts approximately 14 feet square with just over eight feet of headroom inside. A total of 12 crew members were required inside each mount to serve the two guns. The 10 mounts

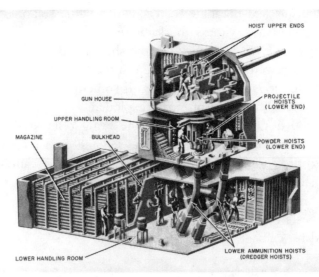

The five-inch gun mounts required three levels of the ship. These guns served double duty. They offered antiaircraft firepower like the 20s but also participated in bombardments of enemy islands like the 16s. Diagram originally from Naval Ordnance and Gunnery, NAVPERS 16116-B, September 1950.
COURTESY OF BATTLESHIP NORTH CAROLINA COLLECTION

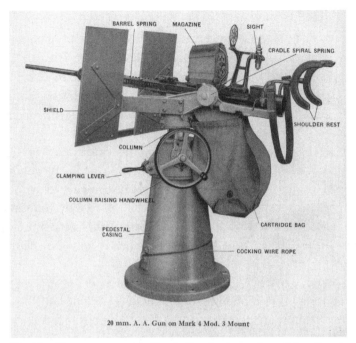

were centrally located, five on each side of the ship, staggered two on the main deck and three on the next level, the boat deck. They were numbered one through 10, the even numbers on the port side of the ship and the odd numbers on the starboard side.

While the actual gun and all its components were located inside the mount with just the barrel protruding, the powder and projectiles were stored in other compartments below deck and hoisted up to the mount as needed. Crew inside the lower handling room, two levels down from the mount, received the powder cans from an adjacent storage room and sent them up one level to the upper handling room, directly below the mount. There, the outer aluminum protective cans were removed and the unprotected brass containers were hoisted up a shaft into the mount. The projectiles were stored in ammunition magazines and sent up to the gun mount through the same handling rooms. When a projectile was sent from the upper handling room to the mount, the shaft holding it rotated to set the fuse. It was ready to fire.

Like the 16s, the fives could be fired from within the mount, but when all equipment was working properly, the alignment and firing were actually controlled inside a director on a higher level of the ship. Inside the mount, the 12 men sharing less than 200 square feet of space with an enormous amount of machinery could prepare the guns to fire 15 rounds per minute per gun—one every four seconds.

For weeks, Wieser and the other members of the five-inch gun crews practiced on a loading machine on the deck. It was not encased in a mount, and the ammunition and powder did not come from handling rooms below and did not look exactly the same, but the machine simulated what each member of the crew must do and in what order each action must take place. It was the most effective way for the crew to train safely.

As powder man, Wieser had to lift the powder charge—about two feet long, five inches in diameter, and 30 pounds—when it came up through an opening in the floor directly between his feet and place it in the loading slot. Almost simultaneously, the projectile man was retrieving the projectile, which he laid in the tray ahead of the powder can. The powder charge must be in place first, if only by a split second. When the gun was fired, the 12-pound empty brass casing that had contained the powder ejected backwards and, depending on the elevation of the gun, automatically slid down a chute and out of the mount through a small opening at the base or was caught by the hotcase man and thrown out a similar opening about waist-high. When in place, the load could be compared to a shotgun shell in separate parts. The tray resembled the area on the shotgun where the shell is inserted, only on a gigantic scale. After the gun fired, the gun captain slapped a lever that released the spade so it dropped back into place, essentially recocking the trigger, and the loading process began again.

During the tests of the guns, a gunnery officer was required to be inside each mount the first time it fired. The boys had been waiting inside mount seven for quite some time when the left hatch creaked open and the gunnery officer entered and slammed the hatch behind him.

"Okay, boys," he said. "Let's see what she can do. Either it'll work like it's supposed to or else we'll all be blowed to hell."

Wieser could feel the bumps rise on his arms. He struggled to focus and forget what the gunnery officer had said.

"Stand by," the mount captain ordered.

Each man took his assigned position at his gun and planted his feet, ready to take action. Wieser stood to the right of the loading tray near the end of the left gun, straddling the round opening in the bottom of the mount where the powder charge would appear.

"Commence firing."

Wieser looked down. When he saw the shiny brass charge of the powder casing appear, he realized this time it was for real. The powder was real; the ammunition was live. His heart pounded, but the extensive training kicked in, and the crew worked in perfect rhythm. Wieser lifted and placed the powder keg, saw the projectile loaded, and closed his eyes just as the ammunition rammed into the gun and the first loud crack of powder split the air. He felt himself jump a bit and hoped no one else noticed. Again and again, he lifted the powder, placed it in the slot, saw the projectile, and squinted his eyes in perfect concert with the explosion. He never saw the gun recoil but instinctively knew when to open his eyes and retrieve another keg of powder. The noise inside the mount was deafening, not just at the moment of discharge but from the constant din of motors and gears required to make the gun work properly.

"Stand down," the mount captain ordered. They had passed their first test.

29 August 1941

When the 16-inch and five-inch guns had passed their initial firing tests, the *North Carolina* steamed farther north for the final leg of the trial run, away from the city so that the concussion from the upcoming history-making tests would not shatter windows in the buildings ashore. Ears stuffed full of cotton and eyeglasses safely tucked away in pockets, officials and media nervously awaited the grand finale. General quarters sounded, creating a

The evening sky glowed as the North Carolina *continued to make history. After each of the guns was tested separately, the ship fired a 19-gun salvo—all the 16s and all the fives on the port side simultaneously. The ship responded magnificently to the enormous blast.*

COURTESY OF BATTLESHIP *NORTH CAROLINA* COLLECTION

pounding stampede of thousands of feet as the sailors manned their battle stations. Once inside mount seven on the starboard side of the ship, Wieser could only watch and wait and pray.

The *North Carolina* had already broken barriers of size and speed. She was poised to attempt something that no other ship had ever done. No practice sessions existed by which to gauge success, no previous attempts by which to learn and correct mistakes. Thousands of tons of gunpowder and projectiles sat inside the turrets of the 16s and the handling rooms of the fives—enough to virtually vaporize the ship if it all exploded at one time. What kind of structural damage could occur from the impact of 19 big guns firing in unison? The world was about to learn.

The preliminary order sounded loud and clear over the PA system: "Now hear this. Stand by for firing. All guns on the port side will be fired in one minute."

Three huge turrets rotated to port, their nine 16-inch guns elevated to 45 degrees. Five mounts trained their 10 guns at the invisible target. In one thunderous display of fire and smoke and noise, all 19 guns fired simultaneously, sending 12 tons of metal soaring into the sky. The ship lurched sideways away from the force as her guns belched, and crew members grabbed hold of anything they could to stay upright. But the ship's structure proved itself sound, with little more than a few broken light bulbs, a loose rivet or two, and some very clean ventilation shafts to mark the momentous occasion.

30 August 1941

Bearing the master headline "Newsmen Honor Ship's Paper," the 21st edition of the ship's newspaper, the *Tarheel,* featured articles by nationally known journalists who had been aboard the ship for the gunnery trials. The staff's note said in part, "We of the *Tarheel* staff take great pleasure in thinking ours is the first and only ship's paper that can lay claim to having so many famous names appearing in one issue. We might go so far as to say that no paper, be it a ship's paper or metropolitan newspaper ashore, can boast of this, and we ask our closest competitor, the USS *Washington's* *Cougar Scream,* to take notice."

Media who had witnessed the history-making 19-gun salvo from aboard ship included correspondents from the *New York Mirror*, the *New York Times*, the *Washington Post*, International News Service, the *Chicago Daily News*, *Transradio Press*, McGraw-Hill Publishing, and the Mutual Broadcasting System. Each wrote an article for that week's edition of the *Tarheel*.

The power of the *North Carolina* and the capabilities of her crew—from experienced officers to young, green enlisted men—astounded the media. In an article entitled "Reflections," Pat Henry of the *New York Mirror* wrote of the difficulty the press faced in trying to express the full ramifications of that moment in history they had shared: "Every officer down to the last enlisted man so performed his duty that the hard boiled news and radio men were amazed. Men accustomed to sitting at a typewriter and dashing off front-page stories of the happening of the day, sat at their typewriters waiting for a 'lead.' What was the big story to tell? How would they get the first big splash to the world of what they had been allowed to witness exclusively?"

But it was perhaps the offering by W. W. Chaplin that best described the crew's own underlying knowledge of what they were meant to be:

Looking Seaward
By W. W. Chaplin, International News Service Correspondent

I'm a land-faring man and what I know about the Navy couldn't be measured with a micrometer, but I've had occasion to study the fighting men of several countries in three wars and I guess fighting men can be assayed about the same way wherever you find them, afield or afloat.

So, I'll say this about the *North Carolina*, or rather the men who are the heart and soul of the *North Carolina*.

The assorted brains aboard for this cruise from the Bureau of Ships and the Model Basin and the Naval Arsenal can tell you the hidden meaning of the roar of the turret guns, the crack of the auxiliary batteries, and the snap and rattle of the 1.1 and the fifty calibers; it's just a lot of Fourth of July to me.

But I heard one noise that makes more sense to me than any super-salvo ever fired, and it may have passed unnoticed to a lot of folks aboard who had cotton in their ears. That noise doesn't make any more rumpus than a snap of your fingers, but it's one of the most important sounds in life.

It's the click of a big organization when order suddenly takes the place of chaos. It's the click that changes a green football team into a winning unit. It's the click that comes at dress rehearsal or the play is doomed. It's the click that turns a new army into a fighting force.

I heard that click before the Argonne engagement in the world war and you know what happened there. I listened for it in France in the days before Dunkirk and didn't hear it, and you know what happened there. I didn't hear it in Ethiopia and that's history, too.

But when the big guns roared on the *North Carolina* I heard that click, and when the call comes I have little doubt as to what accounting this ship will give of itself, because that peculiar transformation has taken place which turns a crowd into a crew.

CHAPTER FOUR

America at War

★★★★★★★★★★★★★★★★

*"I had duty this weekend and was asleep in my top bunk
when the word came. 'This is not a drill. The Japanese have
bombed Pearl Harbor. We are in a state of war.' We went
to general quarters and started setting up guard posts
throughout the ship. I was given a .45 caliber automatic
and duty belt and stood watch outside a lower five-inch
handling room. Some patrolled the opening to the Navy Yard
in our launches, watching for anything that might float in
that was suspicious. I had no idea where Pearl Harbor was,
and knew little about the Japanese. I soon learned."*

Former crew member William R. Taylor,
diary entry, 07 December 1941

September 1941

Basking in notoriety following her successful broadside salvo
that splashed headlines across the front pages of newspapers and
thrilled anyone connected with building or operating the ship, the

North Carolina left New York headed south for more extensive training and further testing. Her first destination was Chesapeake Bay, Virginia, where she would meet up with her sister ship, the *Washington,* for the first time. When the BB55 entered the harbor, her band was topside playing "Anchors Aweigh," the standard port entry selection. As the *North Carolina* passed the *Washington,* her band struck up "Here Comes the Show Boat" from the musical *Show Boat.* Even though done in jest, the greeting solidified the nickname, and the *North Carolina*'s crew began to consider it a term of endearment. She became the "Showboat."

For the next three months, the Showboat traveled up and down the Atlantic coast testing the equipment and training the crew. She steamed from Chesapeake Bay to Hampton Roads, Virginia; to Guantanamo Bay, Cuba; down to Kingston, Jamaica; and back again. She then made various runs between New York and Virginia, sometimes accompanied by the *Washington* but always accompanied by destroyers to protect her from submarine attack by the Germans, which had become a growing problem along the Atlantic coast.

★★★★★★★★★★★★★★★

Paul Wieser's girlfriend, Jean Coddington, had given him a pen-and-pencil set, and he used it to write to her almost daily. Even though the ship was most often in New York and he was able to go home on liberty, just the fact that he was in the Navy seemed to make their relationship more important. While he was in boot camp, he confessed to Jean how difficult it was but asked her not to inform his buddies because he had told them it was "swell." During the months that the ship was out to sea for training and practice, he wrote, "I am writing this letter in the middle of nowhere, water all around us." He told her about his battle station and his job on the five-inch gun: "I throw a forty-five pound powder can into the gun. If I hit the back of the can, she'll go off and blow us to kingdom come. I wouldn't want to go that way. If I do go while I'm in the Navy, I want to be a hero."

Each time the ship returned to the Brooklyn Navy Yard, her crew was excited to be back and anxious to take liberty. Wieser, from just across the river in New Jersey, always went home. He anticipated see-

Paul Wieser first told his girlfriend, Jean Coddington, that he loved her by using flag language called semaphore on this second page of a letter—one of more than 600 he wrote and she saved.

ing Jean and finding out if their relationship had really progressed as much as their letters indicated. He first told her he loved her in small drawings of himself spelling out the words with semaphore, the flag language he was learning aboard ship.

Japan's military leaders knew that the Americans would be a formidable force if war between the two nations developed, so despite the guise of negotiations, they went on the offensive. In the predawn hours, six Japanese carriers launched 181 torpedo bombers, dive bombers, horizontal bombers, and fighters heading for Pearl Harbor in the American territory of Hawaii. While the enemy planes were winging their way toward attack, an American destroyer, the USS *Ward,* spotted and sank an unidentified submarine near the entrance to the harbor, but the report was taken lightly by officials. An Army radar operator located the approaching planes on his screen, but superiors dismissed them as a group of American planes expected to arrive.

So the Japanese achieved complete surprise, and the result was a fiery, bloody, devastating blow to the American fleet. The first wave of enemy aircraft bombed and strafed planes on the airfields and torpedoed and bombed ships in the harbor. A second wave of 170 Japanese planes followed 30 minutes after the first. As ships burned and sank, enemy gunners dipped in low and slaughtered sailors with machine-gun fire.

When the attack subsided less than two hours after it began, 21 American ships had been sunk or damaged, including all eight battleships located in the harbor; 188 aircraft had been destroyed and 159 damaged. Loss of life was high—2,403 killed, including 68 civilians. And 1,178 military personnel and civilians were wounded. The harbor was in shambles, and the nation was in shock.

★★★★★★★★★★★★★★★

Many of the BB55's crew had weekend liberty, and others were out for the day. No one was due back at the ship until midnight. Walter Ashe went to a football game at the Polo Grounds in New York. During the game, a voice came over the loudspeaker telling a specific colonel to report to Washington, D.C., at once. Ashe and his companions wondered briefly what that was all about but quickly directed their thoughts back to the game. Later, as they exited the stadium, newspaper boys were on the corners.

"Extra, extra!" they shouted, waving papers in their hands. "Japanese bomb Pearl Harbor."

Ashe thought to himself, *Must be some publicity stunt. Where do they get this stuff anyway?*

His thoughts were quickly interrupted by shore patrol.

"Sailors, report back to your ships immediately."

Many sailors on weekend leave heard the call on the radio for all military personnel to report back for duty.

Wieser was on duty that weekend, so he had not left the ship. He was standing at his locker about midafternoon when the guys on liberty from his division rushed in.

"What are you doing back already?" he asked them.

"Shore patrol sent us back. The Japs bombed Pearl Harbor."

Wieser looked at his shipmates with a quizzical expression. "Where's Pearl Harbor?" he asked.

None of them knew for sure, but they knew it must be important, so they started asking around and talking to other guys until they discovered that it was way out in the Pacific Ocean, part of the territory of Hawaii. And more importantly, they learned that most of the ships of the United States Navy might have been there.

Many of the crew thought the Showboat would leave immediately, but she was not yet ready and had not received orders, so liberties in the city continued. In fact, many were sent back to finish their liberties that same day.

Joseph Smits was lying in his bunk that Sunday afternoon, broke and without anything much to do. He and his equally short-on-money friend in the bunk next to him were just shooting the breeze waiting for chow call. They noticed increased activity and excited conversation in the passageway adjacent to their living quarters and asked what was going on. Smits knew all about Pearl Harbor. He had been stationed there just before transferring to the *North Carolina*. He and his buddy decided to join the activity, so they got dressed, left the ship, and took the subway downtown. When they ordered food at a restaurant, someone said, "I'll take care of that. You boys will be going without for a long time." When they ordered drinks at the bar, the drinks were on the house. They even saw a movie without spending any money. Despite leaving the ship

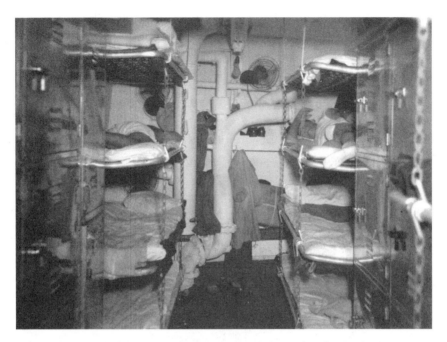

When the boys had nothing else to do, they sometimes lay around in their bunks, known as racks, just to pass the time, write letters home, or read. The racks were often stacked as many as five high. Joe Smits and his buddies were out of money and resting in their racks when they learned that Pearl Harbor had been bombed.
COURTESY OF BATTLESHIP *NORTH CAROLINA* COLLECTION

with practically no cash at all, they had a great time in New York that night.

And their experience became the norm. Life aboard ship, in the shipyard, and especially in New York City changed in many ways that day. Security in and around the shipyard was heightened—more guards appeared, and more of them were carrying firearms. Ship preparation and gunnery training took on a new and more urgent meaning. Prior to December 7, the boys could get free tickets to concerts and ball games and other events through the YMCA, but they had to pay for most things. Dressed in their uniforms, they were not always greeted with open arms. Some people, especially young women's parents, were suspicious of them. But with the country facing war, the boys of the BB55 became heroes even before they left port. Taxi drivers didn't let them pay; they rode the subways for free; bars gave them drinks on the house. In many ways, their uniforms became free tickets to entertainment.

★★★★★★★★★★★★★★

Seventeen-year-old Charles "Chuck" Malvern Paty, Jr., was in his parents' home in Charlotte, North Carolina, listening to the New York Philharmonic Orchestra on the radio when the broadcast was interrupted by a special news bulletin. When he heard that Pearl Harbor had been bombed, he woke up his napping parents, then dashed out into the yard to find anyone he could. He told his neighbor that he was joining up immediately, but when he went back into the house and told his parents, they had other thoughts.

"No you're not," his mother said emphatically. "You are only in the 11th grade. You are too young and too small, and you're not going anywhere except to school."

Chuck Paty
COURTESY OF CHUCK PATY

"I need to join up," Chuck said. "The Japanese bombed Pearl Harbor. I want to join the Navy."

"You need to finish high school," his father said. "Go to college. Then if you still want to join the Navy, I'm sure it will still be there."

"But I need to go now," Chuck argued. "That's way more important than school."

"Nothing is more important than school," his mother retorted. "Besides, you're our only child. You don't need to go running off to join the Navy and go who knows where for nobody knows how long. What if this causes us to go to war? There's no telling where you'd end up."

"But Mama—"

"Besides," his father interrupted, "you're too small. Do you have any idea how hard boot camp would be? You'd just about die every day from being so tired. You're going to want to come back home and get in your own bed, and you're not going to be able to do that."

The argument continued throughout the rest of the afternoon and into the evening. Finally, close to midnight, his parents relented.

"Be ready to leave with me in the morning," his father said. "I'll drop you off at the recruiting station on my way to work."

"Yes," Chuck said triumphantly, then looked over at his mother.

"You're so little you'll never pass anyway," his mother said. "I don't know why I'm so worried. They'll just send you back home."

08 December 1941

Chuck was dressed and waiting long before his father was ready to go. He hugged his mother, then jumped in the front seat beside his father. All the way to the post office where the naval recruiting station was located, Chuck worried that he might be overreacting.

I'm going to look like a fool, he thought. *I'm crazy doing this. There's not going to be another person there.*

His dad dropped him off and told him to catch the bus to school or back home when he was done. The recruiting office was on the second floor of the building. As he climbed the stairs, Chuck saw a wall of guys waiting in line, at least a hundred or more.

"I want to join the Navy," he told the first representative he reached.

"How old are you?" the recruiter asked him.

"Seventeen."

"Get in that line over there."

Chuck walked to the line where the man had pointed and continued surveying the growing lines in the office while he waited. He saw guys of all ages, but most of the men looked older than he was. Some were already wearing uniforms. He learned that they were reservists coming to sign up for full-time service. The lines moved quickly, especially the one for 17-year-olds. The boys were measured and weighed before they even talked to anyone. Five foot three, 110 pounds.

When Chuck reached the recruiter, the man asked him, "Where are your parents?"

"They're not here," Chuck said. "My mother's at home, and my dad's at work."

"You're only 17; they have to sign for you," the recruiter said impatiently. "And you don't weigh enough. Take these forms home and eat a bunch of bananas. I mean a bunch of them. Come back tomorrow with your parents' approval and you might pass."

Chuck caught the bus home and told his parents what the recruiter had said. He decided he wouldn't even eat meals; he would just eat bananas.

★★★★★★★★★★★★★★★

Aboard the BB55, work detail continued as it had, although a noticeably heightened tension permeated the air. Feeding more than 2,000 sailors three squares a day was no small task and required an enormous amount of food. Down in the butcher shop, Lincoln Hector hacked away at the meat all day long. Deck hands took on supplies, which that day included 825 pounds of beans, 680 pounds of lettuce, 825 pounds of cucumbers, 625 pounds of spinach, 1,425 pounds of oranges, 600 pounds of turnips, 1,650 pounds of tomatoes, 600 pounds of eggplant, 1,250 pounds of apples, 2,466 pounds of veal, 1,008 pounds of bacon, 517 pounds of luncheon meat, 840 pounds of cauliflower, 550 pounds of frankfurters, 10,279 pounds of boneless beef, 710 pounds of liver, 1,984 pounds of chicken, 1,020 pounds of butter, 210 pounds of cheese, 500 pounds of onions, 2,076 pounds of pork, 1,000 pounds of sausage, 1,381 pounds of duck, 21,780 pounds of potatoes, 100 pounds of yeast, 213 pounds of headcheese, 833 pounds of turkey, and 940 pounds of white cabbage.

About midmorning, the loudspeakers on the ship crackled: "Stand by for a message from the president of the United States." On deck, the loading and cleaning stopped; in living compartments, the acey-deucy games halted and the craps cards stayed in hand; in the scullery, the dish washing ceased; and in the butcher shop, the cleavers were still. A quiet enveloped the ship and even the Navy yard itself as everyone strained to hear President Roosevelt speak to Congress: "Yesterday, December 7, 1941—a date that will live in infamy—the United States of America was suddenly and deliberately attacked by naval and air forces of the Empire of Japan. . . . I ask that the Congress declare that since the unprovoked and dastardly attack by Japan on Sunday, December seventh, a state of war has existed between the United States and the Japanese Empire."

A cheer, not of jubilation but of support and determination, filled the harbor that morning, then the ruckus of shipbuilding and preparation for war continued with invigorated purpose.

09 December 1941

Throughout the morning, the crew followed normal in-port routine. At 1231 hours, the shrill *Shee-ree, shee-ree* of the boatswain's pipe sounded general quarters. The boys had heard that sound in trials when they were practicing, but never in port. Over the loudspeaker, the call came, "All hands, man your battle stations."

Wieser had just finished lunch and was stashing his tray. His heart began to race, and a lump filled his throat. As he mounted the steps to the main deck, he caught a glimpse of the New York skyline beyond the Navy yard. He climbed the rungs outside mount seven, hoisted himself into the mount, and took his place next to his gun over the powder chute. The hatches closed behind him.

"Stand by," the mount captain ordered.

Wieser planted his feet and readied himself to retrieve the powder charge. He tried to ignore the fearful thoughts running through his head. *How can we fire these guns in port? Every window in New York will shatter from the concussion of the guns. Would the Japs really attack us here?* Fearful moments passed.

"Stand down."

The air attack had been a false alarm. Wieser realized he had been holding his breath and let out a deep sigh.

★★★★★★★★★★★★★★★★

Chuck Paty ate bananas all the way back to the recruiting station, signed papers in hand. He passed the weight test.

"Go home and wait for a notice," the recruiter told the group of about 30 new enlistees. "You'll have to go to Raleigh to be sworn in, and you won't be in the Navy until you take that oath. You can back out now. You can back out anytime before you get sworn in, but after that, there's no backing out. You're in the Navy."

While he waited for his notice, Chuck thought a lot about what the recruiter had said. Several days later, a letter arrived telling him when to report and where the recruiting office was in Raleigh. The letter also carried instructions to bring one change of underwear, a toothbrush, toothpaste, and one pair of clean socks. Other than the clothes he was wearing, that was all he would have. He kept thinking about what the recruiter had said: "You can back out anytime before you get sworn in, but after that, there's no backing out."

His parents dropped him off at the station to catch a bus to Raleigh.

"We'll see you after boot camp," his father said as Chuck got out of the car.

"Yeah, see ya," Chuck replied. He could hardly bear the look on his mother's face. "It won't be long; I'll be fine," he reassured her.

About 40 new recruits were gathered in a conference room and told to stand at attention. It was the first time most of them had assembled in any orderly fashion. Chuck surveyed the group. He saw boys in overalls, some in dress clothes, some in suits and ties, some in everyday work clothes. Chuck had on a jacket, but it didn't match his pants. An officer walked in.

"You are about to be sworn into the United States Navy," the officer said. He read some details and then repeated the offer about backing out that Chuck had heard over and over in his mind for the past few days. Then the officer said, "This is your last chance. If you don't want to go through with this, step forward now."

During the ensuing silence, Chuck surveyed the group again. They were all much larger and heavier, better developed than he. Chuck had never even played sports in high school. He just wasn't very athletic. His father's warning rang in his ears: "You're too small. You'd just about die." Chuck decided that if anyone else stepped forward, he would, too.

But no one did.

"Raise your right hand and repeat after me," the officer ordered.

Chuck raised his shaky hand.

"I, state your name . . ."

"I, Charles Malvern Paty, Jr. . . ."

" . . . do solemnly swear . . ."

No turning back.

After the swearing-in ceremony was over, the new seamen boarded a bus headed for the Norfolk Training Station in Virginia. They arrived several hours after midnight and had not slept at all. They were told to march to the barracks, but exhaustion and inexperience undermined what little coordination they had, and they stumbled more than marched into the brick building. They were assigned bunks and told to hit the sack. Reveille would come early.

Paty learned abruptly after breakfast the next morning that he had forfeited all the privacy he cherished as an only child. Standing in a long line of at least 200 naked sailors, he was poked and prodded and herded from one place to another, then given the clothes he would be wearing for the next few years and instructed on how to wear them properly. He would never again see the clothes that he'd worn into the building that day and piled up against the wall when he stripped. As Paty stood in line for the first of what would be a daily series of shots, the man who had reached the front of the line suddenly fell to the floor. He was a large man, and he didn't crumple into a pile but fell over straight and stiff like a tree that had just been chopped off at the roots. The pharmacist's mate gave a here-we-go-again look, slowly stood, walked around the desk, knelt, and gave the man a few firm slaps on his cheeks to rouse him. For the first time in his life, Paty felt just a slight twinge of needle phobia.

The Norfolk Training Station had a drill field as large as four football fields, surrounded by brick barracks several stories tall. That area was called the quadrangle. At one end, a large mess hall fed the thousands of servicemen training there. The station wasn't far from Hampton Roads, where ships came into port, but as new recruits—"boots"—Paty and the others were not allowed to venture past the quadrangle alone. If they tried, their status could be easily recognized by the one additional uniform item they wore. Since the weather was cold, the required uniform included a dark blue turtle-neck sweater, to be worn underneath a dark blue top called a jumper with a large squared-off collar but no white stripes. The regulation dark blue pants had a U-shaped fly that buttoned all the way around. They did not have bell bottoms, but rather straight legs that could easily be covered below the knee by white canvas leggings called "boots," the distinguishing characteristic of every new recruit. The boys were issued two pairs of black shoes and could choose to wear low-cut shoes or high-tops, which offered better support to the ankles during the intensive drilling process. The winter attire also included a wool peacoat and gloves.

Mornings began with reveille, followed by a huge breakfast of scrambled eggs, fried eggs, ham, sausage, pancakes, and more. The boys ate as much as they wanted, but after three or four hours of drilling, that fuel had been exhausted, and they were ready for lunch. The afternoon routine included training classes on naval procedure and policy. They learned when to salute an officer and when not to

The white canvas leggings worn by new recruits during training distinguished them immediately and earned them the name of "boots" while they were at boot camp. Bob Fennelly, shown here, wore his boots while in training. He joined the ship's crew soon afterward.
COURTESY OF BOB FENNELLY

salute. That was more complicated than Paty expected. The *Bluejacket's Manual* contained a list of 17 different scenarios for saluting and standing at attention. He hoped he remembered them all.

They learned that the chain of command started with the first promotion. They must obey any order handed down by even the next higher-rated man. As new recruits, Paty and the others were apprentice seaman. The next rank was seaman second class, earned automatically by time served. But if a seaman second gave an order to an apprentice seaman, the order was to be followed.

Afternoons also included rifle practice, which Paty enjoyed even though the World War I-vintage rifles they were issued had one hell of a kick. Other drills put them on the water. They marched down to the docks, their cadence steadily improving but still not perfect, and climbed into rowboats to learn not only how to row but to master the nomenclature of the ship. As they rowed, the officer would say, "Turn to port" or "Turn to starboard." Unless each one of the rowers knew which way to turn, their little rowboat wouldn't go where it was supposed to go. Paty rattled the terms around in his brain, drilling himself over and over. *Starboard is the right; port is the left. Starboard is the right; port is the left. Port has four letters; left has four letters. Port is the left; starboard is the right. The bow is the front; the stern is the back. The bow is the front; the stern is the back. If I bow, I bow forward. The bow is the front; the stern is the back.* And those were just the basic directions. Speaking and understanding "Navy" sometimes felt like learning a foreign language.

11 December 1941

The boys of the BB55 lowered her radar mast and headed her toward the Brooklyn Bridge. Crew members topside noticed something different that day as they cruised under the bridge. Police lined the rails and barricaded the lanes, halting all traffic until the *North Carolina* passed safely underneath.

Following a couple of weeks of rigorous training runs, the crew of the Showboat spent its first Christmas as a family anchored at Hampton Roads, Virginia. A few days earlier, when the holiday edition of the ship's newspaper, the *Tarheel*, had been published, the boys had received a stern reminder to send letters home: "What are you going to do for the folks back home? . . . A Christmas letter can bring great joy and it may add much to the happiness at home if there is a bit of folding money inside. . . . Certain of our people fail to write . . . so the lonely hearts of our loved ones are left in anxiety."

Decorations were prohibited for fear of fire, but Christmas cards from home lined the inside doors of the boys' lockers. The crew ate well—turkey and dressing, ham, vegetables, fruits, nuts. Christmas carols streamed through the public-address system. For most of the young men who were away from home for the first time, the holiday was melancholy, but they were encouraged by words from shipmates published in the *Tarheel*: "We can't carry Christmas cheer home; let's keep it aboard. Greet your shipmates with a friendly smile that fills the ship with the warmth of Christmas spirit which is traditional in our Navy, and which conveys to all the message . . . Merry Christmas."

★★★★★★★★★★★★★★★

When the ship was in port as at Hampton Roads, the deck crew lowered all her smaller boats into the water by crane and attached them to the ship with lines tied to a boat boom extending off the side of the *North Carolina*. The boats stayed in the water for the duration of the anchorage, ready to transport liberty crews or work crews or officers wherever they needed to go. The boats were transports, not lifeboats. Although the ship had three supplied rafts on each side, she had no lifeboats. When the time came for the ship to depart, as she did near the end of December 1941, those 14 wooden boats had to be reloaded and restacked inside each other, seven on each side. In great weather, the job was an enormous task.

But when the weather was bad, the job was miserable and could become dangerous.

Rain pelted Wieser in the face, and the wind threatened to knock him and the other boys of the deck crew off their feet as they attempted to retrieve the boats. The storm roughened the waters of the harbor, which splashed over the sides of the rocking boats. While others climbed down the ladder and moved from one boat to the other, hooking the hoist each time it was lowered over the side, Wieser handled multiple duties on deck. The wind was biting cold, and Wieser's eyes burned from the elements, straining to see through the rain. As the cranes lifted each boat out of the water and up above the deck of the ship, he helped guide it into its cradle, unhooked the hoist so it could be lowered again, located the skids for the next boat, placed them inside the hull of the boat already loaded, and then guided the following boat into place when it came over the bow rail. The boys wore their winter blues, their peacoats and gloves, but they had no rain gear, and the unrelenting downpour soaked them to the skin as they worked. When the chore was finally completed, Wieser changed into dry clothes, but it took hours for the chill to leave his body.

The next morning, the ship headed south as part of Task Force 17, which in addition to the *North Carolina* included the battleship *Washington*, the carrier *Hornet*, and the destroyers *Hogan*, *Noa*, and *Stansbury*.

09 January 1942

Boot camp was scheduled to last 90 days, followed by at least 10 days of leave. Paty had been in Norfolk only about a week when he learned that his group's training would be shortened to two months. But less than a month after they arrived, an officer came into the barracks and said, "Pack your sea bags. We're leaving at dawn."

The bags were big and, when packed, contained every possession a sailor owned. After packing uniforms and towels and shoes and toiletries, Paty had to learn to wrap his hammock around the bag so that it could all be carried at one time. Completed, it weighed in excess of 75 pounds—at least two-thirds Paty's body weight. As the boots packed their belongings that night, they wondered among themselves where they were going. They talked about what they would do on their leave time. If boot camp was over, it was time for leave, right?

The recruits prepared to depart the next day with no idea where they were going. Paty looked at his sea bag standing there against his bunk. It was more than half as tall as he was and had no straps, no means to grasp it except some puny drawstrings and the cords from the hammock wrapped around it from top to bottom. He grabbed the cords as tightly as he could, bent his knees, positioned himself in front of the bag, and moved both hands up over his shoulder, hoping that when he straightened up, the sea bag would come up off the floor and balance on his back.

"Fall in," the command came, and the apprentice seamen lined up and began to march.

Balancing that bag on his back while standing still was one thing,

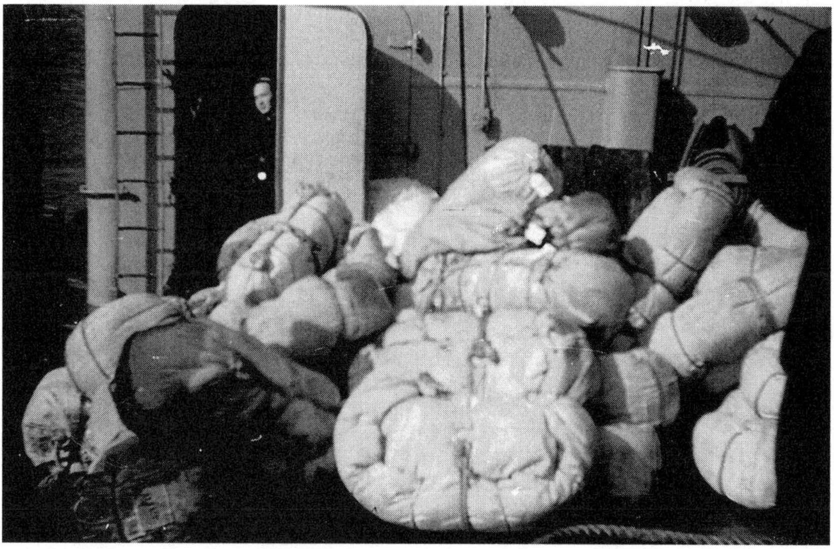

Navy sea bags were piled up during transfer of gear and crew from boot camp to the ship or from one ship to another. The hammocks wrapped around the bags from top to bottom made them even more difficult to carry.

COURTESY OF BATTLESHIP *NORTH CAROLINA* COLLECTION

but marching with it there was something entirely different. Paty struggled, but he kept pace with the bigger, stronger guys. Still, after they had marched farther than he could imagine and his arms began to burn, he thought, *I sure wish one of those big guys would carry mine on his other shoulder for a while.*

They loaded onto a bus, which carried them downtown to the Southern Railway station. The train was waiting, the engine puffing, but they didn't load right away. They stood on the platform and waited, and waited, and waited. For a while, at least, Paty didn't have to keep balancing that sea bag on his back. It leaned against his side.

During the nearly two hours that Paty's group of about 40 seamen stood waiting, other troops continued to arrive. They came by bus; they came by truck. They came until about 400 young men and sea bags were gathered on the loading dock. They kept asking any new person they saw, "Where are we going?" None of the boys knew, and the officers who did know would not say. By the time the train left the station, darkness had enveloped them. No one could even tell what direction they were traveling.

Paty tried to sleep, but the seats were uncomfortable and did not recline. He thought about what his father had said: "You're going to want to come back home and get in your own bed, and you're not going to be able to do that." He dozed fitfully.

The morning light revealed familiar scenery. The train traveled through the suburbs of Charlotte, North Carolina, and pulled into the Southern Railway station downtown. Paty was very close to home. When the train stopped, he stood. He wanted to call his parents and tell them he was there so they could come see him while the train was at the station.

"Where do you think you're going?" a porter asked him.

"I'm going to find a phone and call my parents," he answered. "I live here."

"Nobody gets off the train," the porter said.

At that moment, Paty realized he probably wasn't going to get any leave. Wherever they were headed would take him farther and farther from home. He wondered when or even if he would see his parents again. He watched the scenery fly by as the train continued south. The boys traveled through South Carolina and Georgia and into Florida, through Jacksonville and Daytona Beach, and when the bridge to Key West appeared, Paty figured they couldn't go much farther. The recruits departed the train and, after eating at a small café, loaded onto a fleet of Greyhound buses that carried them across the bridge to the Key West Navy Yard. They marched down to a pier where two old four-stack destroyers were waiting. *This is it?* Paty worried.

They stood there for hours. Word passed that they would be divided into two groups. They wouldn't stay on the destroyers, they learned, but they still didn't know where they were going. Paty was quickly realizing that, with the Navy, the old adage "Hurry up and wait" rang true. As the light began to wane, their superiors told them to grab their bags and march. The entire group of 400 marched to the airport on the base, where they were fed and told to find a spot in the hangar, unwrap their hammocks, and go to sleep. The canvas hammocks were designed to hang between two stanchions, but none existed in the hangar, so Paty spread the one layer of canvas on the cement floor and tried to sleep. At least the temperature was pleasant enough that far south, so they didn't have to worry about the cold keeping them awake.

12 January 1942

The large group of sailors ate a hot breakfast and marched back to the docks. Paty was prepared to begin the waiting game again, but it wasn't long before someone started calling out names and dividing the group of 400 into halves. Paty's group boarded the destroyer *Stansbury*, which had a regular crew of 180. That day, 200 additional sailors and their sea bags went aboard. They couldn't go below deck, and there was barely enough room topside for the boys and a mountain of sea bags. The sun strained to peer through a gray veil, and the seas tossed teasingly, as if to say, "So you want to be a sailor?" Some of the boys answered with violent attacks of seasickness. Paty felt it coming but was able to hold onto his breakfast. Word spread through the group that they were going to the battleship *North Carolina*. Paty was thrilled. Since the ship was named for his home state, he had heard the facts and followed the news reports about her. But facts could not adequately prepare him for what he was about to witness.

Through the haze and fog, the land quickly disappeared behind them. Paty wondered how far they would have to go, standing almost shoulder to shoulder, struggling to keep their balance, dodging sprays of salt water and seasickness. He stared straight ahead, peering through the mist, trying to see something, anything. When the destroyer arrived within sight of the *North Carolina*, Paty felt his jaw drop. She looked like a massive gray wall rising out of the water and into the sky. The destroyer, dwarfed in her presence, stopped a good distance away.

Motor launches from the *North Carolina* approached the *Stansbury* for transfer. Rough seas tossed the small launches, which rose and fell at least six feet with the swells. Aboard the destroyer, the new recruits, in their dress blues and peacoats, readied themselves for transfer, their sea bags tossed over their shoulders. The boys were instructed to wait until the swells brought the launch to its maximum height, then toss their sea bags into the launch, climb down the heavy rope netting hanging over the side of the destroyer, and drop into the launch. The deck was crowded, the process was slow, and each launch would hold only about 50 of the 200 new crew members.

Paty's anxiety began to build as he edged closer to the side and his turn became imminent. He struggled with his sea bag, fighting to maintain his balance while he waited. When he was close enough to the edge to watch what was happening over the side, he saw one of his counterparts make a bad judgment in timing. He waited too long to let go of the net, and the launch dropped out from under him when he jumped. He landed in the bottom of the launch like a sack of potatoes. Paty heard him hit and hoped his own timing would be better. He prayed he would not be the first to miss the launch completely and find himself in the rough ocean.

Paty stood at the edge. He concentrated on the movement of the swells, watching the launch dip. As soon as it started back up, he tossed his bag, climbed over the side, and leapt out with faith.

The launch rose to meet him, and he landed on his feet.

But that was only half the battle. The launches puttered along toward the huge ship. As they got closer, Paty noticed a ladder hanging over the side—not one with rungs going straight up, but more like a staircase protruding outward from the hull with the steps at a right angle to the ship. At the bottom of the accommodation ladder, a small platform became the target for off-loading from the launch. Sea bag in tow, and once again synchronizing movement with the rise of the swells, Paty successfully climbed from the launch to the platform. Ascending the stairs was another struggle, but he arrived safely at the top and felt an overwhelming rush of pride when he stepped on that teak deck for the first time.

Upon arrival, the new crew members gathered below deck in the mess hall. Roll call assured the officers that all had transferred safely. Then came the task of assigning each of the seamen to one of 21 divisions, which would determine the seaman's job and living quarters.

Paty was shocked to hear he had three choices. *I get to choose?* He began to think of what he enjoyed doing and how that might fit in with jobs on a ship.

"Paty," the officer said. "What is your first choice?"

"Photographer, sir," Paty answered, thinking of how much he had enjoyed taking pictures from the time he was a child. He had his own camera at home and had become quite adept at capturing images.

"And your second?"

"Printing, sir," Paty said. His high school was equipped with a print shop, and he had attended printing class every day.

"Third?"

He couldn't help having noticed guns of every conceivable shape and size everywhere on the deck, so he answered, "Gunner's mate, sir."

"Very well," the officer answered.

After all the boys had been polled, the officer handed down assignments.

"Paty," the officer said. "You are now a radioman."

Paty knew absolutely nothing about radio transmission. He knew nothing about electricity, and he certainly didn't know Morse code. But he would learn. Paty joined the other three boys assigned to the CR division and followed the officer to the Marine berthing compartment. Radio was on the third deck, partially below the water line, but those living quarters were full, so the new seamen would bunk with the Marines for a while.

Early the following morning, Paty and the others in radio began classes in Morse code. Every day, they went to school in the admiral's quarters and studied until lunchtime. The instructor brought in his sound box and key and tapped out letters for the radiomen to type. The goal for excellence was to copy 50 words per minute, but for proficiency, the radiomen could fall just below that. Failing to copy the minimum of 25 words per minute would be cause for dismissal. At any speed, mistakes spelled doom. One small mistake could destroy the message. The messages did not come in plain language or ordinary words, so the radio gang could not readily tell if they had made a mistake. Each series of taps designated a specific code group of five letters and numbers. Only after it was passed to the officers, including Ensign Herb Weyrauch, in the decoding room would the content of the message be known. If the radiomen made any mistakes, the decoders could not match the code group to anything by which to decode it.

Training also included radio theory, how radio worked, the function of each component of the radio, and what each part was named. Early on, the boys had only minor instruction in radio repair, but as Paty rose in rank, he would learn more and more about the equipment and how to keep it in top working condition. Efficient operation of the ship and readiness for action depended on fast, complete, and accurate communication.

The large group of radiomen—the few who came on with Paty and the others who were already aboard—dwindled quickly under pressure. Some of them simply couldn't catch on to Morse code. During the two months of intensive, repetitive daily training, Paty surprised himself at how quickly he grasped the concept and learned the code. He never quite reached 50 words per minute, but he could consistently and accurately copy at least 40.

The radio gang spent mornings in class and afternoons tending

Radiomen like Chuck Paty listened to messages and typed them in code, to be passed on to officers like Herb Weyrauch for deciphering.
COURTESY OF BATTLESHIP NORTH CAROLINA COLLECTION

to the equipment and other daily duties. The apprentice seamen always drew the jobs that no one else wanted—the ones on which the seamen second class and higher had already paid their dues.

One afternoon after Morse code training, a warrant officer approached the apprentice seamen and said, "I want three or four of you guys to follow me."

Paty followed. Carrying rope and rags and small containers of liquid, they followed the officer up the stairs three levels above the main deck to the signal bridge. Then they began to climb the rungs in the ladder well all the way to sky control at level 010, the highest-numbered level on the ship. As they stood there with the officer, Paty had an ominous feeling about what was coming next. Above them, the fire-control radar antenna squeaked back and forth. At that height, the tropical air whipped around them. And as huge as she was, the *North Carolina* still responded to the rise and fall of the swells, especially when she was moving at significant speed.

"All right, men, you see these two yardarms that stick out over here and over there?" the officer said, pointing in both directions.

Paty didn't see what he was talking about at first, but when he moved to the edge, he saw one, sticking out just at the base of the sky-control platform barrier.

"There are insulators out there that get dirty. All this salt spray from the rough seas gets stuck on them. It could short out the electricity. Use this rope to tie yourself off, take these rags and cleaner,

The radar insulators that Chuck Paty crawled out to clean were located at the end of the yardarm just below and to the right of the bedspring antenna at the very top of the ship. Sailors on the boat deck and the main deck below appeared very small from that height.
COURTESY OF BATTLESHIP NORTH CAROLINA COLLECTION

and go out there and clean those insulators."

Paty looked over the side past the yardarm to what he would hit if he fell. Several levels of the superstructure jutted out here and there, but the main deck was about a hundred feet down. He never had cared much for heights. The yardarm itself was eight to 10 inches wide and flat on the top. It extended at least 20 feet out into space, and the insulators were on the end.

Paty tied one end of the rope to his waist, and the officer secured the other end to the bulkhead. Paty stuffed the rag in one pocket and the small container of cleaner in the other, then pulled his Dixie Cup hat tighter on his head to keep it from blowing off in the whipping wind or falling off as he leaned over to clean the insulators. He lowered himself over the edge and onto his eight-inch balance beam. A small wire supported by stanchions ran the length of the yardarm at about waist height, forming a weak and wobbly handrail. Paty walked out carefully, then slowly eased himself down so he straddled the beam while he cleaned the insulators. He shinnied back carefully when his job was done, scared he would fall if he tried to stand back up.

Not until he had safely returned to the radio room and had his headphones over his ears did his knees begin to shake.

★★★★★★★★★★★★★★★

"Hey, Geo-orge. How's Goergina?" one of the boys asked Conlon, slurring his first name into two syllables.

"She's great," Conlon said, waving the letter in his hand. The boys could tell their buddy was smitten. "She said yes! I've got three days' leave coming up when we get back to New York, and I'm going home to marry her."

Conlon dreaded telling Goergina that he had heard the ship would be leaving for possible battle, not just training like the boys had been doing. The German battleship *Tirpitz* was causing problems in the North Atlantic. Scuttlebutt had it that they were probably going up there with the *Washington* to guard the shipping passages and take on the enemy battleship if necessary. Leaving was inevitable, he knew. The ship had passed all her tests and was ready for battle, and a war was raging.

"You've never seen New York?" one of the radio gang asked Paty.

"No," he answered, but he had been thinking about it for days.

"Man, you're in for culture shock," someone else said as the radio gang talked and laughed about what they had done and seen in New York City.

A few of them actually lived in New York, and they had advice for Paty: "Make sure you're topside when we get there."

Fortunately, Paty was not on watch that day, so he found a perch up on the superstructure as high as he could climb and waited for the sights of New York to appear through the haze. He hardly felt the cold winter wind whipping around him, his excitement so intense that it warmed him from the inside out. When the Statue of Liberty broke through the haze with the Manhattan skyline silhouetted in the background, Paty could hardly breathe. New York City. He was there. For a sheltered 17-year-old from Charlotte, North Carolina, nothing in his history books began to do justice to what he was seeing at that moment. As the ship entered the harbor, 12 tugs snuggled up to guide her into Gravesend Bay, where she would anchor for the night.

Crew members were assigned liberty days according to their location on the ship—port one day, starboard the next. While they were in New York, they would enjoy liberty every other day. Since the ship was still in the testing stage, she was moved to dry dock for inspection and repairs.

The night before Paty was due to go on liberty, he spent hours in preparation for his first excursion. When he approached the officer of the deck for pre-liberty inspection, he wanted to pass. He used his blacking kit to shine his shoes until they glistened. He wanted the officer of the deck to be able to see himself in them. He had always taken pride in well-shined shoes, so this was not new to him, but for this occasion, he spent a little extra time on the shine.

When he had come aboard ship and transferred his uniforms from his sea bag to his locker, Paty had been careful to fold them correctly. The weight of the uniforms on each other naturally pressed them. At boot camp, the boys had been taught to fold their uniforms inside out. The only crease on the legs of the trousers should be down the side of the leg with the valley of the crease showing. To fold his jumper, Paty turned it inside out, held it up so the collar hung down, then laid it flat on his bunk. He folded the outer edges of the collar toward each other so they met in the middle. Then he folded the entire jumper over once lengthwise. He folded the sleeves down across the body, then back over so they fit in the width of the folded shirt. Then, starting with the collar, he made three folds to form a compact pile. Trying to sleep that night before liberty, he hoped his fold job had worked.

New York in January was cold, so the liberty uniform was dress blues, flat hat, and peacoat. The dress blues had white stripes on the collar and the ends of the sleeves. As an apprentice seaman, Paty was still a one-striper. Promotions earned more stripes. Liberty began at 1100 hours and lasted until midnight. That morning, in a flurry of activity and excitement, the radio gang prepared for liberty. They retrieved their dress blues from their lockers, brushed them off, and checked the stripes for dirt.

Paty had not worn his dress blues much, so his stripes were clean. Had they not been, his toothbrush would have doubled as a stripe scrubber. After his shower, he borrowed a mirror on someone else's locker to comb his hair. He didn't have a mirror of his own yet. He pulled on his trousers, buttoned the U-shaped fly, and checked the crease down the legs. It pointed inward. That was good. When he unfolded his jumper, he checked to make sure the collar creases followed regulation. Three sharp creases pointed outward when the collar hung down. That was good. He pulled it on and tied the black silk neckerchief, adjusting the knot so that it hung according to regulation. Taking one last look in the mirror, he placed his flat hat square on his head. He could tilt it later, after inspection. The wide band read, "U.S. Navy." As he prepared to leave his compartment, he took one more glance at his shoes. Not a smudge.

He hurried up one flight of stairs to the main deck, located the exec's office to draw his liberty card, and then took his place for the first time in the liberty line. His heart pounded from the excitement of actually going ashore and from fear of not passing inspection. His peacoat over his arm, Paty stood in front of the officer of the deck and saluted him.

"Permission to go ashore, sir," Paty said.

The OD surveyed him carefully, starting at the flat hat and working his way down. As the officer leaned his head slightly to the side to check the trouser creases, Paty fought to control his shaking knees.

"Turn around."

Paty could almost feel the OD's eyes burning into his back as he checked the collar folds, surveyed the white stripes for any sign of dirt. Paty held his breath.

"Permission granted."

Paty breathed, turned toward the stern of the ship, saluted the flag flying off the fantail, and walked down the gangway. When he passed the Marine guard and stepped onto the dock, he was actually in New York.

The shipyard itself was a fascinating place with its eclectic mix of civilian tradesmen and military personnel. But Paty wanted to see the city. He strolled straight to the huge iron gates and asked one of the guards how to get to Manhattan. The guard gave him directions to the closest subway station, and Paty walked out the gate.

Only one destination on his mind, he hurried down Sand Street with no intention of stopping at any of the tailor shops, restaurants, bars, and what he saw simply as hotels. The women smiled at him, but he just kept walking, intent on the list of things he wanted to do. Paty had not made any close friends to that point—no friends good enough to share liberty with, anyway—and was quite content to take this grand adventure on his own. He hopped the subway for a nickel and headed for Manhattan. He disembarked at 42nd Street. The sidewalks bustled with pedestrians. The marquee lights sparkled even in the sunlight. Broadway shows were free to the military, so he saw his first one that day. But most of the day and into the night, he simply walked the streets of Manhattan, straining his neck as he looked upward, amazed at the height of the buildings, enjoying the attention his uniform commanded from the young ladies he passed.

On subsequent liberties while the ship was in New York, Paty would see more Broadway shows, hear Frank Sinatra sing, and spend one entire liberty seeing how far he could go on the subway for a nickel. He rode all over New York, out to Long Island, and back to the Bronx, never leaving the subway except to change trains. He must have logged over 150 miles that day.

07 March 1942

The ship anchored in Hampton Roads, Virginia, having departed New York and completed yet another successful series of training runs. Deck hands busily replenished the ship's supplies and reloaded ammunition reserves. One of the most difficult jobs in ammunition storage was lowering the 2,700-pound projectiles for the 16-inch guns. They were maneuvered using chains and pulleys. A trunk line for loading powder and ammunition for the 16s extended from the main deck all the way down five levels to the very bottom of the ship, where the powder-handling room was located. It was accessible from several sides through vertical hatches on each lower level. A horizontal hatch on each deck could close off the trunk line from the next level up or down. Those hatches were about three feet by four and the actual trunk line about five by six. A metal ladder welded to the bulkhead ran up the inside of the trunk line; a narrow catwalk ran around the hatch opening. Crew lowered the projectiles using large crab-claw loading tongs at the end of a heavy chain.

Joseph Smits and some of his buddies from the fire gang finished standing the four-to-eight watch. They were sleepy and tired, but mostly they were hungry. They stood watch in the fireroom, far below the main deck, where they practically lived—working there, standing watch there, manning general quarters there. They had quickly learned they could take a shortcut to the mess hall by going up the trunk line for the 16-inch gun turrets. They went that way every morning—when food was involved, the fastest way to get there was the best way.

Standing with his buddies at the vertical hatch that opened into the trunk line, Smits waited his turn. He watched as one, then another boy checked the chute to make sure nothing was coming down, then disappeared several levels up the ladders to breakfast. When it was his turn, Smits not only looked but listened, then reached in, grabbed the rungs, hustled up the ladders, and was sitting down enjoying breakfast in no time at all.

Waiting his turn behind Smits, Tommy Thompson could almost taste all that good hot food. The ship never skimped on breakfast. A good hot cup of coffee and a platter full of food, a shower and a nap, and he'd be a new man. He watched Smits disappear, then stepped through the hatch into the trunk line and onto the narrow walkway that surrounded the opening to the next level down. Climbing from level to level, he always double-checked each time he stepped onto the catwalk to access the next ladder.

Tommy edged his way around to the ladder to the second deck and breakfast, reached for the rungs, and hoisted himself up. He had almost reached the top of the ladder when he heard a loud clanging noise. Horrified, he looked up and saw the loading tongs hurtling toward him, free-falling. They were massive, the handle three feet long with huge metal claws large enough to encircle the massive projectiles. Tommy froze; escape was impossible. The tongs struck him in the head, broke his grip on the ladder, and carried him bouncing against the edges of the hatch openings from the second deck to the third deck to the first platform. He landed on the second platform, his skull crushed from the impact.

Smits was finishing his breakfast when one of the guys he'd left behind walked up to the table without his food.

"Where you been?" Smits asked. "You not eating?"

"Tommy's dead," he answered. "Damn tongs busted his head and knocked him all the way to the bottom."

Smits was dumbstruck.

Having come aboard at commissioning like Smits, Thurman "Tommy" Thompson was a "plank owner," an honorary title bestowed upon enlisted men and officers who were aboard as crew

The 2,700-pound shells for the 16-inch guns were lifted and moved by these heavy metal loading tongs. Tommy Thompson was killed when the tongs broke loose in the trunk line, hitting him in the head and carrying him several decks down.
Courtesy of Battleship *North Carolina* Collection

members on the day of commissioning. He had already attained the rank of water tender first class. Smits and the other guys enjoyed being around him; he was just a nice guy, recently married, they thought. He was the first casualty aboard the USS *North Carolina*. But Smits knew he would not be the last.

CHAPTER FIVE

Changing Oceans

"I noted with satisfaction and pride the splendid spirit shown by all hands in accomplishing the very hard work which was necessary to get the ship ready for sea on time. . . . However, we have many new officers and men on board, and much intensive drill at battle stations will be necessary in order to insure our readiness for action at an early date. The Japs are good fighters. We must be better. Let's go!"

Captain G. H. Fort,
USS North Carolina *commanding officer,*
1 June 1942–5 December 1942

17 March 1942

The War Diary for USS *North Carolina* is started this date in accordance with orders of the Commander in Chief, United States Atlantic Fleet. . . . The ship is at anchor in Casco Bay, Maine, having arrived at that anchorage yesterday morning after an uneventful but foggy passage from Hampton Roads, Va. The day's operations consist of casualty drill on battle stations and ship's work. On information that the *Tirpitz* had gained the high seas, the ship was put under two hours sailing orders and liberty stopped. This order was canceled by the Captain at about 1600.

Walter Ashe wasn't too worried about the German battleship *Tirpitz*. He and his storekeeper buddies—Svenningsen, Stephenson, Sohl, Davis, and Perrin—were ready to go ashore just as soon as liberty was restored. They huddled down in the motor launch as the sea spray stung their faces and soaked their uniforms. With the ship anchored out in Casco Bay, the launch ride was nearly 30 minutes long. Maine was cold in March, but the bay, with nothing to block the winds coming across the water, was almost unbearable. Sometimes when it was really bad, the boys would gather in the shore-patrol waiting room after they arrived on shore just to thaw out and let the ice crystals on their peacoats melt before continuing with liberty.

A short distance outside Portland, Ashe and his buddies found a place called the Lighthouse Café, where they could enjoy drinking and dining and dancing, but mostly drinking. When they had been there a few hours, their tables were covered with glasses and bottles. Ashe sat at the table and watched his shipmates out on the dance floor. He was bored.

"Hey, Stephenson," Ashe said. "You want to see some excitement here tonight?"

"Sure," Stephenson answered.

"You mind if I start it?" Ashe asked.

"No, go ahead," Stephenson replied.

Ashe looked around at the couples on the dance floor swinging to "In the Mood." He glanced over at the girls talking to the sailors sitting at the bar. He stood up. For a few moments, he swayed to the saxophone solo and smiled, contemplating his next move. When the trumpets introduced the softer segments of the song, he swept the table clean with his arm in one continuous motion, sending glasses and bottles flying and breaking across the dance floor. He dashed over to the bar, picked up a tray of silverware, and flung the contents into the air just as the trumpet blared into the grand finale. Forks and knives and spoons rained down on the crowd. Amid the shrieks and screams of the people in the diner, the boys ran out the door and down the street in different directions, trying to avoid being caught by the police.

Running out of the café, Ashe yelled, "Oh, my god, they cut my head!"

He ran down the street, stuck out his thumb, and hitched a ride back toward Portland. The vehicle had not traveled far when a police car pulled up alongside and motioned for the driver to pull over and stop. The officer told Ashe to get out of the car. By that time, the excitement had sobered him up enough to obey.

"Yes, sir," Ashe said. "Is something wrong?"

"Take off your hat," the officer replied.

Ashe did as he was told.

"Let me see your head."

Ashe obeyed the officer and bent his head so the officer could see it. Nothing was wrong with his head.

"I'm sorry," he said to Ashe. "We're looking for a sailor with a cut head."

Ashe arrived back at the ship to find none of his buddies there.

"What happened to the rest of the storekeepers?" the division officer asked Ashe.

"The last time I saw them, we were running," Ashe said. "I don't know what happened to them."

All five of the other storekeepers had been arrested and thrown in jail. They were released the next day when the café owner decided not to press charges.

21 March 1942

Seventeen-year-old Bob Fennelly stood in line at the recruiting station in Baltimore. He had to get away from Govenstown. People probably thought he was just making excuses, but it really did make

Bob Fennelly, 1942
COURTESY OF BOB FENNELLY

a difference when he had diphtheria and missed so much school. He was fine now, but he had just never been able to catch up after that. He hated school, dropping out when he was 16. He was not lazy or dumb. He knew that. He had worked his way up from delivering newspapers on his bike to owning his own corner location, where customers came to him. Just that one move almost quadrupled his newspaper income for the same number of papers. But he felt that he was an embarrassment to his family, and he had to change that. He'd really messed up when he started hanging out with those older boys, and he knew his mother was disappointed in him. He hadn't wanted any part of stealing gasoline for those cars the guys were building. He really hadn't. But they got caught. His dad tried to help him out, got him a job as an electrician. He was doing pretty well at that, but this would be better. He would make them proud of him.

The lines at the recruitment office were fairly long, and each prospective recruit had to pass a standard physical exam. Bob was one of about 30 accepted for boot camp that day. They were told to line up, then step forward when their names were called. The recruiter went down the list, calling name after name. Each guy stepped forward in turn. Bob watched and waited, listening for his name—Robert Fennelly. He would be a sailor. But the roll call stopped with Bob and several other boys still standing in the back line. Bob wondered what was wrong.

"Go home," the recruiter told the ones whose names had not been called. "You'll hear from us in a week to 10 days."

So Bob went back to Govenstown once again. He waited. A week passed and he heard nothing. He worried. But on day 10, the phone rang.

Bob dressed in his new brown tweed suit that he had purchased with his own money. He styled his thick, black, wavy hair and put his comb in his pocket with his toothbrush. He didn't need shaving supplies. His young face was still slick. He shoved a little bit of money he had saved into his pocket. He figured he wouldn't be needing too much of anything. The Navy would provide.

The new recruits loaded onto a train in Baltimore. The trip to Newport took all day. Rhode Island could have been in Europe and Bob wouldn't have known any more about it. Upon arrival at the train station in Newport, the boys transferred to a bus for the trip to the Newport Naval Base. There, they were herded into a large, very cold building. Off came the tweed suit and everything else. For five or six hours, the boys underwent physical tests and endured embarrassing questions as they walked totally nude from one medical checkpoint to another.

"Bend over and spread your cheeks," one medic said.

Bob had never been naked around a bunch of guys before—except for the time he and his buddies went skinny-dipping. But those were his pals, and he was younger and at home and knew them.

"Did you ever sleep with your sister?" another medic asked Bob.

By that time, he was pretty fed up with the humiliating commands and ridiculous questions and wanted to shout back, "No, asshole, did you ever sleep with yours?" But he held his tongue. Maybe it was a test. He was determined to pass.

As each part of his body was checked, the medics placed a mercurochrome mark beside it to indicate success. So by the time the Navy knew that Bob could hear and see and walk and talk, his body was painted up like an Indian ready to go into battle. When the barber finished with him, he looked like he'd lost that battle. The razor scalped all his thick, black, wavy hair in long, quick strokes.

When the total body inspection was over, Bob joined others in the communal shower—a long wall with many showerheads protruding from it. Any modesty he might have had was lost forever. He received his clothes for boot camp—dark blue serge pants with a 13-button front, matching long-sleeve top with a wide squared-off collar, black neckerchief, white socks, skivvies, black shoes and canvas leggings, a wide white belt, and a white Dixie Cup hat. He also received his bed—a canvas hammock that would become a permanent part of a sea bag he would have to learn to roll properly before he could graduate from boot.

In the dormitory, the young recruits strung up their hammocks from post to post on metal hooks. The groups were divided into sections, the boys taking turns standing watch. Not only were those on duty charged with making sure that no unauthorized persons were roaming the grounds, they were also on snore patrol. Absolutely no snoring was allowed, so if a sleeping sailor let one slip, the person on patrol used his nightstick to whack him on the butt or the bottom of his feet to stop him.

Reveille rousted the guys from their hammocks, and a flurry of teeth brushing, face washing, showering, and dressing had them ready for chow in no time at all. The washrooms were in the same building as their dormitories, but the food was across the parade ground, about the length of a football field away. In the chow line, the guys grabbed a tray and presented it forward to whichever cook was serving up the stuff they wanted to eat. A typical breakfast would include beans, chipped beef and gravy, scrambled eggs, coffee, water, milk. When Bob pushed his tray forward, the cook slapped a spoonful onto it. At the beginning of the serving line, a sign said, "Take all you want, but eat all you take."

Muster followed chow. Names were called, uniforms checked. The boys learned to be where they were supposed to be when they were supposed to be there and to be dressed according to regulation. For the first five days, they received a shot in each arm every morning. Then they started drills. Their arms already sore, learning semaphore became a challenge. Handling the rifles was even harder. Bob was a natural at the firing range with his Springfield .22. The instructor asked him if he'd like to stay behind and give instructions, but he declined.

Every day, the recruits marched and marched and marched. One day, they started marching in one direction and never turned. They just kept marching and marching. Newport is on an island, so they eventually arrived at the seashore. Their drill leader never said halt, and the recruits kept marching across the sand dunes and down to the water. He never called halt. Some recruits marched right out into the ocean.

"Halt!" the drill leader yelled. "Relax. I'm going to talk to you like I was your granddaddy. This was an object lesson. When I didn't call halt, you didn't have to go into that water. A time will come during your service when you will be faced with something that is beyond your reach of duty. If you want to risk your life, that is your decision, but yours alone."

In three short weeks, Bob and his classmates became seasoned boots and were ready for their assignments. His family came to Newport for his graduation. Bob greeted his brothers and sisters and father. When he looked down into his mother's face, she smiled.

Bob Fennelly shared with his mother the happy occasion of his graduation from boot camp in Rhode Island. Her smile let him know that she was proud of him.
Courtesy of Bob Fennelly

Winter in Casco Bay had been very difficult for the sailors. Although they had no contact with the German battleship and had not engaged in battle, they rigorously prepared every day for the inevitable. They knew they would play a major role in the war at some point, they just didn't know where or when. They spent their days in the North Atlantic in gunnery practice, trying to maintain their assigned areas of the ship, and taking care of their guns despite the snow and the freezing rain and the storm-tossed ocean. When they were anchored in the bay and had the opportunity to go ashore for liberty, many didn't. The time spent in Portland just wasn't worth the misery of the half-hour ride in the open skiff, sea spray drenching them and ice crystals forming on their coats and hair. Their days froze together as they fought monotony and struggled to perform their duties.

Even into spring—April and the first part of May—the weather remained dreary and cold. Realizing the toll the winter had taken on the morale of his crew members, the captain, with the help of Portland citizens who appreciated the sailors, arranged for a special party at Casco Point. The boys would go in shifts—half at a time—for a clambake on the beach.

Joseph Smits and his friends were excited about the chance to go ashore and taste fresh Maine seafood. When they arrived on the beach, food and drink were abundant. The cooks dug holes in the sand, filled them with fire. They covered the hot coals and clams and oysters with seaweed so the shellfish smoked and steamed open. Large pots sat on open fires boiling lobster and shrimp. The boys had their pick from an abundance of beer and soft drinks. Citizens joined the sailors for the party.

After Smits and his buddies had eaten until they could hold no more and drunk enough beer to toss caution to the wind, one of them had an idea.

"Let's check out some of those vacation houses in the woods."

"We're not supposed to leave the beach."

"Don't be a spoilsport. We won't touch anything. Won't even get close."

"Yeah, we could walk into the woods a little bit so we can see how the rich people live. What harm can there be in that?"

The boys each grabbed another beer and made their way through the crowd, across the sand, and into the woods. They had not even walked 50 feet when they saw clothing hanging from the limbs of the trees and strewn around the sand, as well as busted-up furniture and other household items. The summer home in front of them had been broken into and trashed. The boys did not think to turn and run. Smits picked up a bright blue necktie and pulled it around his neck.

"Hey, I've forgotten how to tie these things," he laughed.

One of his buddies tried to help him, and he couldn't do it either. They had tied their neckerchiefs so many times they couldn't remember how to tie a real necktie.

"Let me try," another one said, and pulled a red necktie from the limb of a nearby tree. "Hell, I can't do it either!"

The boys laughed at each other, oblivious to impending trouble until shore patrol walked up. Then the laughing stopped. As innocent as they were, no amount of denial could convince shore patrol that they were not the culprits who had destroyed the home.

"You should be ashamed after what these people tried to do for you. You're a disgrace to your uniforms."

The officers carted the boys off to the town jail. The *North Carolina* was not the only ship in the harbor, and Smits thought the winter must have taken its toll on a lot of sailors. The jail filled with drunken sailors, some beaten up and bleeding, others just sleeping it off.

The next day when they returned to the ship, the boys faced captain's mast, the ship's abbreviation of trial by judge. The officer in charge was furious and got right in Smits's face, yelling at him and demanding that he admit what he had done. Smits knew he should not have been there, but he had not trashed the house, and no amount of yelling and screaming and threatening was going to make him admit to something he hadn't done.

"Ten hours extra duty in the laundry." Punishment for the crime.

Smits had a friend who worked in the laundry, so every night he took his own clothes down, washed and dried them, then took them over to the steam press and ironed them. For the 10 days of his extra duty, Smits was one of the best-dressed sailors aboard. Even though he hadn't trashed the house, he felt bad that it had happened and especially that he had gotten caught in the middle of it. Those folks had been really nice, and he worried that the incident would change their impression of all the sailors.

17 May 1942

After graduation from boot camp, life continued unchanged for a while at the base. Then one day, Bob Fennelly and his fellow apprentice seamen were called to muster with their sea bags. They started marching, arriving at a stake-body truck with a canvas cover. The seamen climbed into the back of the truck and began the next leg of their journey. They did not know where they were going. The ride took hours—long enough that they stopped for lunch along the way. They arrived and disembarked in Portland, Maine, on a cool, drizzly, foggy spring day. A 60-foot motor launch pulled alongside the dock to pick them up. It had a canvas awning so that when the men were seated, they could not see very well what lay ahead.

Fennelly was immediately interested in the bells and how each sound or combination of sounds had obvious meaning. He watched the coxswain watching the compass and setting his course. When Fennelly felt the boat turn, he stuck his head out from below the awning. Before him, lying in what he later learned was Casco Bay, was the USS *North Carolina*.

My god, that thing is as big as an island! Fennelly thought.

The boat pulled alongside the accommodation ladder of the *North Carolina*, bumping gently against the wooden fender. The seas were calm that day, making the transfer relatively easy. Still, climbing out of the launch and up the ladder was no simple feat with a sea bag over his shoulder. The newest members of the crew were sent down to the mess hall, where they swung their hammocks from hooks overhead. It would be their temporary home until they were assigned to specific divisions.

Fennelly had done some electrical work before joining up. Being an electrician was sort of a family tradition, and he enjoyed it, so when asked what division he would like to be assigned to, he asked for the electrical division.

"That division is full," he was told. "We'll put you in the deck division until an opening in electrical becomes available."

That opening did not occur until two years later, and by that time, Fennelly was settled and happy in Fifth Division.

★★★★★★★★★★★★★★★★

By the end of May, the threat presented in the Atlantic by the German battleship *Tirpitz* had waned, so the *North Carolina* headed south, leaving the *Washington* to guard the waters farther north. The ship arrived in Hampton Roads, Virginia, just in time to begin a new month with a new captain. On the first day of June, Captain George H. Fort relieved the ship's commanding officer, Captain O. C. Badger. With the ship at anchor in the harbor, the crew dressed in whites and stood at attention at quarters. Captain Badger heard the official orders read and descended the accommodation ladder on the starboard side of the ship. He off-loaded into a waiting boat rowed by the department heads. As the boat headed to shore, the massive 16-inch guns, their turrets trained toward starboard, waved up and down to tell the captain goodbye.

The ship made a brief stop in Norfolk, then headed south. The boys had been south earlier for firing practice, but they knew this was different. Their official destination had not been divulged. In his diary, Ashe wrote, "Destination unknown—hoping for West Coast."

The crew had worn their undress blues during the frigid winter days in Casco Bay, but in warmer climates, the uniform of the day changed to undress whites. Then on June 8, as they steamed southward, another change of uniform indicated other changes were imminent. The new uniform of the day became dungarees and blue chambray shirts. The boys were instructed to dye one of their white Dixie Cup hats blue so they would be less visible to planes flying overhead. The next day, the ship entered the Panama Canal Zone for the first time. She was changing oceans.

As the ship entered the locks of the Panama Canal, Charlie Rosell and Joseph Smits were down in the firerooms controlling the steam to the boilers. The ship had less than two feet of clearance on either side, and they could feel a bump and hear a scrape each time the massive battleship hit the canal walls as she passed through. When the ship entered the fresh water of Gatun Lake, the crew used that opportunity to give their lady a bath. Although they scrubbed the decks and cleaned all parts of the ship as a daily routine, they used salt water through their hoses. She had never been in fresh water before. Midday in Panama in June, the heat soared, so for a few moments, the crew once again became the boys that they were, not only spraying the ship with the fresh water streaming from their saltwater hoses but spraying each other as well. Their laughter filled the air.

For security purposes, the numbers on the front of the ship and on her airplanes and the name across her stern had been covered for the passage, but when the boys went ashore, they were greeted with "How are you guys from the *North Carolina* doing?" The ship's notoriety and uniqueness could not be masked with a few drapes of canvas.

When she completed her passage through the canal, the Showboat became a part of America's battered Pacific Fleet. The ship had received orders to proceed to Pearl Harbor, but those orders were changed, and she headed to California to join a different task force. Few of the crew knew there had been any changes at all, but Chuck Paty down in radio and Herb Weyrauch in the code room knew. Paty wondered why.

For the next few days as the task force steamed along, the ships participated in gunnery practice. The guns of the main battery, the huge 16-inch cannons, fired on the *Quincy* using live ammunition but offsetting their sights so that to score a hit, they didn't really shoot the ship. Planes from the *Wasp* sped off her flight deck, flew away from the formation, then headed back in to simulate dive-bombing and torpedo attacks. One of her pilots crashed over the *Wasp*'s bow, and his body was never found. The BB55 Kingfishers were catapulted into the air and practiced dropping depth charges on a spar towed by one of the destroyers. During subsequent dive-bombing and torpedo-bombing routines, another of the *Wasp* pilots crashed, but he was rescued.

When the *North Carolina* entered San Pedro Harbor on June 19, seven old battleships were anchored there. The long column of ships was a sight most of the crew had never seen except perhaps on newsreels. For the young and inexperienced Paty and Weiser and Fennelly, the scene was magnificent.

The ship traveled north to San Francisco, and the boys got their first taste of liberty in a large West Coast city. From June 24 to July 5, 1942, the ship remained in port in San Francisco. The crew was within walking distance of downtown and enjoyed taking in the sights and sounds and smells of a new town. On the Fourth of July, the ship sent two detachments—one of Marines and one of sailors—to march in the Independence Day parade and participate in other celebratory activities.

Before the ship left the West Coast, all her 14 beautiful wooden boats were removed except for one whaleboat on each side that would be used for the captain's gig. The elegant wooden gangways were replaced with steel ones, some wooden furniture was removed, and, as the ship sailed southward, crew stripped the shiny red linoleum from below decks, revealing steel floors. Wood and linoleum were considered too flammable. As the Showboat steamed toward Pearl Harbor, she left a trail of red on the ocean floor—red linoleum. During the six days required for the ship to reach Pearl, the crew also stripped all the oil-based paint from the bulkheads and repainted those interior walls with water-based paint. They were preparing for battle and undoing things that had proven on other ships in other battles to be too dangerous.

07 July 1942

Robert L. "Bob" Palomaris loved baseball. He lived baseball. But he hated the Japanese, and he wanted to kill every last one of them. Bob was 16 years and four months old in the summer of 1942 when he went to the naval recruiting office at the YMCA in his hometown of Pasadena, California, and joined the Navy. His mother signed for him, and he couldn't go to boot camp until he was 17 the following March, but in the meantime, he reported one weekend a month to San Pedro, where the Navy prepared the boys for boot camp. They watched movies about life in the Navy and the dangers of venereal disease. They did calisthenics to get in shape, but Bob thought that was a waste of time for him, since he was already in top athletic form.

Bob finished the 10th grade, then started playing professional baseball, Class C and Class B in the minor leagues. He also formed a semipro team in south Pasadena called the Pasadena Pirates, but the boys disbanded in 1942 and went to work, Bob as a riveter on the Vultee Vengeance wing sections at the Vultee plant near Long Beach, California.

11 July 1942

Being in the deck division, Fennelly worked topside long before the crew was called to quarters. Six days had passed since they last saw land. In the distance, he noticed a dark spot on the horizon. Gradually, Diamondhead increased in size, appearing black and sharp, rising majestically out of the ocean. The ship rounded the southern end of Oahu, and Fennelly studied the landscape, the rolling green hills of the island a stark contrast to the bluest water he had ever seen. The beauty was overwhelming for the teenager who, until he joined the Navy, had never left Maryland. The ship slowed, maneuvered closer to the island, and entered the channel, passing torpedo nets guarding the mouth of the harbor, opened so the Showboat and her two destroyer escorts could enter.

Paty found a spot to stand on the starboard side of the ship. He knew he would have to move to the port side when the crew was called to quarters, but for the time being, he was enjoying the sights with nothing between him and the island but water. He marveled at the size of Diamondhead, saw Hickam Field and the naval hospital come into view. Like so many of the crew, Paty saw each place visited as an adventure, but the excitement of going to Pearl Harbor was overshadowed by the anticipation of what he would see there. Seven months had passed since the Japanese attack, and he did not know what to expect.

Men standing watch in the signal tower on the island, catching the first glimpse of the Showboat as she approached, used their lights to flash the news, which traveled by semaphore flags flapping and crew members shouting. A flurry of anticipation spread throughout the harbor.

Stationed aboard one of four fleet tugs assigned to escort approaching ships into the harbor, Kenneth Dews and the 16 other members of the tug crew were awestruck when the *North Carolina* appeared. Dews reveled in her width, her length, her heavy armament as she steamed slowly and smoothly toward him. The sun glistened off her gray hull, shiny and sleek. He could see her crew members in their stark white uniforms, such a contrast to the dark and dingy denim smudged with oil and grime worn by the sailors in port, who were working day in and day out to clean up the harbor and repair the damaged ships. No matter how clean they started out each day, the very nature of their task quickly dirtied their clothes and hands, but even worse, the months of struggle left smudges of grief and despair on their hearts, minds, and souls. To Dews, the arrival of the *North Carolina* brought a ray of hope to the war-weary sailors at Pearl.

When quarters sounded aboard the BB55, crew members lined the rails and stood at their assigned positions, creating a great white wall on the main deck and the ascending levels of the superstructure. The ship proceeded past the south end of Ford Island, which sat in the middle of the harbor. Even from his vantage point on the port side, Paty could see the airplane hangars and the landing strip on the island, dark smudges where fire had scorched the ground.

On board the heavy cruiser *Pensacola*, moored inside the harbor beside two other rusty old cruisers, Ben Blee heard word pass down from the signal bridge that something amazing was standing in the channel. Anxious for anything uplifting, the *Pensacola*'s crew excitedly scrambled topside to see what was happening. Blee climbed up high to the signal bridge in an effort to get the best possible view. By that time, the BB55 was on the west side of Ford Island, and even from his vantage point, all Blee could see above the palm trees and airplane hangars on the 450-acre island was an immense tower foremast gliding slowly up the other side of the island. As word spread from ship to ship in the harbor, crew scurried about, scaled masts, climbed on top of turrets and gun mounts, finding whatever vantage points they could to get a glimpse of what was causing all the ruckus.

For the boys of the BB55, the first true realization of the havoc wreaked by the Japanese was the capsized wreckage of the torpedo-stricken battleship *Utah*, her hull gouged open and jagged, blasted apart by explosions. Fennelly stared and wondered about the sailors who had been aboard. The remnants of the hull were riddled with bullet holes where Japanese pilots had swooped in low, strafing sailors struggling to survive.

On Ford Island, workers streamed from inside the machine shops and airplane hangars to view the Showboat as she passed. When the ship met others in the harbor, they exchanged salutes. Each ship lowered, then raised its flags. Upon command, the crew saluted: "Right hand, salute, two"—the word *two* being the exact moment that each sailor raised his hand. A brief bugle blare meant the salute was over. Salutes were repeated over and over as the ship steamed slowly down the west side of Ford Island. Bands aboard the ships honored the *North Carolina* with the strains of "Anchors Aweigh."

Wow, Paty thought. *This kind of welcome never happened in New York or Virginia or even San Francisco.*

But the greatest honor for the crew was the reception they received as they reached the ravaged part of the harbor. When the ship rounded the north end of Ford Island, Blee thought she was the most beautiful thing he had ever seen in his entire life. The *North Carolina*, her flags snapping in the wind, gleamed with new paint and powerful armament and a well-trained complement of fresh young sailors. Blee and the others in the harbor saw beauty and promise and hope. They were thrilled and inspired and uplifted, felt a new surge of determination and possibility.

The *North Carolina* came into full view, and the low drone of excitement erupted into cheers and celebration; all work in the harbor ceased, people streaming out of the naval hospital and shops.

"Aren't you glad she's on our side?" Blee heard someone say.

From the decks of the *North Carolina*, the boys saw the carnage that infamous day in December had caused. They thought back to the outpouring of patriotism they had enjoyed after the president declared war, how they could go into New York City and eat and drink and party with little or no money at all. They heard the cheers of the men who had survived the horror, the explosions, the fires; the men who had watched their buddies blown overboard, had felt their ships sinking, had dodged bullets. The Showboat passed the wreckage of the *Arizona,* sunk upright with only the top part of her superstructure visible, and the *Oklahoma,* mutilated and capsized. Sailors stood cheering and waving. The boys wondered why—why did they deserve such a rousing welcome, why all this gratitude? They had not yet fired a single shot in battle.

The ship moored in Berth 12, and work in the harbor proceeded with a new and invigorated purpose. Immediately, the *North Carolina* deck crews began taking on stores of ammunition and supplies. The boys would be leaving soon and did not know where they were going or when they would return.

Paul Wieser watched as the crane operator lifted the whaleboat, swung it out over the side of the ship, and lowered it into the water. No words were spoken; just the various sounds from the

Sailors aboard the Showboat began to realize the extent of devastation the Japanese had wreaked upon Pearl Harbor when they passed mutilated ships like this one in July 1942, seven months after the infamous attack.
COURTESY OF BATTLESHIP *NORTH CAROLINA* COLLECTION

boatswain's pipe could be heard. When the coxswain needed to take damage control around the ship to measure how she was sitting in the water, Wieser went along. Every day, he studied the actions of the men ranked higher than he, preparing himself for promotions as they came available. He walked across the boat boom, climbed down the hanging ladder and into the launch. He was within touching distance of the debris still floating in the water. The little skiff plowed through the thick oil and floating trash as it slowly skimmed along.

The wreckage of the *Arizona* was sunk so deeply into the harbor that the level of the captain's cabin on the superstructure was even with the water line. A United States flag flew defiantly from the mast. The skiff rounded the bow and slipped around the side, the wake rippling the water and moving one of the *Arizona*'s porthole covers slowly back and forth, creaking as it swung. Wieser shuddered. Bumps ran along his arms, and the hair on the nape of his neck rose. Inside the wreckage, he knew, lay the body of his teenage idol.

Back in New Jersey, when Paul was in his early teens, his gang, The Batch, hung out on the streets about a block from the Polish National Hall wearing their signature black jackets with gold sleeves. They didn't get any closer to the hall because they were afraid the adults would run them off. Besides, one member of the gang lived a block away. When the boys weren't busy hanging out on the street in front of his house or going down to the candy store, they liked climbing up the support beams of the billboard behind his house and jumping off.

The Polish National Hall had a bar, offered regularly held dances, and was a center for activity in the town. Paul and his buddies watched the people going and coming, including Henry Schroeder. Henry looked nine feet tall to young Paul, but he probably measured in just above six. He would strut down the street in front of The Batch wearing his dress blues and would usually acknowledge the boys with a nod or a smile; sometimes, he would speak. Most everyone in the neighborhood recognized Henry and knew he was assigned to the *Arizona*. They later learned he was buried with her.

As the small boat rounded the massive wreckage, Wieser wondered what the future held for him.

12 July 1942

When liberties began, Paty was ready to go. He and a couple of his buddies in the radio gang wanted to see Waikiki Beach and would do whatever was necessary to get there.

The first interesting sight they saw when leaving the shipyard was a large pink hotel, the Royal Hawaiian. They were not allowed inside, however, as it was reserved for officers. They caught a cab to the beach but were disappointed by the sight of barbed wire strung up and down the shoreline. People on the island could still get to the water but must have considered it too much bother. Paty saw few people sunbathing or swimming. The lack of bathing beauties disappointed him.

At the Waikiki Hotel, which was reserved for the submarine crews, the boys were allowed to sit on stools at an outside bar and enjoy their first taste of tropical booze. Paty never drank much, but of course it didn't take much, considering his size and experience.

"Hey, let's take some pictures," one of the boys suggested.

None of them had a camera. They soon discovered, however, that the island catered to men in the military and that things could be rented. The boys rented a camera and some bicycles and biked around the island taking pictures and enjoying the sights. Everywhere they went, they saw men in uniform—Navy, Army, and Marines. Paty saw the Waikiki Theatre and promised himself that he would take in a movie on his next liberty.

Back inside the Navy yard, he walked down to the dry dock and saw the *West Virginia* being repaired. She had been hit by no fewer than seven torpedoes, and Paty tried to imagine what it must have been like to be on board, down in the radio room, when those torpedoes hit.

The BB55 left her berth and started out of the harbor. Ashe took his diary from the drawer in his storeroom desk and began to write: "0830 steamed out of Pearl Harbor where not many months before the Japs had literally rained bombs on the practically helpless battleships. The main mast of the USS *Arizona* still protruded high above the water, flying their colors defiantly to that nation who had struck that savage blow on Dec. 7. A voice seemed to drift across the waves from the bodies of the many men that gave their lives on her burning decks saying 'With you go our hopes for a victory—give the enemy the same defeat that we suffered here. But don't stop till every flag of the rising sun has dipped her colors beneath the blue waters of the Pacific.' "

During the months since the attack on Pearl Harbor, the Japanese had taken the Philippine Islands, the Solomon Islands, New Guinea, New Britain, Singapore, and other smaller islands in the Pacific, working their way across the ocean closer and closer to the United States territory of Hawaii. Japanese subs had even shelled an oil refinery off the coast of California. But their aggression was soon to be halted, as the United States prepared to go on a major offensive.

On her way to the action somewhere in the South Pacific, the Showboat was assigned to Task Force 16, a group of ships that included one battleship, the *North Carolina*; one aircraft carrier, the *Enterprise*; and a group of nine cruisers and destroyers. One of the lessons learned from the attack on Pearl Harbor and the battles in the Coral Sea and at Midway was the change in the part battleships would play in the war. Battleships were designed and built to slug it out with other battleships on the open seas. That was the main purpose of the 16-inch guns. But the Battle of the Coral Sea in May 1942 was the first in modern naval history in which battleships did not fire on each other. The Japanese had changed the direction of the war, using planes for air attacks as their most effective weapon. So aircraft carriers became the first line of attack and defense for the United States Navy, and they needed to be protected. The battleship *North Carolina* became a guardian angel for the carrier *Enterprise*.

En route, Task Force 16 joined up with four other task forces, creating a powerful mass of ships heading for direct contact with the Japanese. Fennelly mounted the superstructure, and in every direction as far as he could see were American ships. He knew they were going into battle, but he didn't know where. He didn't know what would happen but was confident the boys knew their jobs. They had fired those guns at nothing more than sleds pulled behind destroyers and targets towed through the air by their own planes, but the gun crews had trained relentlessly for months, and Fennelly was sure that if someone went out a mile and threw up a grapefruit, they could shoot it down.

But he did worry about the .50 caliber machine-gun operators, especially the ones assigned to the gun between five-inch mount three, where he worked, and mount seven, where Wieser fought. The gun was centered between the mounts with only a few feet of clearance on either side. The fives were powerful guns, and the noise emanating from them when they fired was a shrill, high-pitched, thunderous, repetitive clacking. Not even the louder, deeper boom of the 16s affected human ears the way the fives did. And those guys were expected to man a gun and fire at the enemy while being sandwiched between the mounts, rounds going off from all four guns every four seconds. Fennelly did not know how they would survive.

CHAPTER SIX

Baptism by Fire

"We became men. The maturity of our seamen and our officers after that, the change in maturity and attitude and the way we approached problems, was entirely different. We had grown up in seven minutes."

Rear Admiral Julian T. Burke,
former BB55 officer

Immediately following the attack on Pearl Harbor, the Japanese invaded and took control of island after island across the Pacific until nothing except ocean was left between Japanese-held territories and the United States territory of Hawaii. The dominance continued for months. Not until the summer of 1942 did American troops begin to slow the advance by successfully defending against Japanese attacks during the Battle of Midway. The tiny United States base at Midway Atoll, just northwest of the Hawaiian Islands, was strategically important for the future of the war, both as a line of defense for the West Coast of the United States and as an offensive base for American forces. Although damaged by the Japanese attack, the base remained operational and became a vital part of subsequent American attacks.

By August, with the *North Carolina* as part of the fleet, the Americans were ready for an all-out offensive, beginning more than 3,000 miles from Hawaii at Tulagi and Guadalcanal in the Solomon Islands. The capture of those islands was vital in the effort to keep shipping lanes open from Australia to the United States. But the Japanese Navy remained a superior power in the Pacific, and victory for the American and Allied forces would not come without great loss of life.

24 July 1942

The *North Carolina* anchored briefly in the bay at the island of Tongatabu to refuel. No liberties were granted, but Walter Ashe had been there before and knew he wasn't missing much—very few women and little to drink. Chuck Paty, however, had not seen the island and was interested. By that time, being in radio, he had made friends with the sailors on the signal bridge. They had to learn Morse code, too, but they had a much grander view than the guys down in radio. Heck, radio had no view at all; it was partially below the water line. Up on the signal bridge, powerful glasses were part of the standard equipment, so Paty went up to take a look. He was a little disappointed at what he saw. The natives were dressed in normal clothes; they didn't look like the natives he had pictured. But they were beautiful people, Paty thought, with light golden brown skin. A few of their houses were grass huts on stilts, but many of them were just plain wooden structures sitting flat on the ground. Missionaries had settled the island over a hundred years earlier, so more development and modern ways of living prevailed than Paty expected.

When the ship steamed away, Ashe followed the daily progression toward impending battle in his diary.

25 July 1942

This afternoon we combined our forces with other U.S. and British task forces—as far as the eye can see is ships—the deadly aircraft carriers—their decks nested with the formidable torpedo bombers and swift fighter planes, low sleek cruisers and fast maneuverable destroyers are seen everywhere—some just barely visible on the distant horizon. Troop ships plowing steadily through the rolling seas—the count all told is set at 120. A mighty fleet of ships such as few of us has ever seen massed together before—this is no drill, no summer cruise or maneuvers, this is the long awaited Allied Naval offensive, when the American eagle shall swoop down and bestow a deadly vengeance against her treacherous foe.

26 July 1942

It's hard to realize that we are sailing towards an eventual battle, to kill or be killed. Everyone seems so calm and unconcerned that the actual reality does not come to the surface. There is a war correspondent from *Colliers Magazine* aboard ship, a Mr. Frank Morris. He seems interested in my drawings. He offered to write a letter to *Colliers Magazine* for me enclosing one of my cartoons. It would be the surprise of my life if they were accepted.

03 August 1942

Today we passed the island of New Caledonia—distance and time is shortening. We have jokingly made plans for after the battle—a golden dragon ring will exchange hands if the present owner doesn't come through—there's a little friendly discussion on who will get my new suit of tailor made blues. There's watches, billfolds, scrapbooks, etc. that have been willed. It is all symbolic of the general unconcern and courage that prevails amongst the crew.

05 August 1942

The ship is being cleared for "action"—down below the armored deck go the supply department records, typewriters and important files. . . . All hands were requested to bathe and put on clean clothes tonight, a precaution against infection if injured.

08 August 1942

Just eight months to the day after the Japs bombed Pearl Harbor we launched our first offensive against the Japanese. The planes from our carriers could be seen passing over this ship heading for the dawn attack on the airfield on Guadalcanal Island.

The sailors of the *North Carolina* trained day in and day out, going to general quarters at dawn and dusk, standing watch four hours on and four hours off. They knew the war was raging, but they often felt like spectators on their Showboat. They were playing a vital role in the Solomon Islands as part of the task forces making raids on Guadalcanal. They were there when the Marines invaded Tulagi on August 7, 8, and 9, meeting little resistance. They watched the planes come and go from the carriers, knew the pilots were engaging in battle, shooting down the enemy. But the only guns fired by the sailors of the *North Carolina* to that point were in practice, trained on targets pulled by their own aircraft or towed by accompanying destroyers. The sailors did not have a death wish, but they wanted to do their part. They were trained; they were on the newest, biggest, fastest battleship America had ever built; they were ready.

After all the entries he had written in his diary about impending battle, Ashe was frustrated. At his desk in the storeroom, he used the artistic talents that had promised him a job with Walt Disney to express the feelings he shared with many of his shipmates. With his pen, he drew an arched streamer across the top of his sketch pad, writing inside, "Excursion trip to the Solomon Islands." Beneath the lifelines he drew around the deck, he wrote the ship's nickname—Showboat. He sketched a sailor on the deck of the Showboat with a bullhorn making this announcement: "We are now passing the island of Tulagi. In the distance the Marines are landing, our bombers are attacking the Japs, etc. etc. Souvenir post cards of the battle will be passed out before our return to the states." He finished the scene by hanging a sign on the 16-inch guns saying, "For target practice only." On top of the turret, a sailor lying back wearing headphones looks up at several gulls and says, "Sky control! Unidentified birds overhead!" Ashe's cartoon included a sailor

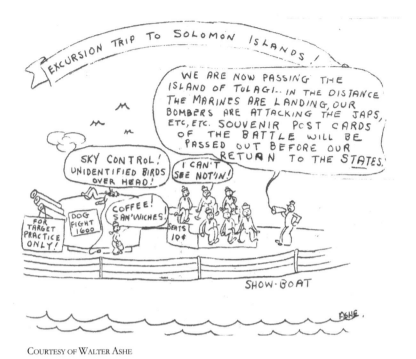

COURTESY OF WALTER ASHE

with bucket in hand calling out "Coffee, san'wiches" to the sailors sitting on bleachers, one of whom says, "I can't see not'in!" The cartoon appeared Wednesday, August 12, 1942, in the *North Carolina Radio Press News*, published by the supply office.

For the next couple of weeks, the *North Carolina* took on fuel and supplies and passed them on to other ships. Fueling was a dangerous and tedious job. The *North Carolina* not only received fuel from tanker ships, she also delivered fuel to destroyers, sometimes simultaneously. To take on fuel at sea, the BB55 slowed to about eight to 12 knots and the tanker pulled alongside starboard. The Fifth Division deck crew, which included Bob Fennelly and Paul Wieser, manned the fuel lines on the starboard side, attaching the ships to each other with a series of lines and hoses. Wieser operated the crane from the superstructure, while Fennelly operated the after-winch on deck. Maintaining the same speed and constant, accurate distance was crucial to success—too close and the ships would bump into each other, too far apart and the hoses would rupture, sending fuel oil flying.

The night gave way to a brilliant blue sky, sunshine, and unlimited visibility. The sea was moderate with scattered cumulus clouds towering overhead. The *North Carolina* continued operating as part of Task Force 16, serving along with six destroyers and a couple of cruisers as protection for the aircraft carrier *Enterprise*. They traveled at a relatively slow speed of 12 knots. Throughout the morning, Task Force 16 communicated with Task Force 61, led by the carrier *Saratoga*, as they launched and recovered airplanes, making contact with the enemy.

At 0934, radio contact reported one enemy destroyer and two small launches sighted northeast of Gizo Island in the western province of the Solomon Islands. At 1005, another plane reported four more enemy ships. A few minutes later, a search plane bombed an enemy submarine, but it submerged without apparent damage. The fleet increased its speed to 15 knots. Another enemy cruiser was spotted at 1020.

Paty listened as the radio crackled.

"Enemy cruiser Lat 8 Long 158030 course 210."

"Two CL's! DD Lat 5-57 Long 158-55."

"Have striking group ready as soon as possible. Report when ready."

One minute after an enemy plane was shot down near the formation, a pilot made radio contact.

"Attacked by aircraft fighting plane type Zero. I am returning to base. Time of arrival unknown. No casualties."

Communication continued at intervals of every minute or two. Just after noon, Task Force 16 reported its fighter attack group ready.

Radio contact from plane: "Attacked by three cruiser seaplanes. Returning to base. One pilot injured badly."

Communication continued. Paty took messages as rapidly as he could. At 1259, Task Force 16 turned into the wind to launch planes. The *North Carolina* moved in unison with the *Enterprise*, turning when she turned, zigzagging as she did, maneuvers to make the ships less likely to be struck by torpedoes underwater or by planes above.

In anticipation of possible action, officers on board the *North Carolina* had the midday meal served earlier than usual. This precipitated a flurry of anticipation among the crew, but things aboard the Showboat continued as usual. After lunch, Ashe stretched out on top of turret three for his daily sunbathing. From his vantage point, he heard an explosion and viewed a pillar of smoke rise into the sky on the horizon. Spectators again.

An enemy task force was spotted 250 miles from Task Force 16. Within minutes, fighters shot down an enemy plane 18,000 yards off the starboard beam of the *North Carolina*. General quarters sounded, followed by the ear-piercing shrill of the boatswain's pipe and the loudspeaker order, "Man your battle stations."

Ashe scurried from atop turret three and headed for his battle station in the clipping room for the 20-millimeter guns on the starboard side of the main deck. The Marine detachment headed for the 20s on the bow of the ship. As the ship picked up speed, waves crested the bow, sending sheets of water down the deck, soaking the gunners and making footholds precarious.

Wieser didn't have far to go to get to his battle station inside mount seven and was there in seconds. He climbed up into the mount and took his position over the chute where the powder kegs would appear. As usual, nothing happened immediately, so the boys began to relax. Several of them even stretched out on the floor for a nap. They had done this so many times now that it had become routine—didn't mean anything, really, never had.

In their respective engine rooms, Joseph Smits and Charlie Rosell concentrated on keeping the engines running smoothly, increasing steam to speed the ship up as the *North Carolina* kept pace with the faster carriers and destroyers. Deep within the ship, the only contact they had with what was going on outside came from the boilermaker, whose battle station was on the superstructure watching smoke. If one of the stacks started smoking, Stubblefield would report down to Rosell's engine room to let the men know what color the smoke was so adjustments could be made. He would give the boys in the engine room a play-by-play of the action if it ever took place.

Paty's battle station was in the base of sky three on the starboard side of the ship. He shared an eight-foot-square compartment with a huge transmitter that occupied at least a third of the enclosure and a ladder taking up much of the remaining room. Wiring cables connected his transmitter to the actual scopes of the radar, located in the five-inch gun director 50 feet above him. Paty's job was to keep an eye on the voltage and amperage gauges for the radar.

As the hours passed and the temperature inside the compartment climbed to a hundred degrees or higher, Paty struggled to stay awake and focus on the instruments in front of him. Each time he began to doze, nightmares of being shot at dawn for failing to stay awake at general quarters startled him back to consciousness. After two hours of monotony, Paty heard the unmistakable motion of the five-inch gun mounts just outside his compartment. The noises indicated that the guns were tracking something. Paty called up to sky three high on the superstructure, where lookouts with glasses could see everything.

"What's going on?" he asked.

"Shut up! Keep this line open" was the only response he received.

For two more hours, his anxiety rose, the sweat fell, and he struggled to keep his eyes open and concentrate on the gauges in front of him.

George Conlon, Lester Tucker, and the others in aviation faced a very different four hours from the boys below deck or closed up inside gun mounts or directors. Topside, the deck became very slippery from the overwash. Conlon was the loader for E. L. Henson on the 20-millimeter near the Kingfisher catapult on the fantail of the ship. Tucker, his loader Coates, and his trunnion operator Stone were manning the 20-millimeter just 10 feet forward. When the waves splashed over the side, Tucker advised his gun crew to duck behind the gun shield. They spent the first four hours at general quarters dodging water instead of bullets.

During those long, hot hours of tense waiting for the boys aboard the BB55, the pilots of the *Enterprise* planes were shooting down enemy craft and continually reporting an enemy task force moving toward their home base.

At 1701, the call came once again to prepare to repel air attack. A minute later came this: "Bogies appear to be attempting torpedo attack. This may be both a bombing and torpedo attack—stand by."

After months of waiting, training, and anticipation, the boys of the BB55 were facing their first air attack. The reality sank in; adrenaline pumped through their veins; their hearts pounded in their chests. But the training took over. At 1712, the first group of 15 dive bombers began its attack on the *Enterprise;* the five-inch mounts on the port side of the *North Carolina* opened fire. The *Enterprise* began radical course changes; the *North Carolina* followed.

Down in the engine room, the air temperature approached 120 to 130 degrees. Although Rosell could not see what was going on outside, he realized something big was happening when orders came to continually increase speed until the ship was running at her maximum of 27 knots. As the ship zigzagged to follow the *Enterprise*'s diversionary tactics, the metal monster creaked and groaned. Rosell called Stubblefield on the phone.

"Hey, Stubby, what in the hell is going on?"

"I don't know; I'm inside the conning tower," Stubby answered.

"Well, get out there and tell us what's coming in!" Rosell said.

"Who the hell is going out there? You crazy? A guy could get hurt out there. I'm watching smoke. I can do that from the inside."

Within the first minute of the attack on the *Enterprise,* the *North Carolina* became a target herself, 10 dive bombers swooping in toward the starboard bow.

Inside five-inch mount seven, the mount captain commanded, "Stand by."

The boys jumped to their feet and positioned themselves next to the guns. Enclosed in the mount, the sailors could see nothing but each other. Wieser fixed his eyes on the mount captain's face. His chest tightened when he saw the officer's expressions change. He saw the red light above the guns light up. His heart slammed against his ribcage. Wieser thought about his mother back home, the person he always relied on for advice. She couldn't help him now.

"Commence firing!"

When a bomb exploded aboard the deck of the aircraft carrier Enterprise *during the Battle of the Eastern Solomons on August 24, 1942, the blast killed the photographer who took this picture. The battle was the* North Carolina*'s introduction to combat.*
COURTESY OF BATTLESHIP NORTH CAROLINA COLLECTION

Wieser reached for the powder keg that came up through the opening at his feet, just like he had done scores of times during drill without one misstep.

Do I really want to kill somebody? he asked himself.

The keg slipped from his hands and clanged against the steel deck.

If you don't kill him, he'll try to kill you, he reasoned, grappling for the explosive can of gunpowder rolling around on the floor, the brass charge exposed and vulnerable. Time seemed to stop. Wieser argued back and forth with himself while trying to grasp the powder can. He finally lifted it and placed it into the tray. The loader set the projectile, and the gun fired. For the first time, Wieser watched the gun recoil without flinching or squinting his eyes closed like he had done throughout training.

A spiraling rainbow split the sky—enemy planes bursting out of the cover of high clouds, streaking through the glare of the afternoon sun. Their dark fuselages were decorated with stripes of varying shapes and colors. The torpedo bombers, their loads hanging beneath their bellies, had white or yellow stripes running the full length of their long, sleek fuselages. Their canopies were long and low, window-pane glass. The hatches of the thicker dive bombers blended into their fuselages. Red rings encircled the tails, and the wings, spitting machine-gun fire, were tipped in red. Wheels on the planes were bright yellow.

The attackers came in closer, and the five-inch gunfire was joined by the automatics, the barrage of fire rattling the ship. Inside his battle station, Paty watched his gauges jumping erratically. He frantically twisted and turned knobs, struggling desperately to keep the voltage and amperage of the radar transmitter at proper levels.

The antiaircraft 20s had a range of only about 2,000 yards. The aviation boys knew that when enemy planes were within striking distance of the guns they manned, accuracy was a must. They would have no second chances.

Tucker strapped himself into his gun, the U-shaped brace wrapping around each shoulder, and his loader began feeding in the magazines. Each barrel-shaped drum carried 60 rounds of ammunition, each projectile designed to explode upon contact. The loader worked at a rate of one 63-pound drum every seven and a half seconds. Four hundred and fifty rounds per minute from each of the 20s burst into the sky toward the advancing enemy. About every fourth round was a tracer, so Tucker watched the explosions to train his gun toward his targets, remembering the gunners' directive—"Lead, damn it, lead!"

Three bombs dropped by the first group of enemy planes barely missed the *North Carolina*, one about 75 yards out, the next at 50 feet, and the third on the port side so close to the ship that it flooded the main deck in that vicinity and knocked one case ejector chute off five-inch mount 10.

As another wave of enemy aircraft washed over the *North Carolina*, four bombs splashed nearby, one so close it knocked the automatic-weapon gunners down and flooded the deck with about a foot and a half of water.

A third group of bombers dipped out of the clouds preparing

to make a horizontal run across the BB55. Six to eight heavy bombs crashed into the seas between the Showboat and the *Enterprise*.

The *North Carolina* was simultaneously attacked on all sides from every angle. Nearly all her antiaircraft guns were in action at the same time—20 five-inch guns, 16 one-point-ones, 40 twenty-millimeters, and 26 machine guns, for a total of 102 guns firing a barrage of explosives that sent fire and smoke streaking through the air. At the height of the encounter, the *Enterprise* radioed.

"*Carolina*, are you afire?"

During the heat of battle, the sounds of the planes and gunfire were deafening, and talking was next to impossible, so Tucker, realizing he was down to about 20 rounds, kicked his mesmerized loader, Coates, in the rear to get his attention. When Coates turned and bent over to pick up another drum full of ammunition, Tucker and his trunnion operator opened fire on a Nakajima. The gunners fixed their sights on the enemy, one pilot flying in so low they could see his face. He had pushed the arched window-pane canopy back on his plane and was face to face with the Americans. He rounded the stern, turned in toward the starboard side of the ship, pulled the trigger, and sent a stream of machine-gun fire across the deck of the *North Carolina*. Bullets split the air around Tucker and his loader, one whizzing over Coates's back just as he leaned below the height of the shield to pick up the drum of ammunition. One knocked the snaps off the cartridge-bag container, slinging the top open, while another ricocheted around in the empty cartridge bin, sending cartridges falling around Tucker's feet and ankles.

The *North Carolina* gunners made contact, and the enemy spiraled into the ocean.

Conlon felt a hot rush pierce his belly as he fell backward to the deck. He thought of beautiful Goergina. They had so many plans. He thought about his mother. He knew she was worried about him, still her baby boy. Who would tell the women he loved? Who would take care of them? He felt himself being lifted and became weightless.

During a brief respite from the onslaught, Tucker glanced back toward the aviation-shop hatch. He saw his friend Conlon lying there. He could tell he was unconscious, could see the hole in his abdomen, but was surprised at the lack of blood.

Pharmacist's Mate John Egan rushed to the aid of Conlon but found nothing he could do for the young man. The bullet had ripped open his abdomen near his spleen. Egan stuffed part of a battle dressing into the wound and headed back to his station to take cover. But on the way back, he saw ammunition carriers plastered against the overhang of turret number three, perhaps frozen from fear, so he grabbed the ammunition and carried it back to the guns where Conlon had been hit. He made three trips back and forth before the battle ended.

Inside mount seven, Wieser heard the command, "Cease fire."

A battle that seemed to last for hours was over in nine minutes. When the smoke cleared, the boys of the BB55 had expended 841 five-inch, 1,067 one-point-one, 7,425 twenty-millimeter, and 8,641

The Showboat's deck was covered with expended shell casings following the brief battle that claimed the life of a crew member during the ship's baptism by fire in the Solomon Islands on August 24, 1942. Crew spent the next few hours cleaning up the aftermath. This sailor stacked five-inch shell casings.

George Conlon, 1942

fifty-caliber rounds. As the gunners climbed out of the turrets and mounts, piles of empty shell casings littering the soaked deck told the story of the battle they had not seen. Paint peeled from the ends of the five-inch gun barrels, blistered and melted by the intense heat of rapid fire.

Fennelly opened the hatch to mount three and looked out. His ears were ringing from the constant crack of the five-inch guns. Leaning back against the bulkhead behind mounts three and seven, two gunners from the .50 caliber machine guns stood in shock. Blood ran from their ears and noses.

"Call a medic!" Fennelly yelled back to his mount captain, who was inside with the headphones. Fennelly remembered how often he had worried how anybody could man those guns placed on the main deck between two five-inch mounts. At least the gunners had survived.

When the five-hour general quarters ended, the aviation boys returned to their workshop. They wondered and talked about Conlon, not yet knowing his fate. They recalled how excited he was that Goergina had transferred with the phone company and would be in San Francisco when the ship went back to the West

Coast. They hoped he would recover and could get back there to see her. But their worst fears were realized when the call came for quarters on the main deck at 2130 for Conlon's funeral.

The boys didn't know what to expect—it was the first time they had lost a shipmate in battle at sea. Six of the aviation boys were selected to carry the body. The pharmacist's mates had completed their task, preparing Conlon's body for burial, sewing it up inside a canvas bag with two projectiles from the five-inch guns so it would quickly sink to the bottom. Nothing was visible to Conlon's shipmates except the shape of his body underneath an American flag as he lay on the stretcher board.

The boatswain's pipe shrilled, and over the loudspeaker came the call, "All hands bury the dead."

Conlon's fellow aviation boys lifted the stretcher board and led the procession on the main deck just aft of mount seven. The funeral procession included Chaplain Francis Lee Albert, a bugler, a firing platoon of Marines, and a small entourage of the ship's band.

The band played softly as the procession advanced, then stopped at a section where the lifelines of the ship had been lowered. Sailors not on watch came from all divisions of the ship, climbing on the turrets and on top of the five-inch gun mounts, lining the rails of the upper decks, absorbing the realization of what had happened that day.

Standing near the body of the young Catholic boy, the chaplain faced the living and spoke words meant to assuage their grief.

"Out of the depths have I cried unto thee, O Lord: Lord, hear my voice. Let thine ears be attentive to the voice of my supplications. . . . Let our hearts . . . be deeply moved at this sight of death, and while we consign the body of the deceased to the deep, let us be mindful of our frailty and mortality. . . .

"All hands, please join me in the Lord's Prayer."

As darkness enshrouded the ship, the low drone of young male voices descended upon the burial party.

"Our Father, who art in heaven, hallowed be thy name . . ."

"May he rest in peace. Amen."

The bugler sounded attention.

"To thee, O Lord, we commend the soul of thy servant

George Conlon's canvas-shrouded body slipped from beneath the American flag to its everlasting grave at the bottom of the Pacific Ocean. Two five-inch shells were placed in the bag to carry the body downward.

COURTESY OF BATTLESHIP NORTH CAROLINA COLLECTION

George. . . . May Christ receive you, who hath called you, and may the angels escort you into Abraham's bosom."

Lifting the end of the flag, Conlon's shipmates tilted the stretcher and watched his canvas-shrouded body slide into the ocean and be swallowed up in the churning water rushing past the moving ship.

"Eternal rest grant unto him, O Lord. Let perpetual light shine upon him, and may his soul and all the souls of the faithful departed through the mercy of God rest in peace."

The ship's colors, which had been lowered for the service, once again rose to full staff. The sailors climbed down from their perches and wandered off to their quarters to pick up a game of acey-deucy, shoot some craps, or reread that last letter from home. The aviation crew taped a picture of Conlon outside their workshop. When others came by to ask about Conlon, they declined to talk. While they could mention him within their own small circle, they could not bring themselves to talk about him with others.

★★★★★★★★★★★★★★★★

When the executive officer, J. A. Crocker, sat down in his stateroom to write his report, he reflected on the performance of the crew of the BB55:

> When the attack approached this Task Force, the fire of the anti-aircraft batteries of this ship was spontaneous. The volume of fire was maintained at a very high rate. The action was rapid and lasted only nine minutes, but all automatic weapons and 5-inch batteries were directed with flexibility and speed. Gun crews were not distracted by the approach of enemy planes, but repelled them with greater vigor. Whether deluged by water or knocked down by the detonation of near-miss bombs, or hampered by the gun blast of our own 5-inch batteries, they immediately resumed their stations. . . . Throughout the ship, the officers and men were calm and eager to engage the enemy, and this spirit prevailed before, during and after the action in every department. There was no exception, no single case of absence of this spirit of determination to destroy the enemy. The general performance was gratifying without personal incidents deserving praise or censure. Every man knew his job and stuck to it.
>
> However, it is considered that the Gunnery Officer, Commander Thomas B. Hill, U.S. Navy, deserves special commendation for having so effectively organized and trained his officers and men for battle that the air attack was deliberately and successfully repelled the first time that this vessel was under fire.

Of the 30 to 40 planes that directly attacked the *North Carolina* that day, BB55 gunners shot down seven confirmed and 14 possibles. For the remainder of August, the ships refueled and regrouped. The *Enterprise* had been damaged severely enough in the August 24 onslaught that she had to return to Pearl Harbor for repairs. On the last day of August, a torpedo slammed into the starboard side of the carrier *Saratoga*, and she was towed away toward home.

CHAPTER SEVEN

Torpedo Junction

"We must have been in a nest of Jap subs, because torpedoes were coming at us from every direction. The area was rightly named 'Torpedo Junction.' "

Leo O. Drake, former crew member

01 September 1942

Sixteen-year-old Bob Palomaris received an invitation to Wrigley Field to try out for the Los Angeles Angels of the Pacific Coast League, a farm team of the Chicago Cubs. The Cubs played winter ball near his home in Pasadena, and he sometimes played with them—men like Lou Novikoff, Peanuts Lowrey, Bob Sturgeon, and Louie Stringer.

Following tryouts, the manager handed Bob a contract. He was elated; the offer was the highlight of his young life. But then he remembered that he couldn't accept it. Palomaris was in the Navy.

06 September 1942

Hornet pilots lieutenant J. J. Lynch and ensign W. D. Carter completed their search mission for the day. On the return leg of their flight, they spotted a surfaced submarine about three miles away, heading toward the task force. The two-plane unit must have been spotted by the enemy, for as the pilots started toward the sub, she picked up speed and began a crash dive. By the time Lynch was in position to attack, only the top two feet of the conning tower were still visible. He dropped a bomb that landed about 20 feet in front of the sub, and when it exploded, the sub partially surfaced again. Carter, positioning himself for attack just as the sub appeared, dropped a depth charge, then flew in low to strafe the periscope. The submarine disappeared with seemingly no forward motion, and although there was no proof, the pilots believed she had been sunk. They did not know the sub had already released several torpedoes.

Lookouts aboard ship spotted a torpedo wake heading for the *Hornet* at about 300 yards. One of her pilots dropped a bomb in its path. The bomb exploded, followed by two consecutive concussions—two torpedoes taken out with one bomb. As the ships made a hard turn to starboard, lookouts spotted another wake passing parallel to the port side of the *North Carolina* at about 400 yards. It never reached a target. That day, the ships passed unscathed, but the task forces were alerted to expect sub-infested waters as they journeyed toward Guadalcanal.

Since the battleship's most important job was protecting aircraft carriers, the way she and the other ships traveled reflected that duty. The task forces formed concentric circles, with aircraft carriers being the center, battleships and heavy cruisers forming the next ring, and the smaller, faster destroyers offering the first line of defense in the outer ring. While steaming forward toward their destination, the ships also zigzagged to decrease the chances of being struck by a torpedo. Erratic motion made them more difficult targets.

Traveling at speeds from 15 to 25 knots, the task forces performed an ocean ballet. The carrier in the center of each task force led the choreography. If she turned, they all turned, keeping formation, changing direction, advancing. This maneuvering took tremendous coordination and concentration—especially in the dark, when blacked-out ships could easily collide with devastating effect.

The task force protecting the carrier *Wasp* was traveling in co-ordination with the force surrounding the carrier *Hornet*, which included the battleship *North Carolina*, her duty having been shifted away from the *Enterprise*, still in Pearl Harbor for repairs. The task forces traveled within view of each other—about eight nautical miles apart, as measured from carrier to carrier.

15 September 1942

For the crew aboard the *North Carolina*, the morning began as most others—early. At 0336, reveille rang out for all hands. At 0356, general quarters sounded, followed by the ear-piercing shrill of the boatswain's pipe and loudspeaker orders to "man your battle stations." Dawn and dusk were considered the most likely times for attack, so the crew stood battle ready a couple of hours each day before the sun crested the horizon to intensify the tropical heat. The young men, exhausted from the oppressive heat and humidity and the rotating four-on, four-off shifts, rolled out of their bunks and stumbled to the head, their "go-aheads"—shower shoes—scuffing along the metal deck of their compartments as they walked. Wearing little more than dog tags and skivvies, if that, they sometimes bumped into each other in the close confines and narrow corridors, a few curse words flying, directed more at their situation than each other. Most quickly donned daily work attire—dark blue denim jeans, long-sleeve, light blue chambray shirts, and black leather shoes. The blue dye on their white hats had begun to be bleached out by the intense sun, and the hats appeared more gray than blue. Those who worked in extremely hot areas of the ship like the laundry didn't bother with clothes at all. They worked in their underwear.

These crew members on laundry detail worked in their skivvies trying to survive the intense South Pacific heat, which was almost unbearable anywhere below decks but was intensified in areas like the laundry, the galley, and the engine room.
COURTESY OF BATTLESHIP *NORTH CAROLINA* COLLECTION

General quarters passed uneventfully that morning, and by 0700 hours, crew members were having breakfast. The entire crew of more than 2,000 was fed in less than an hour, the routine repeated at lunch. Everyone in the crew's quarters rotated mess duty. Bob Fennelly was on mess duty that day and had just finished cleaning up after the whirlwind meal. He slid the mess tables and benches into their overhead racks and sat on one of the stools bolted to the floor in front of the side tables attached along the bulkhead, intending to catch a wink or two.

When the sailors were not in battle, their day revolved around four-hour shifts. When they were off, they were free to shower, write letters home, play cards, sunbathe on the deck, go down to the barbershop for a haircut, or catch up on missed sleep. When they were on, they worked in various divisions of the ship. Some stood watch close to their battle stations but were free to pass the time doing trivial things like playing acey-deucy, a favorite board game.

Around noon, the *Wasp* sent up her planes in response to enemy aircraft sighted 15 miles west of the formation. The pilots successfully shot down a four-engine enemy seaplane. As the planes returned to the carrier, the task forces simultaneously turned into the wind, taking a southeasterly course so the aircraft could land safely.

★★★★★★★★★★★★★★★

At least a dozen Japanese submarines lurked in the waters, stalking their prey, hidden beneath the white-capped ocean. Forty-year-old lieutenant commander Takaichi Kinashi of the Imperial Japanese Navy was destined to become a hero that day. At about 1250 hours, the submarine's hydrophones detected movement, a massive gathering of sounds that could only mean a large group of ships—a task force, a prize possibility. Kinashi ordered the I-19 to periscope depth, confident the 20-knot trade winds would cause enough turbulence on the ocean's surface to disguise the small wake of the periscope. The view through the periscope offered nothing.

Nearly an hour later, the periscope once again broke the surface. A *kidobuti*, or task force, appeared through its sight—one aircraft carrier, one heavy cruiser, and several destroyers. The aircraft carrier *Wasp* changed directions and slowed to launch and recover aircraft, placing herself at the perfect angle within desired striking distance. Upon Kinashi's orders, six deadly 21-inch no-wake oxygen torpedoes, each carrying almost half a ton of highly explosive picric acid, sliced through the waters seeking their targets.

★★★★★★★★★★★★★★★

In the soda fountain on the second deck of the *North Carolina*, which the men called a "gedunk," several guys, including Walter Ashe, were standing in line for ice cream. They seldom forgot how lucky they were to have their own ice-cream maker aboard ship, and for Ashe, a Coke float was a delicacy he cherished. Standing in line and shooting the bull with the guys around him, he could already taste that smooth, cold, creamy confection sliding down his parched throat.

Paul Wieser stood in line as well. He had already finished cleaning every inch of his crane up on the third level above the main deck. He kept it clean and oiled and in good working condition. He had no immediate supervisor in the area, was pretty much his own

Some Showboat sailors passed their free time playing chess. Many sailors were off duty and relaxing when the torpedo attack began.
COURTESY OF BATTLESHIP *NORTH CAROLINA* COLLECTION

boss, but he knew he was supposed to stay at his work station for his whole four hours. But the thought of some vanilla ice cream had enticed him to disobey. He had eased down two levels of ladders, slipped over to the port side of the ship where he was less likely to be recognized, and negotiated the steps down to the second deck. He was a little worried to see such a long line, but the ice cream called.

In the forward-most part of the ship, Mike Marko sat on the commode enjoying a little bit of privacy. Enlisted men had very little of that. Most of their toilets were actually long metal troughs with slats to sit on. The men sat elbow to elbow. Sometimes, things heated up when a practical joker sailed flaming newspaper wads down the trough, burning the bottoms of unsuspecting squatters. Occasionally, someone would open the valve that fed the trough

Mike Marko

with salt water and create a swooshing rear-end wash.

One day, Marko had discovered a head on the third deck offering that rare commodity of privacy he missed so much. It was in the forward part of the ship—actually as far forward as possible, past Second Division living quarters and through a maze of narrow corridors encircling the level of turret number one called the "barbette," where sailors worked to feed projectiles up to the 16-inch guns above. The combination of compartments formed a U shape around the circular barbette. On each side was a washroom with long metal sinks, a water closet with two showers, three urinals, and a long metal bench. They were joined by a corridor at the very front of the ship with a continuous line of at least 15 stalls—no doors, but real commodes with full-length walls on each side. Marko called it a godsend. He often stayed longer than physically necessary. That day, he did not. As he walked down the corridor, he heard the shower and envied the sailor there. He wished the showers in his compartment were that nice.

Fresh water aboard ship was scarce, so the sailors had strict rules—wet down, soap up, rinse off, turn the water off during the soap-up phase. Leonard Pone turned off the water and soaped up. He scrubbed his head and rubbed the soap around on his face. The heat was unbearable, not like the cool air back home in New Jersey. He hated getting so sticky and sweaty. He turned the water back on just a second, then off again, then scrubbed the rest of his body. One of the things he looked forward to most when he got back home was being able to take a whole shower and just let the water run until he was finished.

Marko stepped through the first hatch to the narrow 40-foot-long corridor that led back to Second Division living quarters. He stopped to talk to a guy kneeling there with a contraption Marko had never seen.

"What are you doing?" he asked the well-built, brush-cut blonde.

"Putting an air test on the void compartments," Ingwald Nelson told him. "Name's Inky."

"Marko," he replied, offering his hand for a solid shake.

He watched as Nelson connected a tube from the large box by his side to a small opening in the lower outside wall of the corridor, then checked the gauges for readings. After a bit of small talk, Marko continued walking—aft one compartment, over to the starboard side, through the machine shop, and to his living quarters, where he got up on his bunk for a break.

The underwater part of the ship had a series of slender compartments, some filled with liquid, others empty and referred to as "voids." Thick steel walls called bulkheads separated the compartments. The compartments formed a defense shield against underwater attack, their configuration meant to absorb intrusion and explosion. The liquid-filled compartments held the huge supply of fuel oil needed to operate the ship. The void compartments stayed empty unless the ship was attacked and started taking on water. Those compartments could be filled with seawater and act as a counterbalance to right the ship.

Oscar Stone and William Skelton were taking soundings—measuring the amount of oil in those compartments immediately adjacent to the void compartment Nelson was air-testing. The sailors accessed the fuel tanks through small metal caps about seven inches in diameter, located along the floor of the corridor and also inside each of the storage rooms to the side of the hallway.

The three boys reminisced about home while they worked close

together on a job that many found frustrating and tedious. It seemed that at least one of the voids always had some type of leakage, so they had to find the problem—often just a loose rivet—and fix it.

By that time in September, the weather would be turning cold in Nelson's hometown of St. Paul, Minnesota, and he missed the anticipation of snow. Red tinges would only be starting to kiss the edges of the maple and oak leaves in South Carolina where Stone lived. He had a brother joining the Navy, too, who he hoped might be assigned to the *North Carolina*. The boys knew all about Skelton's large family in south Florida. He was the oldest of five boys, and his brothers said in their letters that they wanted to be just like him, to join the military and serve their country. That made him proud. He missed them and told his buddies often, sharing letters from home and cookies that his mother baked and mailed.

Topside, sailors stood watch, caught a few rays, sat in the shade under the overhang of the boat deck playing cards, leaned back against the turrets and read letters from home. Mail seldom came often enough. Many had read those same letters time and again until the edges became wrinkled and worn from being stuck inside pockets and retrieved again and again. The boys hadn't seen much action since the torpedo scare, other than a reported bogie every now and then that usually turned out to be friendly. Days could get long and boring despite the constant duties required to keep the ship functioning and ready for battle.

★★★★★★★★★★★★★★★★

Aboard the I-19, Commander Kinashi and his crew heard the dull sounds of exploding contact—three hits. They knew their mission had been successful. Fighting the urge to shout with celebration, the crew members retained their composure as the submarine retreated to safety, diving at a 45-degree angle until she reached a depth of 260 feet, deeply and silently hiding beneath the wake of the carrier. They heard and recorded what they thought to be as many as 85 depth charges, but the submarine remained unharmed. Above them, their spread of six torpedoes was doing more damage than even they had imagined.

★★★★★★★★★★★★★★★★

When the task-force formations began the turn necessary to resume their original course, the *Wasp* could be easily seen from the *North Carolina*. Chuck Paty wasn't on duty, so he had climbed up to the signal bridge to visit the guys up there. He was looking into the distance through the long glass and saw smoke rising from the deck of the *Wasp*. The boys took turns looking.

"Must have crashed a plane," one of them said.

But the scene quickly intensified, the smoke darker and thicker, flames licking the *Wasp*'s flight deck. The smoke and flames became visible for miles, and the sailors on the *North Carolina* who had long glasses or binoculars stood in horror as they watched sailors on the *Wasp* pushing planes into the ocean, apparently trying to reduce the risk of the planes' gas tanks exploding on board. Dark billows of smoke mushroomed up 1,000 feet. Fire raged, and repeated explosions sent sailors and planes flying through the air. Crew members on the deck of the *North Carolina* soon realized the *Wasp* had been torpedoed.

The destroyer *Landsdowne* was part of the outside screen for the *Wasp* force and was situated between carriers, where the destroyer circles of the forces nearly met. Junior Deck Officer John W. Gendron on the *Landsdowne* was terrified as he watched a torpedo—obviously set at a greater depth and meant for larger ships—speed underneath his craft.

Radio calls crackled on the *North Carolina*: "Torpedo headed for formation, course 080!" But neither the caller nor the intended recipient was identified.

On the signal deck, Paty saw the destroyer signaling the BB55 by light.

"Look!" Paty yelled, and pointed toward the destroyer.

Another radio transmission, breaking up and incomplete: "Torpedo just passed astern of me, headed for you."

Emergency flags on the destroyer *Mustin*, between the *North Carolina* and the *Landsdowne*, signaled a torpedo, but the radio signals were too vague and incomplete for anyone to know where the torpedo had been sighted.

As the BB55 sailors watched the mayhem unfolding before them on the *Wasp*, they felt their ship lean into a sharp right turn, following the lead of its choreographer *Hornet*. A huge explosion sent water spray skyward off their port side as a torpedo blasted the bow of the nearby destroyer *O'Brien*.

"Torpedo wake!" a signalman standing next to Paty yelled.

General quarters sounded on the *North Carolina*, the shrill call piercing the air and the order "All hands man your battle stations" sending adrenaline pumping through the boys' veins.

They responded immediately, but not before a torpedo slammed into their ship's port side. Paty had taken one step back from the edge of the bridge when the ship jumped out of the water, and he flew up into the air, landing on his back. He opened his eyes just as a shower of water sprayed over him.

Paty jumped up and headed down the ladders toward his battle station in radio two, wondering as he ran if he should go all the way down to his living quarters on the third deck and get his life preserver first, but quickly realizing that if the ship sank, the life preserver would do him no good. He would be trapped far below the main deck in his battle station with all the waterproof hatches closed and latched.

The huge ship shook upon impact, sending sailors flying across the decks, into walls, out of their bunks. The blast shot a geyser of water and oil more than a hundred feet into the air, and a river of oily water rushed down the deck. Although the sailors had been warned repeatedly not to stand near the lifelines, especially in sub-infested waters, several were. All but one managed to survive.

The tremendous force of water washed Albert Geary overboard. Fellow sailors, shocked at the sight but also fighting against the same fate, fixated on the bottom of his shoes as he vanished over the side. Geary was the talker for the group of guns near where the torpedo struck. He left behind a dangling phone line and a broken lead line. He had been aboard the *North Carolina* less than eight months when his family in Pennsylvania received the news that he was missing in action. His body was never recovered.

The torpedo pierced the ship and exploded into the fuel and void tanks below where Nelson, Stone, and Skelton were working. The impact ruptured the third deck in the storeroom, peeling an area of about 30 square feet up into the compartment, the torn area coming to rest at a 60-degree angle. Fuel oil and seawater rushed into the compartments. Fire shot up through the holds of turret one and danced around the ammunition magazine, where tons of gunpowder could be ignited and cause catastrophic damage, but the flames were quickly extinguished by flooding via the sprinklers.

Knocked over by the strength of the blast, sailors scrambled to their feet and ran toward their battle stations. Those headed toward starboard faced an uphill climb, as nearly 1,000 tons of seawater rushed into the jagged, gaping hole on the port side and the *North Carolina* listed five and a half degrees to port.

Down in the gedunk, Wieser chastised himself over and over as he hustled up the ladder back toward his part of the ship. If he had stayed at his work station on the crane where he was supposed to be, he would be topside, close to his battle station in mount seven. Now, he had to fight his way back through the crowds of running boys.

Ashe had finally reached the front of the line. He stood stirring the ice cream up into the Coke, savoring the moment, when the blast from the torpedo shook the ship so hard that all his Coke-and-ice-cream mixture flew right up into his face. He stared down at the empty cup in his hand. When general quarters sounded, his first impulse was to find a place to dispose of the empty cup. The boys had been instructed over and over again not to throw any trash on the deck. He quickly surmised that one paper cup wasn't going to make much difference if the ship was sinking, so he threw it down and hurried to his battle station topside.

That same training brought men running from below decks scantily clad or totally naked. Whatever they were doing when general quarters sounded, they immediately headed for their battle stations. Sailors scurried toward their assigned areas of the ship. One boy's face was lathered with shaving cream, making him look as though he were foaming at the mouth. Another, an extremely hairy man, had obviously been caught in the soap-up phase of his shower. He started running up the port side of the ship toward his battle station in turret one, a mass of suds and hair. When he reached the turret, he learned it had been abandoned due to the fire and water. He started running back the other way, soap suds flying through the air.

Charlie Rosell rushed from topside down to his battle station in number-two fireroom. Other members of that crew, previously lying in their bunks, hurried down in nothing but their skivvies, bare feet burning on the metal-grate flooring. Smoke from the explosion filled the compartments, and Rosell couldn't even see his hands in front of his face. His eyes burned. But weeks and months of rigorous training kicked in as the men followed orders, lighting off pumps, opening valves, giving the ship the power to speed up.

Number-four boiler was off-line, cold. Rosell, earphones on and communicating with an engineering officer in main control, started lighting it off, indicating the speed with which the work was being done.

"You're going to knock the front out of that boiler," the engineer warned.

"It is going to go or blow," Rosell replied.

The boiler was on-line and in service in five and a half minutes.

In less than six minutes, damage control counter-flooded the starboard side of the ship and corrected the list. The *North Carolina*, though damaged by a direct torpedo strike, never lost her position in the formation and picked up speed to 25 knots.

The expediency with which counter-flooding occurred could only be attributed to the foresight of Senior Petty Officer Charles H. Odle of A Division. His general-quarters duty was to counter-flood the void compartments on the starboard side if a torpedo strike on the port side caused the ship to take on water and list in the direction of the damage, possibly causing the ship to sink but certainly impeding her progress and efficiency in the water. The tools needed to accomplish that task included a special, very heavy, two-foot-long wrench for opening the vent valve. He then had to open the locked cage to the hydraulic pump and engage the pump to open the outer valve and take in seawater, filling the void compartments on the starboard side, countering the imbalance caused by water rushing in through torpedo damage on the port side.

During drills and uneventful general quarters, Odle had studied the task before him and realized a flaw of design could impede the process. Speed was of utmost importance. Although the original design was effective, additional bunks and lockers had subsequently been installed that prevented a continuous motion with the wrench. The wrench could be turned only so far before it would bump into the top of a locker. It had to be removed, repositioned, turned as far as possible, removed, repositioned, and turned as far as possible, over and over again. In addition, operating the heavy wrench, held high overhead with the operator's body pressed tightly against the locker, caused severe strain to the arm muscles and resulting stress to the operator.

Odle didn't want to be faced with this dilemma in a true battle emergency, so he found a solution. He designed an extension that allowed the wrench to be operated away from the lockers in a continuous arc, passing between two parallel pipes. Less than six months after he completed his revisions, the design was put to the test when the torpedo struck, and it operated perfectly with no delay.

Another measure of damage control caused heartache for the crew closest to the area of impact. The ship was divided into hundreds of compartments, most watertight, which were separated by hatches barely two feet wide and twice as tall, raised two feet off the deck. The watertight hatches had a gear system of closure—six thick metal prongs called "dogs" on each side that locked into position by the turn of a wheel attached to a gear. This procedure, referred to as "dogging down" the hatches, was the first line of defense in protecting undamaged areas of the ship from flooding. When the boys closed the hatches between Second Division and the corridor where Nelson, Stone, and Skelton were seen working, and near the water closet where Pone was showering, they knew the men were there but were helpless to save them. The ones who tried to look for them were accosted by darkness and quickly rising oily water. They retreated in vain and closed the hatches as they had been trained to do.

No one knew exactly where the three workers were at that time—whether they were killed by the blast or drowned in the rising oily water—but an official letter to Skelton's family said he died

The hatch leading to the torpedo-damaged area, including the washroom where Leonard Pone showered, was shored up by damage control after tons of water rushed into the ship through the huge hole blasted into her side. Beyond this hatch, four BB55 crew members perished.
<small>COURTESY OF BATTLESHIP *NORTH CAROLINA* COLLECTION</small>

"probably instantly from multiple injuries, the result of an explosion." Wherever Skelton was and however he died, the fates of Stone and Nelson were similar.

But Pone was trapped as he showered forward of where the torpedo slammed the bulkhead up into the storage areas and curled the deck of the passageway. He was far enough away from impact to possibly survive. If not rendered unconscious by the explosion, he must have fought his way in the dark through the rising oily water. The closest way to safety was down the port corridor, but the damage from the blast created unfamiliar terrain. He could go forward, around the barbette, and through the line of toilets at the bow of the ship to the starboard side, but those hatches had been dogged down, part of damage-control measures to protect other parts of the ship from the deluge of ocean and oil rushing into the damaged quarters. Still, he must have tried. Shipmates were certain they heard someone pounding, someone yelling. But even if Pone had been able to reach the hatch and release the dogs, the pressure from the rising oil and water would have prevented it from being pulled open.

Damage control quickly began shoring up hatches and bulkheads with large timbers and framing from the carpentry shop. Seven hatches and as many bulkheads were braced to prevent further damage or flooding. Although the *North Carolina* was operable except for turret one, she had been severely damaged and received orders to depart from the task force later that night and head toward Pearl Harbor for repairs. Accompanied by two escort destroyers but leaving a telltale trail of oil slicks in her wake, the ship maintained a speed of less than 20 knots, which made her easier prey for a second attack, should the subs still be hunting her.

Through the glass porthole on the shored-up hatch dividing Second Division living quarters from the damaged area of the ship, crew members could see the oily water sloshing against the glass. Knowing some of their crew mates remained inside the flooded compartments made sleeping nearly impossible. During the nights that followed, many of the boys chose not to return to their compartments below deck to sleep, instead dragging their mattresses topside.

Just one day into their southeast journey, the crew's edgy nerves were tested again as lookouts spotted a submarine late in the day. General quarters sounded, accompanied by the shrill boatswain's call and the order, "All hands man your battle stations." But the submarine, knowing it had been spotted, descended quickly without making contact. A couple of hours later, another submarine was sighted, and the exhausted sailors once again scrambled to GQ, only to be relieved in less than an hour. Amidst the mayhem, Mike Marko pondered fate, realizing he, too, would be dead if he had lingered longer in the forward part of the ship.

During the next few days, the carpentry shop built four wooden coffins.

19 September 1942

The *North Carolina* anchored off the small, remote island of Tongatabu 1,200 miles southeast of where she had been torpedoed. By shifting fluids in the holds, the crew was able to lift the ship's bow out of the water, partially exposing the huge, jagged wound in her side, a hole 32 feet long by 18 feet high. Water, oil, and sludge drained from the flooded compartments, and the recovery effort began.

Members of a damage-control party opened the watertight hatches. Wearing miner-type lanterns on their heads, two shipmates entered the darkened damaged compartment in an effort to retrieve the bodies but soon emerged covered in oil up to their waists, the odor having physically sickened them to the point that they were unable to continue.

Chief Pharmacist's Mate Frank Washburn offered to try. "Give me a shot of bourbon and I'll do it," he said.

Although hard liquor was normally prohibited, the circumstances called for drastic measures, and the request was granted. Washburn and a couple of other men, fortified with bourbon, pulled the miner's lamps down onto their foreheads and entered the dark, oily confines to retrieve four unrecognizable bodies. Four sweltering days in fuel-oil-laden salt water had caused the bodies to swell and begin

The torpedo that exploded in the North Carolina*'s side created a hole approximately 18 feet by 32 feet. The workers in the lower right corner are dwarfed by the damage. The ship returned to Pearl Harbor for repairs.*
COURTESY OF BATTLESHIP NORTH CAROLINA COLLECTION

to decompose. Enlarged well beyond normal size, the bodies appeared to have been partially burned, their hair gone. Pressed into the swollen flesh, their dog tags stood straight out.

Washburn and his men carefully cleaned the bodies of their shipmates as best they could and used dental records for positive identification. They gently wrapped the bodies in canvas, then lifted them one by one and placed them in the wooden caskets in preparation for burial.

20 September 1942

Reveille sounded at 0530—no need for early GQ in port. The plan of the day revolved around services honoring Nelson, Pone, Skelton, and Stone, and also remembering Geary, who had been swept overboard.

Following breakfast, preparations began as church was rigged in number-one mess hall using the equipment that had been dedicated more than a year earlier. It included a Hammond electric organ, a folding altar made of light cast bronze, a triptych, altar ornaments, a cross, candlesticks, flower vases, altar trimmings and linens, a dossal, communion service, and a ship's Bible.

As those preparations proceeded, Chaplain Francis Lee Albert readied himself, selecting scripture and the right words to say. He whispered prayers for the families of the young men, mere boys, who would not be returning home. He knew Skelton well from the ship's Bible class. They were both of the Baptist faith. He regretted not knowing the others as well.

At 0802 hours, the colors were lowered to half-mast and the coffins were transferred over the side into the small boats that would take them to shore. They were escorted by a detachment of ship's company clothed in undress whites with black silk neckerchiefs.

Shipmates gathered on a South Pacific island to bury the dead. Although no positive identification of this ceremony has been made, the multiple graves and the white crosses suggest that it was probably the burial at the United States Army Queen's Cemetery on the island of Tongatabu. Four BB55 crew members killed when the torpedo struck the ship on September 15, 1942, were laid to rest there September 20.
COURTESY OF BATTLESHIP NORTH CAROLINA COLLECTION

Amid the mourning, however, daily chores continued—scrubbing the director towers and stacks, painting topside, scraping and wire-brushing all corroded paintwork, general cleaning in living and berthing compartments, complete cleaning in the medical storeroom located near the damaged compartments in preparation for repairs.

A Protestant memorial service began at 0830. At 0900, three planes were hoisted out for gunnery training and a boat was sent to the island for a Catholic chaplain, since the ship did not have one of its own. Confessions for men of the Roman Catholic Church began at 0930 and were more heavily attended than usual.

Tongatabu offered no recreational facilities. The plan of the day explained, "Men who desire to go ashore will find walking the only diversion. Nothing can be bought—the stores are empty and it is reported that there are no soft drink places or otherwise."

Although many chose to go ashore for the funeral services, others just stayed on board. Ashe went ashore and later recorded his day in his diary:

> Today we had liberty for the first time since July 14th—but not genuine whiskey drinking liberty. We, Hohn, Bailey and my-self, went over in the morning—raining, too, but you can't be particular. Things to do was very limited—bought some bananas and found a native who guided us through the tropical jungles to where we could get some native whiskey called "Huha neu"—not so pleasant tasting but the only thing to drink on the island—the natives are money mad and charge exhuberant [sic] prices for ev-erything—they wanted $3 a bottle for the coconut whiskey but settled for $2. Went over again in the afternoon with Millis, Bidwell and Hohn and Gumm and Burrell. Found another native hut in the tropical jungle selling some coconut "home brew" which was bitter and not palatable at all but those that had not been over in the morning drank it readily. We later found another hut farther in the jungles where they had some very refreshing and tasty home brew—tasting something like cider—Gumm, Hohn and Burrell had turned back by this time and the time was short before lib-erty was due to expire. We drank two pitchers and they gave us two quarts to take with us and did not want to take no money but we gave them $3. We were lucky in getting a ride back on a

Army Jeep or we certainly would have been over leave. Later that night we found out that we did not get no bargain on the last "home brew." It must have been very green—for Millis got a touch of dysentery and I had violent heartburns all night. No more fermented coconut juice for me—I'll wait for the states and the "bottled in bond."

While Ashe and his buddies combed the jungle in search of island brew, the funeral party left the ship at 1300 hours as three planes were once again being hoisted for gunnery training. Officers and CPOs were instructed to wear khakis without coats and crew to wear undress whites with neckerchiefs.

At 1400 hours, as a soft tropical breeze rustled the fronds of the palms, shipmates stood in silent salute amid rows of plain white crosses in the United States Army Queen's Cemetery. The strains of "Nearer, My God to Thee," then "Lead, Kindly Light" wafted through the air as the ship's band paid tribute to fallen comrades.

Chaplain Albert began reading Revelation 7, verses 12 to 17: "Then one of the elders addressed me, saying, 'Who are these, clothed in white robes, and whence have they come?' . . . 'These are they who have come out of the great tribulation. . . . They shall hunger no more, neither thirst any more; the sun shall not strike them, nor any scorching heat . . . and God will wipe away every tear from their eyes.' "

The chaplain spoke individually of each man's courage, the examples each set for his shipmates. He prayed for the peace of their souls and the comfort of their loved ones.

"The three flower emblems used here today have a very special meaning," the chaplain explained. "Green is symbolic of the life we all love. Red is typical of this life, which is short and suddenly cut off. White represents our hope of immortality and our faith in the purity of all redeemed souls."

In standard military fashion, the Marine squadron fired three volleys, the coffins were lowered into the freshly dug soil, and shipmates stood at attention as a lone bugler offered up the mournful melody of taps.

The *North Carolina* once again steamed into Pearl Harbor. As she rounded Ford Island, cheers rose from crew aboard other vessels in the harbor and from civilians and military personnel on shore. This time, the boys didn't wonder why. They were no longer the naïve, untested recruits who had arrived less than three months earlier. They had experienced war; their ship had been attacked and had proved herself worthy of that praise. They had already earned three battle stars. But the war was far from over, and while they were anxious for the opportunity to take a little leave time in Hawaii, many were ready to return to battle. They had a score to settle with the Japanese.

Chuck Paty toured Honolulu and the island on a rented bicycle.
COURTESY OF CHUCK PATY

CHAPTER EIGHT

Liberty
★★★★★★★★★★★★★★★

"Our firing accuracy was very good, but we sure as hell were never satisfied. . . . We had to continually work at it and never did feel that we could slacken up on our gunnery exercises and our training. . . . I'm not going to say we were good enough."

Rear Admiral John E. Kirkpatrick (USNR retired), former BB55 officer

While the ship was at Tongatabu, divers cut away the ripped and dangling shards of metal and measured the damage created by the torpedo, so by the time the Showboat arrived at Pearl, the necessary parts were ready and waiting to repair the 32-by-18-foot hole blown in her side. Repairing the damage could take up to a month, so the crew would have some time to relax. But first, they became part of an all-hands working party—a task in which everyone but the officers was assigned to work detail.

The ship went into one of the dry docks at Pearl, and all the water was pumped out so she rested in a cradle above a cement floor. The work detail descended the gangway, then climbed down the ladders into the cavity where the Showboat sat. From that angle at that moment, she didn't look very fancy.

Being in radio, Chuck Paty had never had to do hard labor—no holystoning the deck, no paint scraping, no loading supplies, just cleaning transistors and keeping the equipment working properly.

"Here are your tools," an officer told Paty and the others. "Your job is to scrape the barnacles from the bottom of the ship."

Paty looked at his scraper and wire brush. He listened as the radio gang was assigned its section of the ship—about a 30-foot length near the keel. Since the ship was 108 feet wide, that gave them over 3,000 square feet of barnacled bottom to scrape. Even at five-foot-next-to-nothing, Paty had to stoop to get under the ship, which rested only about four feet off the cement. He adjusted his body again and again, trying to figure out the best position to take so he could stay on his feet, see what he was doing without getting his eyes full of debris, and still give his right arm enough strength to scrape over his head. When his hat began to feel heavy, he flipped down the brim; debris rained down on his shoulders. He left his brim turned down for the duration of the assignment. Throughout the day, he scraped and scraped, dodging barnacles and rust and paint as it fell, trying not to elbow or be elbowed by one of his radio buddies in the process. With the entire crew working, the nasty job took only about a day to complete. Paty looked at his clothes— his dungarees and chambray shirt—and wondered if they would ever come clean. Then he looked at his hat, decided there was no hope for it, and tossed it in the trash.

In addition to the sea bags, each sailor had been issued what they called a "ditty bag"—something small and easy to carry on leave with just a few things inside. As they prepared to head for Camp Andrews for a few days of rest and relaxation, each packed a bathing suit, a towel, and maybe a toothbrush and some underwear. At the camp, they wouldn't need much. The whites and shoes they wore when they departed the ship would again be worn when it was time to return, but not while they were there.

The boys who wanted to go to Camp Andrews left the ship in large groups, each group spending four to five stress-free days in a place where reveille and general quarters did not exist. When one group returned, another departed.

The sailors caught a narrow-gauge train just outside the Navy yard. Paul Wieser laughed to himself as he saw the tiny little thing come *putt, putt, putt*ing up the two-foot-wide tracks to the station. But the train itself was fascinating. It had several open passenger cars with wooden benches, followed by several empty flatbed cars. Paty, Wieser, and many of the other young men had never seen anything beyond the Navy yard, downtown Honolulu, and Waikiki Beach, so when the little train chugged its way out of the populated area, around the harbor, and into the pineapple and sugarcane fields, the sailors were enthralled.

Riding the train, they viewed the way the locals lived, watched them working in the fields and walking along the dirt roads. They saw children playing. Most houses Wieser glimpsed were constructed of wood, but they had no actual windows, just openings covered in screen. Along the way, the train stopped to drop off empty cars at the pineapple factory and then along the sugarcane fields. The train trip took over two hours, but the ride was interesting and kept the wooden benches from becoming too uncomfortable. The uniforms were hot, though.

The train arrived at the station—an open wooden structure with a bench—in the small town of Nanakule. A few native residents waited to board as the sailors grabbed their ditty bags and jumped off both sides of the open cars. The town was very small, just a collection of a few houses, a grocery store, and a service station. The boys walked into the forest of palms that surrounded Camp Andrews. They were assigned to tents where they would spend the next few days. Off came the uniforms, on went the swimsuits— tight, form-fitting short trunks that would be the only thing most of them would wear for the duration of their stay at the camp. They took pictures of each other standing in a group of palms and climbing partway up the leaning trees.

The tents were semipermanent, secured on wooden platforms about a foot and a half off the sand. The sides could be rolled up or down; most of the boys kept them up because they needed the breeze. Mosquito netting attached to poles could be lowered to

surround them while they slept. They could eat three meals a day if they wanted, but even that was optional. Food was standard Navy fare, with lots of pineapple desserts. The camp had a mess hall and an area where the sailors could purchase candy and chewing gum and other things they might like to have. Each day, they were given the standard two cans of hot beer each. Paty had never liked beer much, so he always sold his to one of the other guys. He didn't like gum either, but Wieser did, and since it was in short supply on the ship, he enjoyed it while he could. Evidently, a lot of the other boys enjoyed gum, too. As he approached the mess hall, Wieser noticed a tree leaning close to the steps that looked really sick. Something appeared to be wrong with its bark. But as he mounted the steps and came close to the tree, Wieser realized that the tree had become a depository for chewing gum. Every sailor going in to eat stuck his gum on the tree, so Wieser added his to the collection.

After lunch, Wieser and a group of his buddies from Fifth Division headed to the beach about a quarter-mile from the camp. Some of the guys carried their mattress covers with them so they could stretch out in the sun. An area of coral caused the boys to ooh and aah and ouch as they carefully walked across it, but Wieser was amazed to see the native children running around in no apparent pain. While most of the adults kept their distance from the sailors, the children seemed to enjoy their company. Many a sailor's baglike mattress cover became a hang glider for the kids as they ran down the beach and the bag filled with air, or became a sled that skimmed across the shallows left by receding waves.

The surf was rough, but the boys enjoyed catching the huge waves and body-surfing them to the shore. Wieser caught wave after wave and enjoyed the carefree atmosphere—when he could let his mind forget. The boys may not have been at war long, but they had seen action, had shot down the enemy, had lost shipmates and buried them at sea, had seen the *Wasp* explode and burn, had been struck by a torpedo, had buried four of their own on an island in the middle of nowhere, leaving them there far from home—so his mind did wander. That proved to be dangerous. A strong wave crashed over Wieser, knocking him off his feet. He felt the current tumbling him along with shells and sand and surf. He closed his eyes and held his breath as he bumped and crashed with the wave. His lungs felt heavy and full. He wanted so badly just to breathe but could not get his footing, could not stand, could not feel the bottom as he surged along with the water. When he thought he would be added to the list of casualties, he opened his eyes and saw daylight. A wave had deposited him on the sand. He emptied his lungs, took a deep breath of fresh air, and scrambled to his feet before the next wave could sweep him away with the sand that tumbled back into the ocean with every crash.

★★★★★★★★★★★★★★★

A mountain rising right next to Camp Andrews caught the attention of radioman Paty. He saw a building up there with antennae and wondered what it was. He stopped to talk to a couple of Navy personnel standing next to a Jeep just outside the entrance to the camp.

"What's that?" Paty asked, pointing up the mountain.

Crew members flocked to Camp Andrews for some rest and relaxation. There, shoes and clothes were optional—except for the form-fitting swim trunks—and reveille and paint chipping did not exist.
COURTESY OF BATTLESHIP NORTH CAROLINA COLLECTION

"Naval Radio Station Honolulu," one of the men told him.

"You work there?" Paty asked.

"Yep."

"How do you get up there?"

"There's a road all the way to the top. We just bring the Jeep down here to get groceries and catch the train to Honolulu."

"What do you do up there?"

"We can transmit anywhere in the world," one of the men explained to Paty.

"Those are some high-powered transmitters up there," the other said proudly.

"There's an office over in Pearl Harbor where the keys and the typewriters are. We just pipe the info down the mountain to them," the first one explained.

"Oh," Paty replied. "You have any officers up there?"

"No, there's a first-class who's in charge and a couple of other rated men, but that's it. We pretty much work on our own."

"I like that," Paty said.

"But if we don't do our job right, you can bet some brass will be up there in a hurry."

"Yeah, I guess they would," Paty replied, but his mind was already working, trying to think of how he could get transferred to that job. *What could be better than that?*

★★★★★★★★★★★★★★★

After their four-day stay was over, the boys squirmed as they pulled their white long-sleeve jumpers over sunburned backs and arms. They tugged on their long, hot cotton pants, put on socks and shoes for the first time in days, and carried their ditty bags with them back to the train station in Nanakule. The little train came puffing along, belching smoke as it neared the station. Paty noticed, as they filled the passenger cars to capacity, that no flatbed cars were attached.

On the return trip, the train stopped at the sugar plantation to pick up some cars. Stalks of sugarcane, wrapped in bundles, had been piled high on the flatbeds. A little farther along, the train stopped again at the pineapple factory. Wooden boxes about three feet tall and three feet square were loaded with pineapples and stacked on the railroad cars. The crates were obviously reused regularly, showing signs of wear, written on again and again, with previous messages marked through. Paty saw a sign that offered tours of the plant and made a mental note to do that one day.

When the boys returned to the ship from their mini-vacation, they resumed their work details, though they could still take liberties in the shipyard and around Honolulu.

Joe Smits never even went to Camp Andrews. He preferred staying in the city and preferred his beer cold, even if he did have to pay for it. A bar in downtown Honolulu served its beer in frosty, frozen mugs—a new mug with each beer. Smits spent a lot of time there, but things had changed since the war began. When he was stationed in Honolulu before the Pearl Harbor attack, the sailors had played touch football on the lawn of the Waikiki Hotel. They couldn't do that anymore. He remembered a time before the war when he had seen Mickey Rooney at Waikiki and also a night when he and his buddies had been the recipients of free drinks all night until the bar closed, paid in full by movie star Broderick Crawford.

But that was before the war.

Honolulu was a military town, its streets filled to capacity with uniformed men in Army khaki, Navy white, and Marine green. And many establishments catered especially to their needs. Along Hotel Street, the men lined up for blocks. That three dollars in their pocket would get them three minutes with a woman. Bob Fennelly got in line one day. He had no wife or girlfriend back home, no one to betray. But from the talk he heard around him while he waited in line, that didn't matter much to a lot of the men. The government provided these establishments because it knew what the men needed, they said, so they intended to take full advantage of the opportunity. After all, none of them knew if they would ever make it back home. No one knew.

★★★★★★★★★★★★★★★

In mid-November, the BB55 left Pearl Harbor headed for Noumea, New Caledonia. While the ship's damage was being repaired, she had also received a new line of defense and attack. The 1.1-inch antiaircraft guns had proven ineffective during the Battle of the Eastern Solomons, so they were completely removed. In their stead, 60 forty-millimeter guns were installed in 15 quadruple mounts. The guns were designed for 15 to 20 men in each mount to fire 12 pound-and-a-half rounds per gun per minute, with an effective range of up to 4,000 yards. Since each clip held only four rounds, the loaders' job was especially important, keeping the clips full and feeding them into the gun. Self-destructive fuses caused the shells to destroy themselves if they did not make contact with a target before maximum range was achieved.

Armed with its new weaponry, the ship headed southwest, holding gunnery practice for the 40s along the way. While en route, the North Carolina received new orders to go to Fiji, where she spent several days. During that time, she was reassigned to a different task force, and Captain Wilder D. Baker relieved Captain Fort. The ship was anchored away from the island, but a boat ran back and forth every few hours so that crew who wished to go ashore could.

Paty enjoyed liberty in Fiji, not because there was anything exciting to do but because it was a new place to see, something new

The 40-millimeter guns replaced the 1.1 antiaircraft guns, which proved useless during early battles. Before the ship left Pearl Harbor following torpedo damage repair, all the 1.1s were removed and sixty 40-millimeter guns were installed in 15 quadruple mounts.
COURTESY OF BATTLESHIP *NORTH CAROLINA* COLLECTION

to learn. The curious youngster wasn't letting any interesting opportunity slip past him.

Fiji fulfilled his preconceived notions of a native island. The houses were small grass huts sticking up on stilts. The people were very dark skinned and wore very little, the women often topless. Their hair was not black but rather bleached yellow or red by the sun. Paty saw a few British troops in the downtown area of the British colony. He found nothing much to do but walk around and look.

The ship left Fiji on December 6 and headed toward Noumea, arriving in mid-December. Noumea was a gathering place for the ships of the fleet—a place where they could regroup, refuel, replenish supplies, and rest before the next mission.

02 January 1943

Each ship had various recreational teams and activities, including boxing and baseball. The battleship *Alabama* had a secret weapon on its baseball team—Bob Feller, a well-known pitcher for the Cleveland Indians. While both ships were anchored at Noumea, the *North Carolina* and the *Alabama* scheduled a baseball game on Shangri La Island in Dumbea Bay. Only a limited number of crew members from each ship were allowed to go. A discussion arose in the radio room.

"Man, I'd like to see Bob Feller pitch."

"He doesn't play, he's just their coach."

"He could still pitch."

"Hell, I don't care if he pitches or not, I'd just like to see the guy."

"We can't all go."

"Ain't that a crock. Plan all these activities and then don't let us go."

"If we can't see it, at least maybe we can hear it."

"What do you mean?"

"We're radio, right? Why can't somebody go over there and broadcast the game back to us?"

"Yeah, why not?"

"Who?"

"Gotta be somebody who really knows how to operate the equipment or it won't do us any good."

"Hey, Paty, why don't you do it? You might be the only one can get permission to get the equipment off the ship anyway."

"Yeah, I can do it," Paty answered. "I can do it."

So Paty requested and received permission to take the small portable radio transmitter and battery pack over to the island to broadcast the game. The low-frequency transmitter wasn't too large, but the battery pack weighed more than the transmitter did, and together they were quite a load for the petite Paty to manage. He lugged them down the accommodation ladder and into the boat that would take him to the island. He left in plenty of time to set up and begin broadcasting.

The baseball diamond was located at the base of a small mountain on the island—more a big hill than a mountain, perhaps 150 feet to its peak. It made a great backdrop for home plate. When

Paty arrived, the players were on the field just tossing the ball around, warming up. He set up his equipment right behind home plate, where he could get the best view and hear the umpire's calls. He tried to raise the ship.

"Paty to *North Carolina*. Do you hear me?"

No response.

"*North Carolina*. Do you hear me?"

Inside the radio room on the ship, the boys who were left behind gathered around the receiver, waiting.

"Why doesn't he let us know something? He should be there by now."

"*North Carolina*. Do you hear me?"

No response.

Paty thought the hill might be blocking his frequency. The transmitter was weak, but there wasn't much distance to the ship out in the bay, maybe half a mile or so. So he lugged the equipment up the hill a little. The view was better there anyway. He could see over everyone's head. He tried again.

"Paty to *North Carolina*. Come in."

No response.

Back on the ship, the boys were getting agitated.

"That game's probably already started. Where is he?"

Paty tried again and again. He moved a little farther up the hill. Still no response. He looked back at the field, and the game had started. He called the ship again. No response. He moved another 15 feet up the hill and tried again. No answer. He moved another 15 feet and tried again. He looked back at the diamond, and the game was going on below him, but he couldn't hear the umpire anymore. He tried again. Nothing. He continued to move in 15-foot increments up the hill, lugging the equipment, which became heavier with every move. The game continued below him. He was so far away he could not even tell who was up to bat. In one last-ditch effort, he carried the equipment all the way to the top of the small mountain. He could see the ship anchored in the bay, but when he looked back down at the diamond, the players were like ants.

"Paty to *North Carolina*. Do you hear me?"

"Paty, that you?" came a very faint answer. "We can't hear you."

He tried again and again but could never get a clear-enough connection for them to hear him or even make a recognizable response.

Paty sat on the top of the mountain, exhausted, disgusted, and dreading to go back to the ship. When he no longer saw movement on the field, he decided the game must be over, dragged the equipment down the mountain, and caught the little boat back to the ship. He didn't even know who won the game.

"Man, we couldn't hear a thing," his buddies complained when he returned to the ship.

"You're a sorry broadcaster, Paty."

He did not argue with them.

★★★★★★★★★★★★★★★★

In mid-January, when a request came in to transfer one storekeeper first class back to the States to put a new ship into commission, Walter Ashe started thinking about home. Seven storekeepers qualified for transfer, and all wanted to go, creating a dilemma.

"This is what I'll do," the supply officer told the group of anxious sailors. "I'll put seven slips of paper in a hat, and you can draw them out. One will have a message from me written on it. Whoever draws that slip gets the transfer."

The boys began to draw. Ashe watched as one, then another, then another drew out blank slips of paper. When his turn came, he closed his eyes and reached into the hat. Even before he opened the slip, he thought he saw ink. Slowly, he unfolded the paper. "Have a beer for me," the message read. Ashe's joyous response was not well received by the married storekeepers, who felt it was unfair for a single guy to rate going home first. Although some voiced their opinions loudly, the lottery was considered fair and final. But the executive officer tried to get Ashe to stay.

"Ashe," he said, "if you give up the transfer and stay on board, I will make you chief storekeeper."

If Ashe considered the offer at all, he did so only momentarily. The only way to go home, he knew, was to get transferred to a new ship being commissioned, like he had done when he joined the BB55 crew. He'd been lucky twice and might not get the opportunity again.

"Sir, I have my sea bag packed, and my thoughts are all for going home."

He boarded the former luxury liner SS *Lurline* and found himself sharing a room with the BB55's butcher, Lincoln Hector. All the way back to the States, they had nothing really pressing to do but eat and sleep. Hector was assigned to help with the cooking, but that just gave him access to all the delicacies he and his roommate could want. They dined well and snacked on ice-cream sundaes and banana splits all the way home.

17 March 1943

Bob Palomaris spent his 17th birthday on a bus headed from Los Angeles to San Diego for boot camp, not playing baseball. A cold box of food furnished by the Navy sufficed for his birthday dinner. The boys had been told they would have nine weeks of boot camp, but that was shortened to 21 days. The highlight of those three weeks was two days of 20-millimeter camp on the ocean, where young Palomaris practiced on a simulator, then actually fired

Bob Palomaris, 1943
COURTESY OF BOB PALOMARIS

the real guns. Next to baseball, he probably loved shooting most. He had a great teacher in his uncle Bill. The child had loaded his own ammunition at 12 and molded his own bullets at 14. He had earned expert rifle and expert pistol medals from the National Rifle Association. So when he had an opportunity to request an assignment, he asked for gunnery school.

Thirty days of planned leave after boot camp disappeared, and the boys boarded a train for San Pedro. Palomaris didn't mind that too much; he was 30 miles from home, and they had been told they would be there from six weeks to as long as six months. But he quickly learned that things in the Navy changed fast. After one day of liberty in San Pedro, the sailors shipped out on the *J. Franklin Bell*, headed for Hawaii.

★★★★★★★★★★★★★★★★

For the first few months of 1943, the BB55 and other ships in the task force stayed close to Noumea and ran training practices every day. Around the middle of March, the *North Carolina* had to make a quick trip back to Pearl Harbor for repairs on one of her giant propellers—15 feet, four inches for the inboard and 16 feet, seven inches for the outboard. Wieser had already decided what he was going to do when he got there.

Correspondence between Wieser and his girlfriend, Jean, had become increasingly serious during his years away. He didn't know when he would ever get back home to New Jersey, but he knew that when he did, he wanted to marry Jean Coddington. He wrote to her every single day. The letters didn't get mailed very often, and he was pretty sure parts were blacked out by the censors, but he wanted her to understand how important she was to him, so even if the letters arrived in bunches, she would know by the dates on them that he wrote every day, no matter what. And she wrote back. Anytime the destroyers brought sacks of mail, he always had a handful of letters.

He didn't care much about liberty in Pearl, didn't drink, so the bars were out, didn't dance—at least not without Jean—so he didn't want to go to the USO for the parties, certainly didn't want to go down to Hotel Street and stand in any of those lines. When he

stood at the bus stop in Honolulu and looked down the street, it made him think of snow, thousands of sailors dressed in white crowded everywhere. That just didn't interest him.

He did want to leave the ship, however, to step onto solid ground, to see something other than bulkheads, teak, steel decks, gun mounts, and water. So Wieser chose yard liberty, staying within the confines of the shipyard. He didn't have to dress up to do that, didn't have to fight the crowds in the streets, but he did find things to do. The yard had a recreation area, and Wieser enjoyed the bowling alley. That was something he and his friends had done back home, although their favorite hangout had been the skating rink. The soda shops offered some variation from what was available aboard ship, so he spent a little bit of money here and there.

Wandering through the PX at the sub base, Wieser found a jewelry case that contained bracelets and watches and necklaces and rings. As he walked slowly along the glass case, one set of rings caught his attention. He leaned over the case and looked closer, then tapped his finger on the glass just above one small box.

"May I help you?" Wieser heard. He looked up.

"Could I see those, please?" he asked.

The clerk reached inside the case and touched one box.

"These?"

"No, the next ones," Wieser said. "To the right. My right."

"These?" the clerk asked, touching the box that had caught Wieser's eye.

"Those," Wieser answered.

The clerk set the small box on top of the glass case and hovered close as Wieser leaned in to take a closer look.

"They are a very small size," the clerk said.

Paul Wieser posed in front of a car bearing a Hawaii license tag—that and the lei were proof positive that he was actually there.
COURTESY OF BATTLESHIP
NORTH CAROLINA COLLECTION

"She is, too," Wieser answered. Jean was thin, very thin. "May I?" he asked as he touched the diamond. The clerk nodded, and Wieser pulled the diamond from its slit in the box. The band was narrow gold, and three delicate prongs supported the sparkling round diamond. It was perfect. Wieser slipped the engagement ring back into its place, then ran his finger across the smooth gold of the matching wedding band.

"I'll take them," Wieser said, then hesitated. "How much?"

The clerk lifted the box and tilted it slightly so he could see the bottom. "One hundred nineteen," he replied.

"I'll be back tomorrow," Wieser said. "Can you hold them for me?"

He hurried back to the ship and checked his locker. He had left most of his pay on the books, but each payday he took out just a little bit and tucked it inside his dress blue uniform in the bottom of his locker. In the South Pacific, the weather was too hot to wear the blue wool, so that seemed like a fairly safe place to hide the money. He hadn't been anywhere to spend it, and most everything he wanted on the ship was provided for him. He went down to the gedunk for an ice cream once in a while, but he didn't smoke like many of the guys did, and cigarettes were probably the most expensive thing that could have taken his money. V-mail was free. He had stuck a little of the money in his wallet when he went ashore, but he hadn't counted the stash in a long time and wasn't sure how much was there. He hoped it would be enough.

He took the little wad of money to his bunk and sat down to count. When he made it to $100 and still had bills in his hand, he let out a sigh of relief. Total—$127. More than enough. He tucked the money back inside the collar fold of his dress blues. Before walking away, he checked the lock two times to make sure it was secure. The money hadn't really mattered much until that moment. He hurried down to the ship's post office to get some V-mail forms, since he had used all the ones he picked up earlier in the week. While he was there, he bought an ice cream to celebrate. The ship made chocolate and vanilla. Wieser preferred vanilla.

When he returned to his living quarters, he walked past row after row of bunks hanging five high in the huge open space. Most of them were empty; everyone who wasn't on work duty or watch was on liberty. He sat down on his bunk and began to write a letter home to his older brother, the one who had protected him from the illegal race-card job, the one who had reached the highest rank in the Moose lodge and was well respected in the community, the one Wieser always knew he could depend on. He told his brother he would be mailing the rings home and asked him to propose to Jean on his behalf. They couldn't set a wedding date because he had no idea when he would return to the States, but at least she would know his intentions.

"Make it special," Wieser told his brother. "Maybe a party or something."

When he went on liberty the next day, Wieser headed straight to the PX and found the clerk who had helped him the day before. The clerk had never agreed to put the rings aside, but they were still sitting in the glass cabinet where Wieser had last seen them. He pulled out his cash, made his purchase, and headed back to the ship's post office.

"Package them really good, please," he requested as he addressed the label to his brother and offered up the letter he had written him. He had two letters for Jean—one from the previous day and the one he had already written that morning. He told her he loved her, in words instead of semaphore flags.

★★★★★★★★★★★★★★★

Repaired again and ready to work, the *North Carolina* headed back to Noumea in early May 1943 with Palomaris among the newest members of the crew.

When the BB55 arrived at Noumea and anchored near the channel, the crew checked out a launch from the boat pool on the island for the ship to use during her stay. The captain's gig was lowered into the water and attached to the boat boom. The 40-foot launch used for transportation of the crew back and forth to the island was also attached to the boom. Fennelly and his crew climbed out the boat boom and lowered themselves into the launch, then motored it to the accommodation ladder on the side of the ship for the liberty party to board.

Wieser knew he didn't want to go into the town of Noumea, but he had heard about another spot, also on the island of New Caledonia, a remote area of beach that had been designated as a place for crew members to take their allotted cans of hot beer and spend a few hours of relaxation. Wieser decided to go. After the boys loaded, the launch motored to a very small pier inside the channel some distance from the capital town. The sailors disembarked and began their journey across the center of the island to the ocean side. A narrow path wound its way through the jungle, twisting and turning to avoid palm and coconut trees and matted sections of voluminous vines. The trail opened onto a sandy spot of beach, but the water was rough, and Wieser decided not to swim. He gave his cans of beer to one of the other guys.

Later in the afternoon, dark clouds began to gather over the island. Rain was imminent. The guys who had shared their beer instead of drinking it were level headed enough to know they should leave. The ones who had been the recipients of the extra beer felt no sense of urgency about anything. Darkness tinged the edges of the jungle as the sun disappeared behind the rain clouds. The sober sailors finally managed to direct the partiers toward the path. They needed to stay in a group and follow each other through the jungle. It was thick and dark, and someone could easily get lost. Wieser berated himself for even going on liberty. He would have been much happier sitting on the boat deck writing a letter home to Jean. He didn't know why he kept trying.

When they reached the dock, he was relieved to climb inside the launch. He had barely found a seat when he looked back at the dock. One of the bigger boys from the ship who had taken advantage of the extra cans of beer came running like a madman down the dock, sprang from the end, and came sailing headfirst into the launch. Wieser unintentionally broke his fall. His joints and muscles hurt for days.

★★★★★★★★★★★★★★★

As junior officer of the deck, Herb Weyrauch spent many hours in the presence of the ship's captain, Wilder D. Baker. Often, as the ship was patrolling, Weyrauch stood watch on the navigation bridge. One day, Captain Baker leaned back in his armchair and motioned for Weyrauch to come closer.

"Lieutenant Weyrauch," the captain said. "I will be leaving soon to become commander of Cruiser Division One."

"Congratulations, sir," Weyrauch replied, trying not to reveal his disappointment that the captain was leaving.

"I've been watching you and am very impressed with your performance."

"Thank you, sir."

"I will be needing a good communications officer on my staff." The captain paused, then placed his hand on Weyrauch's shoulder. "I would like for you to join me and be that officer."

Weyrauch was thrilled. He admired the captain and enjoyed working with him. The prospect of continuing under his command was as exciting as the realization of a promotion.

"I would be honored, sir," Weyrauch said without hesitation.

"Very well. I will instruct the Bureau of Personnel to issue your orders immediately. I will be leaving very soon, but you can join me when your orders are processed and transportation becomes available."

"Yes, sir. Thank you, sir."

Captain Frank P. Thomas relieved Captain Baker on May 27. Weyrauch was detached from the *North Carolina* on May 30 while the ship was anchored at Noumea, but he spent a week at an airstrip on the north end of New Caledonia before a plane arrived that could take him to Pearl Harbor. He then had to await transportation north. Six more weeks passed before he joined his commanding officer aboard his flagship, the *Richmond,* at anchor in the bay of Adak Island in the Aleutian chain of Alaska.

05 June 1943

The Kingfisher OS2U floatplanes aboard the *North Carolina* served as the ship's eyes in the sky, flying scouting missions and spotting for the gunners during shore bombardments. They pulled targets for gunnery practice and also performed at-sea rescues for fighter pilots who had been shot down. The planes were just under

34 feet long and had a wingspan of almost 36 feet. They had a main center float and a smaller float under each wing. The planes could be launched off the ship's fantail along a catapult, or if necessary during a rescue, they could take off from the water. They could land only on water.

Although the planes were not designed to be attackers, they were equipped with firepower for protection. They could carry a hundred-pound bomb under each wing and were also equipped with two .30 caliber machine guns. The front-firing machine gun was synchronized so as to fire through the propeller as it spun without hitting it; when the propeller rotated out of the way, the gun released the bullet. The pilot fired the machine gun by a trigger on the control stick. When the gun was not in use and at the end of every flight, the pilot prevented the gun from accidentally firing by pulling back on a bolt that locked the firing pin about six inches away from the ammunition. Then, when the plane was safely back

Following completion of flight duty, the Showboat's OS2U Kingfisher aircraft landed on the water, taxied to the ship, and were hoisted aboard by a crane. They rested in a catapult on the fantail of the ship in preparation for the next takeoff.
COURTESY OF BATTLESHIP NORTH CAROLINA COLLECTION

aboard ship, ordnance boys could unload the guns.

Seaman First Class Robert Alexander Nelson began maintenance checks on number-two plane sitting on the catapult on the port side of the ship. While at Noumea, the planes often pulled targets for antiaircraft practice. They had not flown in several days but were preparing to go out again the next day. He checked the seams on the catapults to make sure no rivets had worked loose. He checked the catapult launching gears and greased them. He climbed up on the catapult to grease the bearings and check the plane's propeller. Nelson reached up, grabbed the propeller blade in his right hand, and pulled down. The machine gun fired a shot that pierced his forehead, and he tumbled to the deck, dead.

14 June 1943

The day was clear, the sun bright. The tropical heat beat down on the teak deck as Gunner's Mate Lester Tucker double-checked the target containers and loaded them onto the bomb racks of the Kingfisher with the help of his aviation ordnance striker. Inside each of the containers, a 20-foot-long target attached to 900 feet of nine-thread Manila line had been carefully folded so that when the container opened during flight, the target would sail out behind the aircraft and not become entangled in its own line.

Ensign John Burns checked the Kingfisher OS2U aircraft to make sure everything was in order for the flight. All the boys in the aviation division loved and respected Burns. Prior to joining the Navy, he had been in seminary preparing for the Jesuit priesthood, and his training there had carried over into his Navy career, guiding the way he treated his fellow officers and the enlisted men who served under him. He was known not to smoke or drink, and none of the boys had ever heard him use any profane language.

Burns climbed into the pilot's seat, and Tucker took his place behind him as rear-seat crewman. The *North Carolina* was steaming in the vicinity of Noumea, New Caledonia, accompanied by four destroyers participating in gunnery trials. The sea was relatively calm that day as the ship turned into the wind to provide additional lift

for the seaplane as it was launched. The Kingfisher's main float sat cradled in the launching cart of the catapult, a 68-foot-long mini-runway that rotated 30 degrees over the water in preparation for the launch. Burns raced the small airplane's engine and gave the ready signal to his crew on deck. A blast of black-powder charge hurled the cart forward from zero to 60 knots, and as a mechanical device caught the cart at the end of the catapult, the seaplane became airborne.

Burns nosed the seaplane higher and higher, leveling off at about 1,200 feet approximately a mile behind the group of ships. He prepared to begin the session of target practice, the destroyers firing their 20- and 40-millimeter antiaircraft guns at the target sleeve pulled behind the plane. Tucker released the container door, and the target fluttered out behind the Kingfisher just as it was designed to do. Burns received directions to make a run at one of the destroyers located off the port bow of the *North Carolina*. At the current distance of about three-quarters of a mile, Tucker could see the red flag at half-mast on the destroyer, meaning "Stand by for firing." When the flag was two-blocked, or raised to full staff, the corresponding order would be "Commence firing." The plane came within a thousand feet of the destroyer, and Tucker saw the guns leading the target as they were trained to do. But he spotted one of the 20s leading the target at an excessive angle, almost twice that of its counterparts. He saw the flag two-blocked and felt a huge lump rise in his throat as the guns began to fire.

Over the intercommunication system, Burns yelled, "What the hell are they doing down there? Don't those damn fools know what they are doing? Fire a warning signal."

Tucker had already reached for the signal pistol to fire a cease-fire warning, but before he got off a shot, an officer aboard the destroyer ordered the gunners to stop. Tucker counted nine tracers whizzing over the plane's canopy, and since only every third round was a tracer, at least 27 rounds had already been fired by that one gun.

"Damn," Burns said, then regained his composure and finished the training exercise.

Tucker would transfer off the *North Carolina* a couple of months later and return to the States for flight school. He never heard Burns curse again.

7 September 1943

Continued problems with one of the propellers sent the *North Carolina* back to Pearl Harbor for repairs again. Several days later, as she neared the Hawaiian Islands, her destroyer escort group was replaced by the *Burns*, the *Kidd*, and the *Bullard*. The *Kidd* was a brand-new destroyer, commissioned in April and passing through the Panama Canal for the first time in August. Training never ceased, whether the ship was a battle veteran like the *North Carolina* or new to the fleet like the *Kidd*. The ships participated in a simulated torpedo attack at dawn, the *North Carolina* illuminating the *Kidd* with five-inch star shells. Something went terribly wrong, and the *Kidd* took a direct hit from the *North Carolina*. One five-inch illuminating projectile pierced her side just above the water line. The other fell short, ricocheted off the surface of the water, passed through the captain's cabin, and lodged in a landing-force locker. No one was injured, and since the repair party was standing by practicing for a real torpedo attack, the damage was quickly controlled.

The crew of the BB55 felt terrible about the accident and tried to think of a way to pass their apologies along to the crew of the *Kidd*. A couple of days later, the *Kidd* came alongside to refuel from the *North Carolina*. While the ships steamed along at fueling speed, the band from the Showboat gathered on deck and began playing for the crew of the destroyer. A box with a large, square white cake inside was passed over the heaving lines. It had decorative icing around the edges, and in the center, the bakers aboard the *North Carolina* had designed an edible purple heart complete

Bakers from the Showboat made a Purple Heart cake for the crew of the USS Kidd *after the BB55 accidentally damaged her during practice with star shells. The cake was accompanied by homemade ice cream fresh from the Showboat's gedunk.*
COURTESY OF BATTLESHIP *NORTH CAROLINA* COLLECTION

Mail call was a highlight of life aboard any ship that spent weeks, months, or even years at sea. The mailbags were passed from the destroyer or supply ship to the BB55 across a highline. The purple-heart cake was delivered to the Kidd *the same way.*

COURTESY OF BATTLESHIP *NORTH CAROLINA* COLLECTION

with ribbon. They had also written "USS *Kidd*" across the cake. A small American flag rose from the cake just above the medal. Ice cream from the BB55's own ice-cream maker accompanied the cake. The captain of the *Kidd* thanked the *North Carolina* for her own special brand of damage control.

27 September 1943

Henry Julian Kobierski of Salem, Massachusetts, was found dead in his bunk shortly after returning from authorized liberty in Pearl Harbor. He had been treated at the naval hospital for heart problems earlier in the year. Kobierski's death was attributed to coronary heart disease, and he was buried at Pearl Harbor on October 5, 1943.

Richard Fox
COURTESY OF BRUCE THOMPSON

6 October 1943

During the *North Carolina*'s stay in Pearl, many crew members transferred off the ship and new ones transferred aboard. Eighteen-year-old Richard Fox was one of the new Marines who joined the Showboat.

The Fox family was large—12 children—and lived in the small farming town of Newport, Nebraska, population 400. As a boy, Richard had loved hunting rabbits, coyotes, and game birds. When the Japanese attacked Pearl Harbor, he wanted to join the military, but his mother insisted that he finish high school first. Two older brothers joined the Army, leaving Richard behind. But when he finished high school in the spring of 1943, Richard immediately traveled to Omaha to join the United States Marine Corps.

Near the end of boot camp, the new Marines learned what their choices for service would be. Fox chose sea school, which would qualify him to serve aboard cruisers, carriers, and battleships. When that training was complete, he and about 250 other new recruits took a train to San Francisco, then an ammunition ship to Pearl Harbor, where they would receive their assignments. The deck of the ammunition ship was covered with bombs, torpedoes, and beer.

Fox was one of about 20 recent arrivals who marched down to the docks in Pearl to board the carrier *Bunker Hill*, but that ship was already pulling out by the time they arrived, so the boys marched back to the Marine barracks for the night. The next day, they marched down to the harbor again for a new assignment. Fox thought the ammunition ship was big, but when he saw the *North Carolina* moored in her berth at Pearl, he was amazed. He had never seen anything like that before.

10 November 1943

While being repaired at Pearl Harbor, the Showboat received a new paint job—black, light blue, and dark blue—as a means of camouflage in the ocean waves. Repaired, repainted, refueled, and refreshed, she left Pearl Harbor with nine other ships headed for assault operations against Makin and Tarawa in the Gilbert Islands of the South Pacific, about 2,000 miles southwest of Hawaii. Following their defeat at Guadalcanal, the Japanese had immediately begun heavily fortifying the Gilbert Islands, and capturing them would prove more difficult than the Americans anticipated. The balance of power had shifted in the Pacific, but the Japanese were far from defeated and would turn to unconventional warfare in an effort to succeed at any cost.

CHAPTER NINE

Night Attacks

"The Japanese apparently are equipped and intend to attack our carrier task forces at night with torpedoes. . . . The Japanese in this case had ample opportunity to attack in the daytime, but chose to come at night."

USS Enterprise *action report,*
26 November 1943

Preliminary bombardment of Tarawa, which did not include the *North Carolina*, lasted only three hours before the Second Marine Division landed. Dozens of ships participated in the advance on Tarawa, but it was the most heavily fortified island the Allies had encountered, and the bombardment had not been long enough. A coral reef prevented the landing craft from reaching the shore, and the Marines had to wade in across sharp coral. Within the first hour of the landing, almost every Marine in the first wave was killed by Japanese hiding in coconut-log bunkers and a series of tunnels. Rear

Admiral Keigi Shibasaki had vowed that "a million men could not take Tarawa in a hundred years." The Americans proved him wrong—Tarawa was secured in four days by 35,000 men, though 1,500 Americans died. Few prisoners of war were taken; Japanese soldiers committed suicide when capture appeared imminent; a total of 4,800 enemy troops died on Tarawa.

19 November 1943

Dawn general quarters sounded aboard the *North Carolina* at 0430 hours. The *Enterprise* launched 34 torpedo planes for the first strike on Makin Island. Every time the task force turned into the wind for the carriers to launch aircraft, the boys manning the 20s on the bow of the *North Carolina*, including Richard Fox and Bob Palomaris, covered their guns and scrambled to duck behind the gun shield or scale the stairs to the signal bridge. As large and seaworthy as the BB55 was—her bow usually stood 30 feet above the water line—she still dipped low when facing the wind if the seas were rough at all, and sheets of water would wash across the bow, rush down its slope, knock gunners off their feet, and pound them into stationary objects. Most of the time, warnings of the impending turn gave gunners the necessary time to take cover, but not always.

For two days, flight operations were uneventful, but at 0307 hours the third morning, air defense sounded aboard the Showboat to repel air attack. During air defense, only the crews of the anti-aircraft guns—the 20s, the 40s, and the five-inch guns—manned their battle stations, but the rest of the crew knew their call usually followed close behind. Bogies had been contacted by radar at 45 and 52 miles, range decreasing rapidly.

On the bow, Fox, Palomaris, and the other Marines and sailors manning the 20s snatched off the protective canvas covers, opened the ammunition boxes, loaded the first magazine, and waited. Inside each of the five-inch mounts, 12 sailors took their places in the dark and closed the hatches behind them—Bob Fennelly as hotcase man in number three and Paul Wieser as powder man in number seven.

Fennelly shoved his hands and arms into the shoulder-length asbestos gloves. When the guns were aimed at a target requiring less than a 45-degree angle of the gun, the empty powder casings no longer ejected automatically down the chute and through the small door to the deck. As hotcase man, Fennelly had to catch the 12-pound casings in midair as they ejected and toss them out through the smaller opening about chest high in the mount's outer wall. The gloves often slipped, and the hot casings burned his arms.

Wieser stood ready to retrieve the loaded powder casings that came up from the handling room through the chute in the floor of the mount between his feet. Fear pounded in his chest. The boys had never received an air-raid call that early in the morning, and the shrill sound had startled him from a deep sleep. Fortunately, his living quarters were close to the gun mount, and he was at his station in seconds. Inside the mount, the boys were oblivious to anything going on outside. They were a dozen men packed into a 14-foot-square metal enclosure full of gun components waiting for orders from the mount captain as the sweat dripped down their faces. Wieser watched the mount captain's facial expressions—illuminated by only the small red lights on the bulkhead beside him—for any sign of what information he might be hearing through his headphones from the director above and for even the slightest indication of impending battle.

Five minutes after air defense sounded, general quarters roused the remaining crew from their bunks. The waiting game began. At 0426 hours, almost an hour and a half after the first radar contact had been made, the ships of the fleet lost all bogie contact. Half an hour later, new contact indicated a large number of bogies at 73 miles. Within 20 minutes, the enemy disappeared off the radar screen again, and the *Enterprise* launched her planes.

On the bow, Fox and Palomaris could see and hear the planes take off. Inside the five-inch mounts, Wieser and Fennelly knew nothing. The boys inside the mounts grew weary, and some tried to find a place to sit or stretch out and catch a nap as they waited for the mount captain to shout a stand-by warning. Even in the early-November morning, the heat and stuffiness inside the mount were draining. But the gun components left little floor space to even sit, much less lie down, and standing for hours while they waited took a toll on nerves as well as legs.

A bogie picked up by radar at 25 miles was shot down by one of the *Enterprise* pilots. Three hours and 20 tense minutes after the first air-raid warning sounded, the crew secured from general quarters and began what became an uneventful day.

For the next couple of days, the task force steamed in the vicinity of Makin Island, planes from the carriers flying routine patrols. On November 23, the ships moved far enough away from immediate danger to refuel. Task force radar had tracked enemy planes heading south toward Tarawa and returning north about 50 miles west of Makin for several consecutive mornings. When the task force was about 75 miles northeast of Makin, the *Enterprise* launched planes just a couple of hours after midnight in an attempt to intercept these flights. If the Japanese could play night games, the Americans could, too. Although radar picked up enemy aircraft during the mission, they were too far away for engagement.

Near dusk on November 25, radar contacted one bogie flying low, but planes from the *Enterprise* were unable to intercept it. The sun set at 1817 into a gray-black ocean, the tropical sunset spilling across the water like a broken, bloody egg yolk. All carriers recovered their aircraft. The night was moonless, surface visibility 4,000 yards as the ships of the fleet steamed along. Intelligence knew that enemy planes were operating from bases in the Marshall Islands, and the probability was great that the task force had been spotted and tracked during the day; tensions were high as the ships waited for Japan's next move.

The boys did not have to wait long. Shortly after evening enveloped the fleet, a lone enemy aircraft was spotted shadowing the formation. Air defense sounded, and the antiaircraft gun crews manned their battle stations in complete darkness. Visual contact with the target was lost, but radar continued to track it. All hands manned general quarters, hurrying through knee-high hatches, scaling rung ladders or small staircases—up on the port side and down on the starboard so they did not bump into each other as they ran toward their assigned stations on every level of the ship. The lone plane turned and began to climb, then circled the formation at a distance too great for the antiaircraft guns to make contact, seeming to toy with the fleet.

Lookouts spotted a blinking light just beyond the *Enterprise*, and the formation changed course, maneuvering in darkness, collision an ever-present risk. Radar made contact with 10 to 12 planes at 24 miles—the snooper flying low, the group closing in. Then it split into three sections. On the port side, the planes were coming in fast at eight miles, then six. Sky two reported ready to fire—planes dead ahead at 6,000 yards. The planes turned away. During their departure, they dropped two float lights that burned brightly and illuminated the ships. Five flares followed, silhouetting the formation, making the ships visible targets for the enemy.

One plane closed in on the starboard side of the BB55 at less than 200 yards, flying at about masthead height. One 40 and two 20s on the starboard bow opened fire, including the mount manned by gunner Fox and his loader, Ray Horn. The plane broke into flames and crashed into the water.

Inside mount seven, Wieser saw the expression change on the mount captain's face.

"Stand by," he said.

The boys jumped into position; Wieser planted his feet and waited for the next order.

"Commence firing."

Wieser reached for a powder casing at his feet, lifted it, and placed it into the tray, repeating the process again and again. The gun crews worked in synchronized rhythm, mounts seven and nine firing 40 rounds before the cease-fire command was issued. The first target disappeared from the screen in flashes, indicating a hit, and firing shifted immediately to a second target, which turned and flew away, speeding beyond the range of the guns. A third plane zeroed in on the BB55, and the entire five-inch battery on the starboard side opened fire. Fennelly deftly caught and tossed the empty hot casings as they ejected from the gun. The enemy disappeared from all radar screens; a ball of smoke and a large splash in the water were observed.

No other planes of that group approached the formation, but a few minutes later, a large group of bogies was located at a distance of 85 miles. The formation changed course, and the bogies faded from the radar screen—all except one group at 75 miles. The formation changed course several more times during the ensuing hour as bogies were spotted and lost. Exactly three hours after air defense sounded, when all radar screens in the fleet were clear, the crew secured from general quarters.

"This attack was broken up and repelled by the AA guns of the screen," Captain F. P. Thomas wrote later in the war diary. "Planes that pressed home their attacks were either shot down or driven off before they got inside the screen. The performance of personnel and material in this ship's first night action and the first action in over a year was all that could be expected."

But it became clear the following evening that the Japanese intended to continue attacking the carrier forces after dark. As the carrier air-patrol groups landed following their day-long duties, a two-engine bomber was sighted 18 miles from the task force, but contact was lost within 20 minutes. Just prior to sunset, the *Enterprise* launched a three-plane night fighter group. Just when the sun ceased to light the day and the moon did not appear, radar picked up an estimated two dozen enemy bombers at 34 miles. Air defense sounded 10 minutes after first contact, and the antiaircraft gun crews once again manned their guns in complete darkness. The night fighter group from the *Enterprise* intercepted the large force of enemy planes, shooting down two and dispersing the group prior to its attack. When those flashes on the horizon were seen, general quarters sounded, and the BB55 was once again at full battle stations.

The gunners did not have a long wait. Within 10 minutes, the ship was under attack by enemy aircraft, and the five-inch and automatic weaponry on the port side opened fire on the intruders. The formation made an emergency turn, but since the ocean was fairly calm and the winds were low, the 20-millimeter gunners on the bow did not have to desert their stations. The port side ceased firing for five minutes, then bogies were spotted five miles to starboard and closing in. The enemy dropped 25 to 30 flares for illumination, making the ships in the task force easier prey. The five-inch guns on the starboard side opened fire as the ship made an emergency turn, then ceased firing as the port-side battery opened up and the ship made another emergency turn. The starboard and port sides rotated firing as the ship continued following the formation in a series of diversionary moves. An ejected five-inch powder can was still so hot when it hit the deck that it started a fire next to mount three, but the repair party quickly had it under control. The engagement lasted approximately three hours, just as it had the previous night.

When the smoke cleared, the captain stated in his report, "All hands repeated their excellent performance of the night before. Special credit is due the five-inch batteries. In both this and the preceding night's action, enemy planes were either shot down or turned away. . . . No planes that were taken under fire by the five-inch battery of this ship got inside the screen."

The BB55 continued operating in the vicinity of Makin Island in support of the landings there until she received orders to proceed to an area approximately 250 miles south of Tarawa, where she would participate in her first shore bombardment at the island of Nauru. Japan had fortified Nauru and used the two landing strips there to launch air strikes and scouting missions. Although Allied troops had bombarded the island in the preceding weeks, the Japanese continued to launch aircraft from at least one of the airstrips. In addition to the carriers, the newly formed task force for the bombardment included three battleships and six destroyers, their mission to render the airstrips useless.

8 December 1943

General quarters sounded at 0540. Ten minutes later, the carriers launched their attack groups to bomb from the air. The battleships and destroyers formed linear columns, three destroyers in front of and three in back of the battleships in the center. The huge turrets on the *North Carolina* rotated to port, the cannons ready to fire. Mount crews in the five-inch secondary battery on the port side prepared for their first real-life shore bombardment. Wieser and Fennelly, on the starboard side with nothing to do, stood behind turret three and watched.

The seas were calm and the sky clear as both of the BB55's Kingfishers were launched prior to the bombarding—one for spotting and one for antisubmarine patrol. In less than half an hour, the spotter plane reported back to the ship that all salvos had landed on or near their intended targets; the successful bombardment was complete, and the crew secured from general quarters. The Japanese would use the airstrips no more.

★★★★★★★★★★★★★★★★

As the fleet progressed in its Pacific campaign, taking islands from Japanese control, it left behind such previous safe harbors as Noumea. When the Guadalcanal campaign was complete, the fleet advanced to a rendezvous point in Havannah Harbor at Efate Island in the New Hebrides, where the *North Carolina* headed after bombarding Nauru, arriving on December 12. Away from immediate danger, the boys thought often of the impending holidays. Christmas was coming, and theirs would be anything but white.

When the ship moored to a buoy in the harbor, the boys lowered the captain's gig into the water so it would be immediately available for use during the ship's stay. Boats for transporting crew to and from the island were checked out from the boat pool and tied to the boat boom that extended off the starboard side. Often, the water in the harbor became oily from leaky ships, and the BB55's captain's gig grew grimy rings at water level.

Fennelly had instilled pride in his boat crew, and they always kept their boat clean. His best man was Millard Nieman, his boat hook, who helped maneuver the boat when it was in use; he used a hook to pull the gig safely to the gangway when it reached its destination and to keep its bow from bumping too hard against the side of the ship or dock. When the boat was in the water, Nieman often climbed out onto the boat boom, shinnied down the hanging rope-and-rung ladder, and cleaned the boat inside and out, leaning over the side to wipe off grime and oil, even though the swaying motion of the boat, tied only by a line that ran down from the boom, often made him seasick.

One day when the ship was in Efate, Nieman came to Fennelly just after cleaning the gig. Fennelly immediately recognized the hallow, pale look on Nieman's face and the way he held his hand just below his neck. Fennelly knew what was coming.

"Bob," Nieman said. "I gotta go to sick bay. I'm not feeling so good."

Fennelly commanded respect from his crew, but they used little formality, and the boys sometimes called him by his first name.

"Go get fixed up," he told Nieman, knowing the young man would be back as soon as the seasickness wore off. Nieman was a good boy, a hard worker, and Fennelly just learned to deal with the episodes of seasickness.

★★★★★★★★★★★★★★

The boys' second Christmas away from home started at Efate, but before the day was over, they were gone. The ships of the task force were put on four hours' notice to get under way before dark and head to a point a hundred miles west of New Georgia Island and operate in that area until receiving further orders. The strains of "White Christmas" blaring through the speakers, Fennelly felt himself become teary eyed as the boys returned the borrowed boats and brought theirs back aboard ship, preparing to get under way. He didn't worry about getting emotional, though, because he knew he wasn't the only one.

The crew ate well that Christmas day—roast turkey, dressing, gravy, pumpkin pie, lots of vegetables, breads, and desserts. But it certainly wasn't home, and the Christmas songs meant to cheer them often had the opposite effect. They knew they were headed back to action, but they didn't know where or when.

As the ship steamed to locations unknown to the enlisted men, they returned to their regular daily routine—general quarters at dawn, ready to repel any surprise attacks, followed by cleaning duties and watches, four hours on, four hours off. They worked at their regular jobs in the interim, went to general quarters at dusk, then got some sleep before the routine started again. Three days out to sea, the battleships fueled their accompanying destroyers, then two days later fueled them again. The destroyers couldn't carry a huge amount of fuel and had to be replenished often and topped off whenever possible. On the last day of the year 1943, the larger ships fueled from a tanker, then began the new year by supporting air strikes on an enemy task force reportedly heading toward Kavieng, New Ireland. Throughout the next few days, the antiaircraft guns were often manned as general quarters sounded, snooper planes bleeping on and off the radar screens. Then the task force received notice to return to Efate. The strikes had been successful, they learned. Word passed from the carrier force that two Japanese destroyers had been damaged by the air attacks near Kavieng.

When the task force arrived in the harbor three days later, many supply ships were already waiting, and the crew of the *North Carolina* began taking on supplies, ammunition, and fuel. The ship stayed at Efate for 10 days, restocking and undergoing minor repairs. Deep down, the boys knew that surely something big was getting ready to happen. As the ships pulled anchor and left the safety of Havannah Harbor, they steamed into extraordinarily rough seas. Waves slapped against the ship and washed over the bow.

In Fifth Division, Nieman didn't handle it very well.

"Hey, Bob," he said to Fennelly, his face white and his hands clenched.

"I know," Fennelly answered before Nieman could even ask. "Go on down to sick bay until you feel better."

They couldn't do much right then anyway; all hands were sent below deck. On the *North Carolina*, one man had already been injured when the sheets of water sent him sliding down the deck. The destroyer *Lang* and the battleship *South Dakota* each lost a man overboard.

When the seas calmed enough that the crew could resume their duties on deck, Nieman was right there to help out. When not in use, Fifth Division's wooden boat was filled with water to keep the seams tight. Each day, the water was drained, the boat scrubbed, then refilled. Nieman had the process down to the letter, and Fennelly rarely had to tell him what to do. They worked in perfect concert, taking care of the equipment, cleaning their area of the ship. Fennelly didn't talk much about his family or home, and out of respect, perhaps, neither did Nieman, but as they worked or played acey-deucy, wrote letters home or sat down to chow, they developed a bond of quiet understanding and mutual respect.

★★★★★★★★★★★★★★★

The ship was under way for several days, repeating January 20 due to crossing the International Date Line. On the second January 20, 1944, Task Force 37, which included the *North Carolina*, arrived at Funafuti in the Ellice Islands, well southeast of its last target of Nauru and out of immediate danger of attack from enemy forces. There, the *North Carolina* became part of a new group, Task Force 58, under the command of Admiral William "Bull" Halsey. Task Force 58 and Task Force 38, under Admiral Raymond A. Spruance, would continue offensive operations across the Pacific toward the Japanese homeland. Next target: capture and occupation of the Marshall Islands, north of both the Gilbert Islands and the Solomon Islands, which had already been captured.

The next round of shore bombardments began on January 29, and by February 1, troops landed on the Marshall Islands. Capture was complete, and the task force moored in Majuro Atoll during the first part of February to resupply and refuel the ships and the crews. The BB55 was under way again by the middle of the month.

Nieman continued to battle his bouts of seasickness. In fact, he had not been able to completely shake the feeling for days. As the task force rendezvoused for refueling, Nieman was having a hard time keeping up with the work. The deck crew had so much to do, especially with all the ships in the task force fueling that day. Manning the fueling lines was a difficult job. Nieman was not moving as quickly as he needed to, and Fennelly feared he would be knocked overboard where the lifelines had been lowered to accommodate the fueling lines. If he lost his balance, nothing would keep him from falling into the ocean between the ships.

"Are you okay?" Fennelly asked his boat hook.

"I feel real bad," Nieman said.

"I can tell," Fennelly responded. "You go on down to sick bay before you get yourself or somebody else killed."

He had become accustomed to the routine and knew Nieman would be back before long.

Refueling all the ships in the task force and then securing the lines and other equipment required most of the day. Fennelly checked the gear locker to make sure everything was in good repair and organized properly when the work crews retired that evening. He was meticulous, and the gear locker was always well organized. He'd been so busy he hadn't had much time to think about Nieman, but the boat hook's illness had become so routine that Fennelly didn't worry when he hit the sack to catch some sleep before dawn GQ.

Word passed that the task force would be making a high-speed run into the highly fortified island of Truk on the night of February 15, 1944. The day started routinely with an uneventful dawn GQ, then Fennelly went about his regular daily routine. As the day

Rigging the fuel lines was a dangerous job even when all hands were healthy and the weather superb, but with Nieman feeling so poorly, Fennelly feared for his safety.
COURTESY OF BATTLESHIP *NORTH CAROLINA* COLLECTION

wore on and Nieman didn't come back to work, Fennelly began to wonder about him and started to worry a little, too.

"Fennelly," said a pharmacist's mate who came to Fifth Division later in the day. "Gather some of your men for a burial party. Nieman died."

Fennelly felt a pain in his chest and berated himself for not going down and checking on the boy.

"But I thought he was just seasick. He got that way all the time, always got better."

"Not this time. We'll have his body ready soon," the pharmacist's mate replied. "You'll need a total of six men."

Fennelly gathered five of his boys, and they descended the ladders to sick bay to retrieve Nieman's body. He had been sewn inside a canvas bag with two five-inch projectiles, placed on a stretcher, and covered with an American flag. Fennelly wouldn't know for weeks what had killed his shipmate. He only knew it was far more serious than seasickness, and he wished he'd done more to help him.

Fennelly's crew, still dressed in their work dungarees and chambray shirts, were joined by two officers in khaki as they carried the flag-draped body of the young Texan to a spot on the deck next to mount seven. Fennelly had watched other burials at sea, but he had not participated before and hadn't personally known any of the others. Wieser was on watch inside mount seven and looked out through the side hatch. Crew gathered atop the mount and at the rails on every level of the ship as the band played. Dressed in his khakis and tie, Fox joined the Marine honor guard as they prepared to honor Nieman with a 21-gun salute. The chaplain administered a Protestant service for the young boy from Lamesa. As Fennelly tried to listen to the words, he felt the hot South Pacific sun beating down on his back and saw the sun glinting off the water.

09 May 1937

"C'mon, Bob," 10-year-old Dickie Fennelly begged. "Please go with me. It'll be fun."

Bob tried to ignore his little brother and continued adjusting the chain on his bicycle. After all, it was his only mode of transportation. But at 12, he didn't use that bike just for fun like a bunch of the boys did. It was his livelihood. It had to be kept in top working condition.

"Can't you see I'm busy?" Bob said.

He picked up the small metal can and tipped it carefully, watching the oil drip one drop at a time from the slender, curved spout onto the sprocket of the back wheel. Bob was meticulous in everything he did. He placed his left hand on the top of the black rubber and pulled down with a smooth, quick motion. The tire made little noise as he watched the spinning spokes. Bob tried to concentrate on his work, but his little brother stood over his shoulder and begged.

It was Sunday afternoon—Mother's Day 1937. Bob didn't work on Sundays, but he would be up at three the next morning delivering papers before school. The mornings were still pretty nippy in Govenstown, Maryland, in early spring, but the sun felt warm on his back that afternoon. Four hundred and fifty times each weekday, he reached into the satchel on his bike and slung a paper into a neighbor's yard. He felt a sense of accomplishment every time he collected that $3.75 a week.

"Bob, please!" Dickie begged. "Please go with me."

"I don't want to," Bob said, adjusting the chain one more time. "Go ask somebody else."

The Fennelly family was large—three girls and five boys—and Bob was in the middle. He thought one of the older brothers must have let Dickie tag along to the lake before. People were always there walking, swimming, picnicking. Bob suspected all the teenage girls sunbathing on the hill interested his older brothers, but he didn't care a thing about the lake. He couldn't even swim.

"They won't go," Dickie whined. "C'mon, Bob, please."

Bob finally relented, dropping his screwdriver onto the small pile of tools lying next to his bike, which was balanced upside down on its handlebars and seat. He looked back over his shoulder at the unfinished work and picked up his pace to keep up with his younger brother.

The sun glinted off the water as the two boys reached the lake. They walked past the women sitting on blankets reading and the teenage girls lying in the sun. Kids squealed as they ran around playing ball or chasing each other across the grass. Even that early in the year, people were swimming in the lake.

Dickie sat on the grass and started taking off his shoes.

"What are you doing?" Bob said. "We're not going in that water."

"I'm just going to wade in the edge," Dickie said. "I did it before."

"But it's probably cold," Bob said. "I'm not doing it."

Bob stood and watched Dickie stick his toes into the edge of the water lapping softly on the sand.

Dickie squealed, "It's cold!"

"C'mon, Dickie, we need to go," Bob said.

"But we just got here."

"Yeah, but I don't want to get in trouble. I never should've let you talk me into coming. Let's go home."

"Just a few more minutes," Dickie pleaded, and waded a little deeper into the water.

"I said let's go," Bob yelled, but Dickie just kept walking along the edge of the water.

"Let's go," Bob repeated.

Bob followed impatiently along the edge, and Dickie didn't go out any deeper. He just kept walking parallel to the shore, where the water was shallow. Then he simply vanished into the water. One step and he was gone.

"Dickie!" Bob screamed over and over. "Dickie!"

He ran toward the spot where he'd last seen his brother, the shallow water splashing as his feet pounded the ground—until suddenly no earth was there. It just disappeared in one step. The water enveloped him, and he gulped big mouthfuls as he searched frantically with his eyes open underwater. He used the only stroke he knew to pull himself to the surface and yelled when his mouth broke the water. No one seemed to notice the terror unfolding before them. Bob doggie-paddled around and around, going down, swallowing water, fighting his way back up, screaming for his brother. But he never saw him again.

"Unto Almighty God we commend the soul of our brother departed," the ship's chaplain said, "and we commit his body to the deep, in sure and certain hope of the Resurrection unto eternal life, through our Lord, Jesus Christ. Amen."

The boys tilted the board, and the bag containing Nieman's body slipped out from under the flag into the ocean churning below the fast-moving ship. Fennelly was the third man down, too far from the side to see over, but he didn't need to see. The vision was vivid in his mind—someone he loved vanishing beneath the water. He would never see his friend again.

Bob Fennelly (third from left at back) *saluted the flag that had covered the body of his boathook and friend, Millard Nieman, during Nieman's burial in the South Pacific.*
COURTESY OF BATTLESHIP *NORTH CAROLINA* COLLECTION

CHAPTER TEN

Rescue at Truk
★★★★★★★★★★★★★★★★★★

"I never saw the North Carolina *while I was in the South Pacific, but I heard about her. We all had. It made us feel better just knowing she was out there."*

Ray Barwick, USS Roper

The task force increased its speed to 22 knots and headed for Truk in the Caroline Islands, about halfway between the Marshall Islands, which the Americans had already captured, and the Marianas, which would be their next major target. The Americans knew that Truk was extremely important to the Japanese forces and that the enemy presence there was immense. Capture would come later, when other islands surrounding it had been secured, but in the meantime, the ships would take potshots at it every time they passed.

Task Force 58 included several task groups, each operating in a formation of its own, all moving together, like several sets of concentric circles gliding in the same direction. Just before sunrise on February 16, when the huge fleet of ships was about 75 miles from

Flak from antiaircraft fire filled the air as an enemy plane spiraled downward during the battle that became known as the Marianas Turkey Shoot.

Truk, the carriers launched the first wave of aircraft to begin strikes. Air attacks continued for two days, then the task force steamed away from Truk at 25 knots, leaving behind its calling card in the form of 19 enemy ships sunk—two light cruisers, three destroyers, two gunboats, one ammunition ship, two oilers, eight cargo ships, and one seaplane tender—and seven probables—one cruiser or large destroyer, two oilers, and four cargo ships. But the heavily fortified island of Truk was far from being ripe for occupation. The ships would return later to finish the job.

The task force continued westward toward the Mariana Islands with orders to make air strikes on Saipan and Tinian. Constant contacts appeared on the radar screen, and the boys of the BB55 scrambled to battle stations at dusk, where they would remain throughout the night, struggling to stay awake and alert, waiting for an enemy that did not materialize until the next day. The *North Carolina* gunners took out at least one, maybe two, enemy aircraft.

Strikes against Saipan, Tinian, and Guam proved successful—

135 enemy planes destroyed in the air or on the ground, 12 ships sunk or burning, and aircraft installations, fuel-oil storage facilities, and radio installations strafed and bombed. Allied losses totaled six planes.

Having made itself well known in the Marianas, Task Force 58 headed back eastward to Majuro Atoll in the Marshall Islands to rest and replenish. Majuro Atoll was a circle of flat islands with a few palm trees around a lagoon. The water in the lagoon was smooth and the beaches sandy, but between the islands that formed the circle, the water moved rapidly with strong undercurrents. Following days and nights of general quarters, shooting down planes, and dodging the enemy, the boys of the BB55 and the other ships in the task force were happy to set foot on land. Unlike some of the other places where the ship moored and the islands were dirty or thick jungle, Majuro was the paradise they had seen on postcards.

19 March 1944

The sailors left the ship in recreation parties carrying their allotted two cans of beer each. The beer was always hot, and hot beer on hot days didn't appeal to Paul Wieser one bit. He let whoever wanted his have it.

As the crew enjoyed the surf and sand, the water in the lagoon so clear they could see the bottom as they swam, some of the tension from the past few weeks began to dissipate. Bob Fennelly thought often of Nieman. He learned that Nieman had died of septicemia, a staph infection. He wondered how long Nieman had been that sick and they had thought it was only seasickness bothering him. *He must have had a fever and didn't let anyone know*, Fennelly thought. *I should have seen it. He depended on me. I should have known.* Without the constant threat of air attacks and general quarters, the regrets had room to flood his mind.

The lagoon was so beautiful and such a welcoming place that a large group of sailors—black and white—gathered to enjoy the cooling waters and the peaceful atmosphere. The boys were instructed to stay on Peggy Island, where they had been taken for their beer party. The water between the islands was too rough, too dangerous to cross. But one group of guys caught a glimpse of a Japanese gun placement on an adjacent island. They bantered back and forth about what a great souvenir it would make. Wieser heard the talk but had no intention of trying to get it himself. He worried when he heard one of the stewards, Norman Gilliam, say he would go get the souvenir.

Gilliam stepped into the swirling water between the islands and was immediately sucked under. No one knew for sure what happened, whether or not he hit his head, or if he panicked, or if maybe he couldn't swim well enough, or if the water would have been too much for anybody to fight regardless of how well he could swim. His buddies yelled for him; several tried in vain to reach him, but he was gone. Gilliam's body was later recovered and taken back to the ship for burial preparation—a wooden coffin instead of a canvas bag. No need for projectiles to weigh him down. A funeral party left the ship and buried the Baltimore, Maryland, youth on an

Steward's mates carried the body of their shipmate and friend Norman Gilliam ashore in the Marshall Islands for burial following his drowning death at Peggy Island in the Majuro Atoll on March 19, 1944.
COURTESY OF BATTLESHIP NORTH CAROLINA COLLECTION

Norman Gilliam was buried with full military honors in grave number 19 in a United States cemetery on an island in the South Pacific. His resting spot was marked with a white cross and a bronze marker bearing his name.
COURTESY OF BATTLESHIP *NORTH CAROLINA* COLLECTION

Richard Fox and other BB55 Marines participated as the honor guard for an island funeral, possibly Norman Gilliam's.
COURTESY OF BRUCE THOMPSON

island in the middle of the Pacific.

By the end of March 1944, shipmates lost to accident or illness almost equaled those killed in action.

★★★★★★★★★★★★★★★

Three days later, the task force left Majuro Harbor heading west for the islands of Palau, Yap, and Woleai south of Guam, where previous efforts had met with great success. When the task force neared Palau on March 29, the Japanese were waiting. Enemy aircraft approached at sunset, circled within sight of the formation, and disappeared. The night was clear and the moon bright, casting its beams to create perfect silhouettes of the ships, making them easier prey for the enemy. Commanders of the task force were sure the enemy had spotted the fleet, and all hands were called to quarters. It would be yet another sleepless night.

Attack planes began approaching just after sunset. A full moon cast its rays upon the silvery stretch of water. Flying in toward the moon, the Japanese pilots could see their targets as though a great spotlight were illuminating them. But the ships in the task force were ready and immediately shot down two enemy aircraft. Enemy planes appeared on the radar almost constantly, keeping everyone alert and ready. Tension inside the five-inch gun mounts grew as Wieser in mount seven and Fennelly in mount three waited and waited. They could see nothing but their shipmates in the mount, had no way of knowing what was happening outside, could only wait and wonder.

The gunners on the automatics—the 20s and 40s—had a clear view of the moonlit night, ships rising off the dark ocean and casting perfect silhouettes against a silver sky. Conditions were perfect for Japanese torpedo-plane attacks. Less than an hour after dark, a group of planes approached the formation. The gunners on the destroyer *Massachusetts* shot down the first one, then the *North Carolina* opened fire seconds later, taking out one coming down the port side. But the next plane crossed behind the BB55 and started up the starboard side, between the ships in the formation, preventing shots from being fired without endangering friendly ships in the process. The gunners waited nervously for a commence-fire order that never came. Enemy aircraft lit up the radar for three more hours before they all just disappeared.

Task Force 58 continued its strikes against the islands for the next two days. The nights remained favorable for enemy torpedo-plane attacks, and ships in the force were vigilant, ready, and expectant. The Japanese began a series of trick tactics that kept the ships on constant standby. One plane would fly in close enough to be picked up by radar, then a large group of planes would appear on the screen. These phantom attacks became a frequently used strategy, a single plane dropping material that tricked the radar into seeing a group of planes. Another plane dropped flares that burned brightly for long periods of time like the enemy had done prior to previous attacks, but no attacks materialized. The phantom attacks kept the crew at general quarters for hours, grating their nerves, draining their energy.

But Allied strikes on the islands were successful. While the task force lost 25 planes, it destroyed more than 150 enemy planes and damaged 49, sank 29 ships and damaged 18, and sank many smaller craft. Another 26 planes were listed as probables.

The task force steamed east, past the Caroline Islands and Truk, back to Majuro for a brief respite, replenishing, and repairs. Even though the ships in the fleet had not taken any direct hits, they needed maintenance and repair on a regular basis. The crews worked on the machinery in their divisions to keep it in top working condition, but battle took its toll. On this trip back to the atoll, the destroyer *Bancroft* had its boilers and machinery completely overhauled.

7 April 1943

While the ship was in Majuro, Joseph Smits from the engine room received orders to leave the *North Carolina* and report to the *Shangri La*. He hadn't had much reason to need his pay since the ship had been at sea for some time, so when he checked in at the pay office, he discovered he had $800 on the books. He knew the first thing he was going to do when he made it safely to the mainland again.

His trip back to the States took him to Pearl, then to the West Coast. When Smits arrived in San Francisco, he hit the town dressed in his blues with a wad of cash in his pocket. His first destination? A fine-dining restaurant.

"May I take your order, sir?" the waiter asked Smits after he was seated. The waiters were all older men dressed in black tuxedos. Each carried a white napkin over his arm.

"Steak," Smits said. "A big one. Porterhouse. Medium-rare."

"Fine, sir," the waiter said. "And?"

"Salad, lots of it," Smits answered. "Fresh greens."

"Baked potato, sir?"

"Yeah," Smits answered. "Loads of butter."

"And to drink, sir, would you care for some wine?"

"Oh, no," Smits answered. "I'd like fresh milk. Big glass, with refills."

"A pleasure, sir."

Smits leaned back in his chair and watched the men walk from table to table; the tables were round, with white cloths, fresh flowers, and a candle on each one. The men stood erect, proud, the white napkins hanging perfectly centered on their left forearms.

His food arrived. Smits had not one but four waiters, identically dressed, some with hair as white as the cloths across their arms. His steak did not disappoint; it was as big as his plate. His side items were served in separate dishes. The waiters stood at his table and smiled at him while he ate, waiting for any indication that Smits needed anything at all. They refilled his glass with cold milk again and again, brought hot bread and butter each time the plate was emptied. There was no odor of sweaty sailors in the engine room, no roar of machinery, no gauges to watch, no worry about steam pressure, no grated floor beneath his feet, no impending danger. For that night, Smits felt like a king.

★★★★★★★★★★★★★★★

Bob Palomaris heard his buddy Joe Parker coming, could tell who it was long before he saw Parker walking through the mess hall whistling *Rhapsody in Blue*. Parker stepped through the hatch to his living quarters, where Palomaris was standing at his locker with the door open. Parker threw his hat on his bunk, walked over to the lockers next to Palomaris's, and leaned against them.

"Hey, Palomaris," Parker said. "Why don't you have a pinup girl on your door?"

"I just don't."

"Look at this," Parker said, opening the door to his locker, which had a large poster of Veronica Lake taped to the inside.

"That's nothing," one of the other boys offered. "Take a look at this beauty." He opened his locker to reveal a picture of Rita Hayworth kneeling in the center of a bed, wearing a black negligee.

Many of the boys had pictures of their wives or girlfriends taped inside their lockers. Others had posters of pinup girls like Mae West, Dorothy Lamour, Lana Turner, and the all-time favorite, Betty Grable. Some had both.

Betty Grable was the all-time favorite pinup girl for World War II. She was known as "the girl with the million-dollar legs."
COURTESY OF BATTLESHIP *NORTH CAROLINA* COLLECTION

"If you could have anybody you wanted," Parker asked Palomaris, "who would you hang in your locker?"

"Shirley Temple," Palomaris said.

"You're joking, right?" Parker laughed.

"No, what's wrong with Shirley Temple?"

"There's nothing wrong with her," Parker said. "She's a real nice girl. Really knows how to ride a horse, too."

"You act like you know her or something," Palomaris responded.

"I do. If we ever make it back to California, I'll introduce you."

★★★★★★★★★★★★★★

The task force left Majuro and headed southwest, where it launched air strikes and prepared for seizure and occupation in the Humbolt Bay area of the northern coast of New Guinea. Along the way, the ships practiced for what lay ahead; carrier planes exercised bombing attacks on towed targets, while their protectors practiced repelling air attacks. Each afternoon, the *North Carolina* gunners on the automatic weapons expended hundreds of rounds of ammunition during practice. The day before the strikes, the battleships topped off the destroyers' fuel supplies, and on April 21, the carriers launched the first air strikes at Humbolt Bay. The next day, occupation forces met little opposition, but air strikes continued for several more days along the north coast of New Guinea.

During that time, Kingfisher pilot John Burns found time to write a V-mail letter home to his friend Jerome Sullivan in Wynnewood, Pennsylvania. In previous letters, Burns had lamented not being able to attend mass, as there was no priest aboard the ship, but in his letter of April 27, 1944, he had good news: "I am going to make a special effort to attend daily mass during May and invoke Our Lady to give each and all of you any special graces and help you may need at the moment. Yes, we have finally been assigned a priest as one of two chaplains aboard, the first Catholic chaplain this ship has had in its Navy life of three years. His name is Fr. Klass and he is from Texas. . . . As for me, it seems like I'm stuck in a rut until they decide to send someone to relieve me, which I have so far unsuccessfully promoted. As far as aviation is concerned, this type duty is obsolete."

The task force rendezvoused with two squadrons of ships—one for refueling and one to replenish the carriers with planes—then headed toward the islands of the Truk Atoll with nearly 50 ships, prepared to finish what it had started in February. En route, the ships passed the International Date Line, and when they prepared to launch planes for air attacks the following morning, the date was still April 29.

The weather was not conducive to the planned attacks, the skies completely overcast and heavy rainsqualls rendering visibility near zero at times. The carriers postponed launching their aircraft until just before sunrise. Enemy aircraft approached, and ships shot down one of the planes, but the other managed to drop a bomb near the *Lexington*. Bogie contacts were made throughout the day, but no planes came close enough to the *North Carolina* for engagement, although combat air control did shoot down several. Following a busy day of air strikes, the task force retreated southward for the night, steaming in choppy water under dark skies.

Crew manned battle stations for evening GQ and prepared to remain there for most of the night. The enemy still preferred to attack in the dark. Just after midnight, bogie contacts appeared on the BB55's radar screen several times within a few minutes, then nothing transpired for more than seven hours. The rainsqualls continued and the seas churned; poor visibility once again delayed launching of the carrier aircraft until 0800.

The *North Carolina* had rescue duty that day, so pilots John Burns and J. J. Dowdle spent the early hours checking their aircraft to make sure they were ready for duty. Less than two hours after the air strikes began, a pilot needed to be rescued, so Burns and radioman Aubrey J. Gill and Dowdle and radioman R. E. Hill manned their aircraft and prepared for launch.

The ship turned into the wind as the first catapult rotated 30 degrees off the fantail. Ready to open full throttle, Dowdle gave the thumbs-up signal, which was relayed to the catapult operator manning the controls at the very back of the ship. The operator pressed the firing mechanism, igniting an eight-inch powder charge that fired the plane down the catapult and into the air. Dowdle guided his plane up and away from the ship. The exercise was repeated on the other side, firing Burns's plane from motionless to 60 knots in just seconds. When both of the aircraft were airborne, the pilots headed toward the south reef of the Truk Atoll, where a pilot was reported in the water. The submarine *Tang*, also on rescue duty, headed in the same direction.

Dowdle spotted the pilot floating in a raft being tossed helplessly about by the wind-swept seas. He lost visual contact time and again as the raft disappeared in the hollows of the swells, then reappeared atop the crests. Dowdle prepared to land, and Burns circled a safe distance away, looking for other pilots in need of rescue. As Dowdle's center pontoon hit the water, the rough seas twisted the plane, catching a side pontoon and flipping the aircraft. Burns then had not one but three men in need of rescue.

"We're going down," he said to Gill. "Hold on."

Burns skillfully dropped the plane into the rough sea and kept its nose turned into the swells, balancing his pontoons, taxiing first to his shipmates in the water, who climbed aboard, sitting on the wings. Burns then maneuvered his overloaded plane through the choppy water to the original target of rescue, the pilot in the raft, who grabbed hold of the pontoon and hoisted himself up, climbing into the backseat with Gill, trying to avoid upsetting the delicate balance of the plane and causing it to flip in the rough water. Swells were not usually too difficult for a Kingfisher pilot to manage when everything was balanced and the weight load was normal. But choppy seas always posed a threat because the danger was unpredictable. With five men aboard a two-man aircraft, nothing was normal.

The submarine *Tang* was on its way to the scene, its crew surprised to see the Kingfisher in the water with not one but three rescued men. Burns taxied to the submarine and off-loaded his human cargo, then sped up across the choppy ocean and, to the astonishment of the submarine crew, lifted the Kingfisher into the air, heading east to search for other downed pilots reported in the vicinity. The *Tang* sank Dowdle's damaged Kingfisher with 20-millimeter gunfire to keep it from falling into enemy hands.

After flying and searching for some time, eyes trained on the water below, Burns spotted the first of three other rafts he knew to be in the water. Once again, he deftly landed his plane in the tumultuous water and rescued the pilot, who climbed into the backseat and onto Gill's lap. The plane was designed to hold only two men, but now it held three, and more were out there somewhere. Burns began taxiing around the lagoon searching for any sign of other rafts.

For more than two hours, the three men in the lone Kingfisher bounced along in the choppy water until they finally spotted one of the rafts. Burns brought the seaplane close beside the raft; they found three men inside. Those three climbed up onto the wings of the small plane, one in the center next to the fuselage and one holding onto each wing, balancing themselves and the plane. Burns, in radio contact with the *Tang*, was 20 miles away from the sub, which had been rescuing other pilots throughout the day. He knew he could not become airborne again, so he continued across the water. As the *Tang* and Burns headed toward each other, Burns and his five-man crew spotted the other raft, also holding three downed pilots.

"Tie your raft to the pontoon," Burns told the pilots, and they tried. But as he began to taxi away, water drenched the men in the raft and increased the difficulty of keeping the plane balanced enough to stay afloat. The men untied their raft and climbed onto the wings of the Kingfisher, one joining the previous fuselage-hugger and the other two splitting up, one sitting on each wing beside the other grateful pilots who had also been shot down by enemy fire that day. Burns then had a load of nine, including himself, as he continued toward the *Tang*. His fuel supply was low. His excessive load caused the pontoons to squat low in the water, and the constant pounding of rough seas broke into one of them. The tail developed a leak and water seeped in, causing it to dip lower and lower in the sea. The plane listed to the side of the damaged pontoon but continued toward the *Tang* for nearly two more hours.

Burns worried that all would be for naught if they didn't reach the submarine soon. He watched his gas gauge dip below empty and struggled to keep the plane level enough to avoid being tipped by the rough waters. If he ran out of gas, all control would be lost. The damaged pontoon and tail continued to take on water, and Burns feared he would not be able to keep the Kingfisher afloat much longer. At last, he sighted the *Tang*, and the airmen on the wings let out a whoop of joy. Burns breathed a sigh of relief. Just a little bit farther.

The sight of the men sitting on the wings and clinging to the fuselage of the battered two-man plane might have been comical had it not been such a long, grueling day for the crew aboard the sub. They gladly gathered their last load of exhausted but exhilarated airmen aboard their vessel.

The *Tang*'s commanding officer, Lieutenant Commander Richard H. O'Kane, encouraged Burns to follow the rest of the men below deck. He did not want him to watch the gunners sink the remarkable little plane that, unbeknownst to O'Kane, Burns had called obsolete just a few days earlier.

Downed pilots clung to the fuselage and wings of an OS2U Kingfisher after being rescued by Lieutenant John Burns, pilot from the North Carolina.

★★★★★★★★★★★★★★★★

Participation in all task-force strikes during February, March, and April and the operation in New Guinea earned the *North Carolina* her eighth and ninth battle stars. Those duties also took a toll on the ship, sending her back to Pearl Harbor for repairs to her huge rudders, which had become severely corroded; large holes were eaten in the port rudder.

The *North Carolina* was the first battleship to be built with twin rudders. They were each 20 feet, five inches high—about the size of a two-story building—and 23 feet, 10 inches wide and weighed 98,000 pounds. The double-rudder construction gave the ship greater maneuverability for tight turns, which, in addition to her increased speed capability, allowed the battleship to keep up with the carriers as they zigzagged and maneuvered to launch planes and avoid attack. And with two rudders, the ship had a spare if one was rendered useless.

When the Showboat went to port, whether just a safe harbor in the Pacific or an extended period at Pearl, crew transferred on and off for various reasons. The crew often joked that they could tell a new seaman by the bruises on his shins, a result of not knowing how high to step to get through the hatches.

Following the daring rescue at Truk, Burns and Gill returned to Pearl Harbor aboard the *Tang* and were given transfers, Burns back to the States for any assignment he desired. That left the *North Carolina* short one pilot and one radioman.

On Ford Island, the Scout Observation Service Unit (SOSU) served as a pool for pilots, radiomen, and aircraft for the fleet. Nineteen-year-old ensign Almon P. Oliver served as an instructor in the unit. After completing flight training at Corpus Christi, Texas, in December 1943, he had continued with two and a half months of extensive operation training in Jacksonville, Florida. Since most of the pilots in SOSU had not had the additional operation training Oliver received, he was chosen to be the instructor. Approximately 15 pilots and an equal number of radiomen at SOSU trained daily in preparation for assignment, flying long overwater navigation flights. Often flying backseat with Oliver was a young radioman

Eldon Means
COURTESY OF BATTLESHIP
NORTH CAROLINA COLLECTION

Almon Oliver
COURTESY OF BATTLESHIP
NORTH CAROLINA COLLECTION

from Kansas named Eldon Means. Neither had a lot of military experience. Although Oliver had received much more training than Means, he was impressed with Means's attitude, maturity, and self-confidence. So it was with great pleasure that he found Means also assigned to the *North Carolina* when he boarded the night before the ship left for Majuro Harbor.

When the BB55 rejoined the task force at Majuro, the ships prepared for the final air strikes, bombardment, capture, and occupation of the Mariana Islands—Saipan, Tinian, and Guam—bringing Allied-held territories even closer toward the Japanese mainland. But Truk, located between the Marianas and any other Allied-held territories, still belonged to the Japanese, so attacks came from both directions. Enemy aircraft were a constant threat to the ships, more than 300 enemy planes attacking the task force within five hours one day. The event became known as the "Marianas Turkey Shoot." Operations in that area continued successfully through the month of June and into July, the boys always aware of impending attack.

★★★★★★★★★★★★★★★★

In early July, the engine-room crew reported an unusual metallic rubbing noise. Inspection at Eniwetok Atoll found that the number-three shaft, one of four that ran from the engine rooms to the propellers, was in bad disrepair. Repair groups patched up the BB55 temporarily and sent her back to Pearl Harbor, where crew began unloading part of the ship's ammunition allowance to lighten her load for the journey to Puget Sound Navy Yard for repairs. After almost three years away from home, Paty, Wieser, Fennelly, and the other boys aboard the Showboat were going back to the States. Their ship had already earned 10 battle stars, and they had survived.

Crew members waited anxiously on the bow of the North Carolina *for a ferry that would take them across Puget Sound to the mainland. They would then depart to hometowns all across the country, some going home for the first time in more than two years.*
COURTESY OF BATTLESHIP *NORTH CAROLINA* COLLECTION

CHAPTER ELEVEN

Home for a Visit

★★★★★★★★★★★★★★★

"You know it's the hand of God, I guess, why some of us are still here."

Larry Resen, former crew member

The major overhaul was expected to keep the ship in port for almost two months. The sailors would each have 25 days leave when they reached Bremerton, Washington, and liberty every other day during the remainder of their time in port. Paul Wieser drew first leave and wrote home to tell Jean they could get married while he was there.

31 July 1944

Chuck Paty was nervous as he stood on deck waiting to go on leave. *What if they search my bag?* he thought. He had decided not to leave his illegal diaries on the ship, but he worried that might have been a mistake. He was sure the MPs wouldn't search everybody's bag—heck, a thousand guys were standing there. But if they caught just one sailor with something he shouldn't have—like the Colt .45 automatics Paty saw some of the boys stash—he was sure they would all be held up for a very long time. He had not seen his hometown or his parents in almost three years, and he didn't want any delays.

The ship wasn't anchored; it just stopped and floated in the Juan de Fuca Straits. The last time Paty remembered the ship doing that was in Key West when he boarded. The first half of the crew departed the ship at Juan de Fuca to enter Seattle, saving them time before the ship continued up to the Navy yard at Bremerton. As he fidgeted and waited, Paty was surprised to see an approaching ferry, but he did not hesitate to board it for the quick trip into Seattle.

★★★★★★★★★★★★★★★

Bob Palomaris stood waiting on the bow when he caught a glimpse of Joe Parker through the crowd and remembered Parker's promise. He didn't really believe Parker, but he was going to call his bluff.

"Hey, Parker," Palomaris yelled toward his shipmate. "When you gonna introduce me to Shirley Temple?"

"How about Saturday?" Parker yelled back.

"Sure, that'd be great," Palomaris laughed. "Just great."

"No, I'm serious," Parker said, squeezing his way through to stand by Palomaris as they waited. "She always goes to the barn to ride on Saturday. I'll bet you my next pay chit she'll be there."

"Yeah, and she'll know you by name, right?"

"She'd better. I took good care of her horse for two years before I joined up."

"You're really serious!" Palomaris shook his head in amazement.

★★★★★★★★★★★★★★★

Wieser felt lucky to be among the ones granted first leave. Many of the sailors standing there on the bow in their dress blues received that first leave for the same reason he had. They were getting married.

Jean was waiting back in New Jersey making preparations for their wedding. She did not have much time to get ready. The future Wiesers had become engaged by proxy when Paul's brother presented the engagement ring at a party held at their mother's home while the future groom was far away in the South Pacific, but they couldn't set a date until Paul knew the ship was returning to the States. So when the boys arrived in Pearl and learned they were going home, he had sent Jean a letter.

Soon, he would be on his way across the country. Before he boarded the train that would take him to Jean, he contacted naval housing and arranged for one of the small accommodations at Port Orchard for himself and his new bride when they returned.

★★★★★★★★★★★★★★★

Bob Fennelly joined the crowd preparing for first leave. The boys had received instructions about the proper, orderly way to load onto and disembark from the ferry, but a thousand sailors, many of whom had not been home in well over two years, forgot everything in the excitement. They were fairly organized going from the BB55 to the ferry, as the accommodation ladder didn't allow for much deviation, but when the ferry touched the dock, the boys poured off, running up the hill or hopping onto the running boards of cars cruising up the road. The drivers didn't seem to mind, and the boys hung on.

★★★★★★★★★★★★★★★

When Palomaris had said goodbye to one of his girlfriends in the spring of 1943, he had told her he probably wouldn't see her again until the end of the war. She had tipped her head so that her long, dark hair hung below her right shoulder, stared straight at him with warm hazel eyes, and said, "I'll see you next year in August."

Riding along in the Pullman car of the Southern Pacific Railroad that was taking him home to Pasadena, he thought about the way Laura always consulted her Ouija board. When he joined the Navy, he had been told he would be going to Faragut, Idaho, for boot camp. After a little hocus-pocus around the Ouija board, Laura had said that he wouldn't be going to Idaho, he would train at the San Diego Naval Training Station. Palomaris certainly didn't believe that kind of stuff, but she had been right about training, and as he nodded and dozed while the train sped south, he realized it was August and he was going home to see his family and Laura.

★★★★★★★★★★★★★★★

The sailors had been surveyed on their way back to the States and asked where they would be going on leave and what mode of transportation they wished to take. The Navy was footing the bill, so Paty had decided to fly. The flight would be a new adventure for him. He didn't want to waste any time taking the train or a bus.

When he arrived at the airport, received his tickets, and walked out to board the plane, he was a bit surprised to see the small DC-3 waiting on the runway. He ridiculed himself for expecting something fancier. Of course, the military would send him home on a military plane if the Navy was paying the fare. The little transport was a workhorse for the Army, and the fact that it didn't have a pressurized cabin didn't mean a thing to Paty before he boarded. He sat in a window seat and watched the props crank up, heard the motors grinding as the plane gathered enough speed to lift off. When they were airborne, he began enjoying the sights until the plane attempted to gain altitude. The engines seemed to be struggling as the plane crept higher and higher, straining to clear the Rocky Mountains. But the sound of the motors got lost in the ringing and popping in Paty's ears. The higher the plane climbed, the more his head pounded. It hurt so bad he thought he was going to explode. No seasickness had ever come close to the way he felt while the little plane rose above the mountains. He survived, although at times he thought he wouldn't, maybe even wished he wouldn't. After the plane crossed the mountains and settled in at a lower altitude, the pain eased, and he enjoyed the rest of his flight. He made a stop in Chicago, then headed south to Charlotte.

Alerted by a letter home, his parents met him at the airport. His mother, who had never wanted her only son to join the Navy, had not written a tearful letter to him the entire time he had been gone.

She always said she missed him, but it was simply stated. Paty was not much of a letter writer himself, so the correspondence had been slight since the day he left for boot camp, certain he would be home in 90 days. Two years and eight months had passed since then. Paty couldn't help crying at his parents' tearful welcome. His mother hugged him like she would never let him go. At home, she tried to feed him everything she had ever cooked that he once enjoyed. She hovered over him so much that he just wanted to get out of the house. But things had changed during the years he had been gone. Everything was rationed—beef, shoes, clothes, gas—and all his close childhood friends were gone. Most of the boys had joined one branch of service or another. The girls had either left for college or gotten married.

Paty had a gas-ration card that would have been sufficient if he were careful, but he wasn't careful. He drove his father's car around every day looking for someone or something familiar from his past. He was amazed at how everything could change so much in less than three years. His father worked for a company that manufactured and sold trucks, so he rated a higher gas-ration card and let his son use it. The opportunity to ride around Charlotte

Chuck Paty reclined in a rocking chair on his family's porch in Charlotte, North Carolina, while on leave in 1944, his first time home since joining the Navy in 1941.
COURTESY OF CHUCK PATY

drew attention from some of Paty's former acquaintances who were still in town. But Paty quickly realized he had changed even more than things at home had. The carefree, happy-go-lucky attitude of the kids in Charlotte annoyed him. He still had visions of explosions and air attacks and people dying, burials at sea, the red barrels of enemy aircraft bearing down on his ship, the horror of the *Wasp* burning while her crew pushed exploding airplanes over the side, dead shipmates floating in water and oil. He knew a lot of the families in town had sons who had entered the service, and he was sure they understood there was a war going on, but he heard that many had been assigned to stateside duty or to ships that rarely left port. He felt a bit jealous and a lot disillusioned, and those feelings grated on him the whole time he was home—that and his mother's constant hovering. He understood, he really did, but he wasn't a kid anymore. As much as he loved his parents, he was more than ready to return to the ship when his leave was up.

★★★★★★★★★★★★★★★

During his liberty at home, Palomaris played a few rounds of golf and went fishing almost daily. One evening, the family drove over to his aunt's house for dinner. His aunt disappeared into a back room and returned with a recent newspaper article from the *Pasadena Star-News*. It was a front-page article with a picture of the Showboat and a huge headline that read, "USS *North Carolina* reported sunk in the Pacific."

"I was so worried about you," his aunt said, and hugged him for the fourth time. "I worried every time they said it."

That was not the first time the *North Carolina* had been reported sunk. Tokyo Rose kept the rumor hot on her radio program, and newspapers ran the story more than once.

"I tried not to worry," his mother said. "Your letters kept coming."

"But this one was so recent," his aunt said. "I just didn't know. But I'm glad you're here. Now, let's eat."

Laura Jakobson was not the only girl Palomaris had been writing while he was away at sea. He figured the more he wrote, the more mail he would receive in return. He also corresponded with

Nadine Knause, Mary Lou Morgan, and Norma Doll. The following day, he visited Norma where she worked at Nash's Department Store. When he went downstairs to the lingerie department, he saw Norma busily waiting on a customer. She did not see him at first, so he hid behind a rack of nightgowns and watched her for a few minutes. She walked between two counters with an armload of boxes and bent over to put them underneath the back counter. He slipped up to the front counter and just stood there waiting, enjoying the view.

When Norma stood up and turned around, he grinned, but she turned as white as the bras lying on the counter in front of her.

"You! Polly, you're alive!" she screamed, then ran around the counter and hugged him.

"Yeah, I'm alive. Shouldn't I be?" he asked, puzzled. Then he remembered.

"But the paper said your ship sank," Norma said when she caught her breath and the color started returning to her face. "We all thought you were dead."

"Nope, here I am in the flesh," Palomaris said, and turned around in a circle with his arms spread out so she could see how striking he looked in his dress blues.

★★★★★★★★★★★★★★★★

The first thing Fennelly did when he hit the streets of Seattle was locate a tailor shop.

"I need a new set of dress blues," he told the tailor, who then took all his measurements.

"Come back in four hours," the tailor said.

So Fennelly walked down the street and found some food. When he returned a few hours later, he was surprised to see the dark blue wool uniform completed and hanging up, waiting for him to try it on. He carried it into the dressing room and inspected each piece as he took it off the hanger. The bell-bottom pants were completely lined with matching blue silk, and the square front fly had 13 buttons—one for each of the original colonies. The workmanship was flawless, the pants hugging his legs and hips like they had been molded around his body. The jumper was form fitting and fully

lined as well, tailored to his exact measurements. But what pleased Fennelly most were the three white stripes around the large, square collar and at the ends of the sleeves. One stripe he had received for being an apprentice seaman. The second stripe he had earned simply by time served. But the third stripe—the seaman first class rating—had required an abundance of hard work, including studying the books and taking a test. He had passed. In addition to the black silk neckerchief, the tailor added one more item—a flowing white silk scarf.

Fennelly purchased his new tailor-mades and headed to the train station. Only one train was going east, and he wasn't going to miss it. Maryland awaited. Fennelly loaded into one of the back cars with sailors from the *North Carolina* and other ships in port. But the atmosphere deteriorated quickly. The boys had brought liquor aboard, and every time the train stopped, they bought more. Fennelly wanted to drink, but he knew that always made him fight, and he wasn't going to risk not getting home in one piece. As the train traveled across the country and stopped at stations along the way, the residents knew it was coming and arrived at the stops with food and coffee and cookies and chocolate. Fennelly was amazed at the reception the boys received. But the booze made some of them sick, and many became so rowdy that the conductor finally closed off the last three cars and would not let the sailors come forward.

When they arrived in Chicago, many changed trains for various East Coast destinations. Fennelly was heading to Baltimore. He had decided not to let his family know he was coming, wanting his arrival to be a surprise. He hadn't written home like he should have, and Japan had reported sinking the *North Carolina* at least three times by then. He couldn't wait to see the look on his father's face.

In Chicago, Red Cross volunteers greeted the boys and shepherded them into the VFW building, offered them a place to clean up. As the sailors showered, the volunteers cleaned and pressed their uniforms, helping them make a grand impression on the last leg of their journeys home.

Fennelly hopped off the train at the station in Baltimore and caught a cab the rest of the way home to Govenstown. He asked the cabby to let him off a block from the house so it wouldn't spoil his surprise. As he walked up the street and saw his front yard, he thought about all the fun he and his brothers and sisters had there. He saw himself kneeling on the grass working on his bicycle and his little brother Dickie aggravating him. The yard was empty and quiet. Fennelly walked up the sidewalk to the front stoop, looked down to check his new blues to make sure everything was in place, and knocked on the front door.

When his father opened the door, he looked into his son's eyes, then fainted. Fennelly caught his dad on the way down.

★★★★★★★★★★★★★★

The Great Northern train cars were packed with sailors journeying across the country. The seats were straight backed, two in a row. Wieser sat beside his friend Ernie Zietsman, who was going to be one of the groomsmen in his wedding. Zietsman lived in New York. The boys were lucky to have seats, even though they had to sleep sitting straight up. At least they were allowed to move to the

Pullman car for meals. The train was so full that some of the sailors were lying in the luggage racks. But they didn't care. They were what many people called "Asiatic." They had been in the Pacific so long that they were crazy with excitement about returning home.

Winding its way across the country, the train steamed along mountainsides so curvy that Wieser could see both the engine and caboose at the same time. When the train stopped to recoal at little stations along the way, many of the boys hopped off and returned with bottles in their hands, drinking every day of the first three-day leg of the journey. Wieser had never been one to drink, so he just kept his seat. He was intoxicated enough with what the next few weeks would hold.

When the train arrived in Chicago, Wieser and Zietsman switched to the Pennsylvania line for the last one-day leg to Newark, New Jersey. They shared that train with many civilians. The friends, although dressed in their blues, were not wearing their ribbons or campaign bars. Neither felt the need to exploit them. They had hated seeing the guys in liberty towns over the last couple of years wearing all kinds of bars and medals they had not even earned just to make a big impression. Everybody called them "Market Street commandos."

A lady on the train accompanied by two small children kept looking over at the sailors. Wieser assumed she was going into New York City, perhaps on a shopping excursion with her children. He watched her watching them. When the train neared the station, Wieser and his friend decided they should put on their campaign bars. Shore patrol would stop them to make sure they were properly dressed, including their medals. They wanted nothing to slow them down. As the sailors started decorating the left sides of their chests with the bars, the woman watched. Wieser was sure she thought they were phonies. He didn't like how that made him feel.

Jean was waiting at the station. As the train slowed, Paul took in every detail of the woman who would soon become his bride—her welcoming smile, her narrow waistline, her light brown hair gently touching her shoulders. She greeted him with a tender embrace.

The next few days were a whirlwind of activity as Jean and Paul put the finishing touches on the wedding plans, hurrying to make everything happen as quickly as possible, since he had only 25 days' leave and had spent the first four of them on a train. Their wedding would be held in the Catholic church, since both Paul and Jean had attended Catholic school as they were growing up. Paul's brother helped by locating a place for the reception in the local Moose lodge, which he was able to procure at no cost to Paul. They did not plan a dance, just a celebratory dinner to share with their friends.

The groomsmen consisted of one of Paul's brothers who was in the Army, his friend Ernie, and his niece's friend, also in the Army, who had just been released as a prisoner of war. Ernie and Paul wore dress whites, the Army boys their khakis with coats and black ties. Jean chose her sister, Paul's sister, and her best friend as her bridesmaids. They wore softly flowing pastel dresses.

Standing at the front of the church, Paul became misty eyed as the pianist began playing the familiar strains of the wedding march and Jean appeared in the doorway at the end of the long, carpeted aisle. Her formal white dress, lacy and beaded, had long white sleeves that puffed slightly at the shoulders, then narrowed from the elbows down her slender arms to her wrists. The princess neckline dipped below a string of pearls, and the extra-wide waistband accentuated her figure. In her hands, she carried a small bouquet of white daisies with white ribbon streamers; the bouquet dropped petals and leaves in front of the narrow skirt. As she walked toward her future husband, her long, beaded train flowed smoothly with each graceful step. No veil hid her face from Paul as she smiled; it hung simply, pinned to her hair at the back.

Following the wedding and a trip to the photographer for a formal wedding photo, the new Mr. and Mrs. Wieser honeymooned in New York City. They caught the train from New Jersey to New York, but the conductor did not require them to have tickets. They hailed a cab to take them to their hotel, accompanied by a lady they did not know. But she paid the fare. They arrived at the Hotel Imperial near Broadway. Three days later, when they checked out, they were charged for only one night.

During those three days, Paul and Jean walked hand in hand along the streets of New York. They window-shopped and made

Jean and Paul Wieser exuded happiness in a
professional photo taken after their July 1944 wedding.

plans for their future and the family they would one day share. They took in a Broadway show, walked around Central Park, rode the carousel. They enjoyed everything about New York City, but they enjoyed each other even more.

★★★★★★★★★★★★★★★★

Paty knew a couple of buddies in his division who usually got into trouble on liberty. Loker and Kosloski were always together, so Paty wasn't surprised to find them together when he returned to the ship at the end of his leave.

"Let's celebrate!" Ski said. Those two had even taught Paty how to drink.

"Sure," Paty said. "I'll hoist a few with you."

So the boys went into a bar in Seattle, then another and another. Paty, still disillusioned after his highly anticipated but equally disappointing trip home, had more than he was accustomed to drinking. Loker had no trouble supporting his little buddy when they started walking, Paty at five foot three and Loker a huge, burly guy.

"Hey, buddy," Ski said to Paty. "Why don't you stay with us tonight? We've got this hotel suite, a nice one with a bunch of rooms. Had to spend some of that money we've been leaving on the books for so long."

"Yeah," Loker added. "A few of the boys are coming over. I'll pick up some bottles and we'll have a party."

Paty wasn't sure how much more he could take, but he was willing to go along with the guys.

"Okay," he said. "I'll go. But don't expect much partying out of me. I'm going to take a shower and hit the sack." Paty had no trouble falling asleep wherever he found a bed, regardless of what was going on around him. That was a useful trait on the ship.

"Suit yourself," Loker said as he guided his friend along the street toward the hotel. Loker and Ski glanced at each other over Paty's head and grinned.

The boys took the elevator up to the fifth floor. The hotel suite was huge, and several other guys were already there, sitting back drinking. From the center living room, a door opened to the next room, which also opened up into an adjoining room. Down a short hallway, Paty saw a woman breeze by.

"Who's that?" Paty asked Ski.

"A real fine lady," Ski answered. "If you want to go meet her, she doesn't charge much."

"No way," Paty said. "I'm going to take a shower and hit the sack. Which bed can I have?"

"Take that one," Ski said, pointing to a room in the opposite direction from where Paty had seen the woman.

"That's good," Paty said.

Paty went into the room and closed the door behind him. He walked into the bathroom, closed that door, stripped down, and stepped into the shower. The hot water felt good, and he just let it run over his head and down his back, puddling around his feet as he soaped up. He let the water keep running, then soaped up again and still let the water keep running, just because he could. He heard the door creak.

"Who's there?" Paty questioned.

"It's me," an all-too-feminine voice answered.

"What? Who is this?" Paty demanded.

"Let me see you," she said, and jerked the shower curtain open.

Paty tried to cover himself. The woman, who he had to admit was not bad looking, stood there absolutely naked staring at him. She smiled.

"Get out of here!" Paty yelled. "I'm not interested."

"C'mon, honey," she said. "Have a little fun."

"I mean it!" he yelled louder. "Get out."

He jerked the curtain closed and heard her storm out, slamming first the bathroom door, then the bedroom door behind her.

Paty got out of the shower fuming. He dried briskly and pulled on his pants, then walked out into the center room.

All the guys let out a whoop of laughter as he stood there staring at them.

"What are you trying to do to me?" Paty demanded.

The only answer he received was a roar of laughter from the group of boys drinking and having fun, forgetting where they had been and where they would be returning. The woman had already disappeared into another room. Paty was sure she was not lonely. He turned around, walked back into the bedroom, and slept long and hard. When he awoke the next morning and entered the living area, boys were sprawled everywhere, surrounded by piles of beer bottles. He slipped out the door and went back to the ship.

★★★★★★★★★★★★★★★

When his 25-day leave was over and Palomaris returned to the Showboat, he had mail. He anxiously opened the envelope and pulled out an 8-by-10 color glossy head-and-shoulders shot of 17-year-old Shirley Temple, looking absolutely gorgeous in a white V-neck dress. She sat at an angle with her oval ivory face turned slightly toward her right, her dark brown eyes looking off in the distance, her burgundy-lipsticked mouth parted slightly to reveal a soft, sensuous smile. Curly brown hair billowed around her face, a yellow flower perched in the part. The light background blended into her dress in an innocently sexy blur. In the lower left-hand corner, she had written in four lines, "To Bob Polly, all of the best, Sincerely, Shirley Temple."

He smiled as he thought back to the day he had actually met her. Parker lived in Los Angeles, only 17 miles from Palomaris in Pasadena. He was surprised when Parker called him to make plans to meet at the North Hollywood Riding Academy. Palomaris was still skeptical, but he thought it was worth a try, even if Parker could just get them through the front gates and he could catch a glimpse of Shirley Temple.

But everyone at the stables did recognize Parker and told him how glad they were to see him home, including the child star. Palomaris still couldn't believe it—he had actually sat down at a table across from Shirley Temple, shared hamburgers and a Coke, and carried on a conversation like normal teenagers. And here was the proof in his hands. He taped it inside his locker door—his pinup girl.

Palomaris spent his liberty days fishing and playing golf, going into Seattle for dinner or a ball game. One day, he and his friend Joe Ohla found a flyer for a riding academy taped to a window in one of the stores downtown. They caught the streetcar out toward

A personalized note from Shirley Temple made this photo special to Bob Palomaris. She sent the photo to him after the two met through a mutual friend and had lunch together when Bob was on leave while the ship was being repaired at Bremerton, Washington, in 1944. She became his pinup girl.
COURTESY OF BOB PALOMARIS

the address and walked the rest of the way. As they strolled down the long dirt driveway toward the barn, they stopped for a moment, climbed on the three-rail wooden fence, straddled it, and watched a chestnut mare grazing with her baby. The colt ran round and round its mother, bucking spindly back legs in the air, then running again. He was a bay with a dark brown body, black leggings, and a wispy black mane and tail.

"Let's see what they have to ride," Ohla said, and the two sailors jumped off the fence and started down the gravel road toward the long center-aisle barn with a high tin roof. The sides were red cedar, vertical planks with two-by-two stripping at the seams. As they walked through the open double Dutch doors, they could smell the sweet mixture of shavings and hay and horse manure.

"Saw your sign in town," Palomaris said to the barn hand. "We'd like to rent a couple of horses and go riding. You have trails?"

"Indeed we do," the barn hand answered. "Are you experienced?"

"I've ridden before," Ohla said.

"So have I," Palomaris answered. "We can handle them just fine."

"All our horses are well trained," the barn hand said. "Would you like to ride with or without a guide?"

"Without," Palomaris answered. "Just point us in the direction of the trail."

"Let me show you the horses that are available," the barn hand said after they had settled up on the money. "Here, we have Rocket." He was a sorrel quarter horse with a wide white blaze and white stockings on his back legs. But he was barely 15 hands tall, and neither Palomaris nor Ohla was impressed. They walked past several more stalls containing horses that just didn't interest them. "Now, this is Rivera," the hand said, approaching a stall about midway down the barn. "His father was a thoroughbred, and he has a quick step." Rivera was solid black—body, mane, and tail—and held his head high confidently, almost defiantly.

"I like his spirit," Palomaris said. "I'll take him."

Rivera was nearly 16 hands tall, and Palomaris had to rock back on his right heel to lift his left foot high enough to slip it into the stirrup and pull himself up on the horse, his right hand on the back of the saddle and a tuft of Rivera's thick mane tucked into his left hand with the reins. Rivera trotted off quickly, and Palomaris reined him in to wait for Ohla.

Ohla chose a sorrel-and-white paint with a bald face and blue eyes. He had always heard that one blue eye meant the horse had a lot of spirit, but that two blue eyes could forecast trouble. He didn't mind the challenge.

"The path makes a circle through the woods and past a large apple orchard," the barn hand said. "Stay on the path and follow the signs. It should bring you back here in about four hours."

Palomaris clucked to Rivera, barely touching him with his heels. The horse loped off with a smooth rocking-chair gait. The sun beating down on his back and the rhythmic motion of his body in the saddle began to release the tension Palomaris didn't even realize had built up in his muscles from more than a year of constant readiness.

The hilly trail began in a residential section—houses sprinkled through meadows for a couple of miles—then turned into the woods. The towering trees cast shadows on the dirt pathway as the sun strained to peer through the lacy foliage. Palomaris could hear a stream rushing over rocks somewhere below their path. The constant thud of the horses' hooves scattered birds and sent squirrels scurrying out of harm's way. The horses did not spook, even when a loose limb crashed into the brush below.

"Let's walk them awhile," Ohla said, a bit breathless, reining in the paint to first a jog, then a walk. Funny how a rider could get winded when the horse was doing the running.

"Easy," Palomaris said to Rivera, pulling back on the reins in short, clipped motions.

They slowed to a soft, steady walk, and the forest sounds intensified as the horses moved almost silently along the trail. Only the slight squeak of the leather moving back and forth with the riders intruded on nature. Palomaris reached for the canteen slung across the saddle horn and took long, slow gulps of cool water.

They had been riding for almost two hours, and the boys were beginning to feel chow call coming on when the shadowy path opened into bright sunshine. As far as the boys could see on both sides, apple trees hung heavy with their bright red harvest.

"Wow," Palomaris said. "Have you ever seen so many apples?"

"I'm sure they won't miss a couple," Ohla said, and walked the paint off the path into the orchard.

Palomaris followed. He reached up and grabbed a large apple off a heavily laden branch drooping over his head. As he sank his teeth through the crisp skin, juice spurted out both sides of his mouth and trickled down his chin.

"Let's rest a minute," Palomaris said, swinging his right leg over Rivera's haunches and dropping softly to the ground. He pulled another apple from the tree and shared it with his mount. Then he sat down in the orchard and leaned against the trunk of the tree to savor the sensation of biting into the juiciest, sweetest apple he had ever eaten.

When snack time was over, the boys each pulled a couple of extra apples to put in their saddlebags and take back to the ship. They were sure the orchard owners would never miss them.

★★★★★★★★★★★★★★★★

Paty spent his liberty days with his good buddy Joe Klineberger. Over the last few months, they had gotten really close, and Klineberger didn't drink much at all. That appealed to Paty after the fiasco at the hotel.

One day when they went ashore in Seattle, they hopped a streetcar to see where it would take them. The streetcar passed right in front of a high school, where it stopped for students to board. Paty had been in the 11th grade when he quit school to join the Navy, so these kids weren't much younger than he and Klineberger. Two girls, giggling and talking quietly to each other, sat down in the seat right behind the sailors. Paty could hear them whispering. He wanted to turn around and look at them, speak to them, but he was shy. Girls had never paid much attention to him. Klineberger was much more self-confident and turned around in his seat, put his arm over the back, and smiled.

"You going our way?" he asked.

The girls looked at each other, giggled shyly.

"Which way are you going?" the one with long blond hair asked, directing her question to Klineberger, although by that time Paty had adjusted himself in the seat so he was sitting sideways and looking at the girls, too.

"We're riding the streetcar that goes by your house," Klineberger said, adding his best grin and tilting his Dixie Cup hat just a bit.

"Oh," the blonde responded. Paty was afraid Klineberger had gone too far when he saw the shocked look on both the girls' faces, but then the blonde said, "We get off about three blocks that way."

"That's where we get off, too, right, colonel?" Klineberger said. Paty was the only Southerner in the radio gang, and many of the boys called him "rebel." Klineberger was the only one who called him "colonel."

"You're a colonel?" the girl with short, dark hair asked, seemingly impressed.

"No, uh-uh," Paty said, embarrassed. "That's what Joe calls me. I'm Chuck."

Joe Klineberger (left) *and Chuck Paty toured the campus of the University of Washington during liberty while the ship was being repaired at Bremerton, Washington.*
COURTESY OF CHUCK PATY

"Oh, I'm Marian, and this is Alice," she said, pointing to her blond friend.

When the streetcar reached its next stop and the girls stood up, Chuck and Joe stood, too. They waited for the girls to gather their books, then followed them off the car.

Joe and Chuck stood on the street corner and watched as Marian and Alice walked down the street, then crossed over and started down the sidewalk. They walked parallel to the girls on the other side of the street. Every once in a while, Marian and Alice would look their way, and the boys would wave. The girls giggled and kept walking. After a couple of blocks, Joe and Chuck crossed over and began walking on the same side as Alice and Marian.

Marian was tall and wore her hair short in a different style than most of the girls then. Chuck thought she was beautiful. She smiled at him.

The boys walked behind the girls until they turned up a set of steps to a house.

"This is where I live," Marian said. "We have to go in now."

"Okay," Chuck said. "It was nice to meet you."

"Nice to meet you, too," Marian responded.

"Hey, can we see you again?" Joe asked.

"I don't know," Alice said. "What would we do?"

"We could go to a movie or something," Joe answered.

"Or just walk around," Chuck said. "But we can't do it today. We have to get back to the ship."

The ferry ride between Bremerton and Seattle was an hour each way. Liberty didn't begin until 1100 hours, and they had to be back by 2300 hours, including the ferry ride. The afternoon was already gone by then, so they arranged to meet the girls two days later when they had their next liberty. Half of the crew was on leave; the other half rotated liberty every other day so the ship always had a skeleton crew.

"We'll be here around noon," Joe said. "Day after tomorrow. It's Saturday, so you don't have to go to school."

They didn't know where Alice lived, so they offered to just drop by Marian's house. They hoped both of the girls would be there and that Marian would actually answer the door. The girls never did say yes.

"We have to go in now," Marian said. They walked in and closed the door behind them, leaving Chuck and Joe standing on the stoop.

Two days later, the boys were standing on that same stoop again, dressed in their blues, praying they would make a good impression. Joe knocked on the door, and Marian's mother answered.

"May we speak to Marian?" Joe requested.

"Yes, hold on," her mother said, and walked away, closing the door behind her.

"What should we say?" Chuck asked.

"Let's see if she can go to a movie," Joe answered. "If her mother says we can, then we'll go get Alice. I don't think she's in there."

"Okay," Chuck said, "but if she says no, then should we just see if we can walk around somewhere?"

"Yeah, that'll work."

Marian opened the door.

"Can you go to a movie?" Chuck blurted out the minute she opened the door.

"I'll ask," Marian said, and went back in the house.

She returned after only a few moments.

"I can't," she replied, "but Mother said we could walk around in the neighborhood for a little while if you want to."

"Great," Joe said. "Where's Alice?"

"She lives a few blocks from here. I'll show you."

The trio started walking, Marian in between the sailors.

When they arrived at Alice's house, she had no problem getting permission to go with the group and was out the door in seconds.

"We can walk over to campus," Marian said. "It's where I'm going to school when I graduate."

"Sure, that'll be great," Chuck said.

They seemed to partner up naturally, Joe with Alice and Chuck with Marian. As they strolled around the campus of the University of Washington, Marian talked about music.

"I'm in the high-school band right now," she said. "I'm just a junior, but when I graduate, I'm going to come to school here and get a degree in music. I love music."

"I do, too," Chuck replied. He was beginning to think he'd like anything Marian said she liked.

"Do you prefer Bach or Beethoven?" she asked.

"Hmm, I'm not sure." Chuck hesitated. "But I really like Sinatra."

Popular music was his favorite. Sometimes, he had listened to the New York Philharmonic Orchestra on the radio, but when Marian talked about classical—about learning to play the violin, the flute, the piano, about learning to conduct—he loved just listening to her. The foursome spent the afternoon walking around campus, taking pictures with the camera that Chuck had brought back with him from Charlotte. He could get the film developed in Seattle before they went back out to sea. Chuck was surprised at how quickly time passed and how soon they had to walk the girls home, catch the streetcar back to the dock, and board the ferry for the long ride to the ship.

Chuck continued to visit Marian every other day during his liberty at Bremerton. The long ferry rides became routine. He spent the morning trip anticipating what he would say to her, the time returning in the evening wishing he'd said something different. But she kept inviting him back, and his polite Southern manners must have made an impression on her mother.

"Would you like to stay for dinner, Chuck?" Marian's mother asked him one day.

"Yes, ma'am," he answered. "That would be nice, thank you."

Marian's father worked as a guard at the Boeing plant. She had a younger sister who was about 14. They all sat down to dinner together in the formal dining room with a white tablecloth and real silverware. Chuck watched Marian to make sure he used the right fork, placed his napkin across the lap of his dress blues, and did his best to appear mature and sophisticated. He wanted them to like him. No girl had ever paid that much attention to him before.

★★★★★★★★★★★★★★★

Paul Wieser's leave was nearing an end, so he and his new bride boarded the train to travel back to the West Coast. It was Jean's first trip away from home and family. When the Wiesers arrived in

Sailors could not leave the ship without a liberty card. The cards were divided port and starboard so that no more than half the crew was gone at any given time.
PHOTO BY THE AUTHOR

Washington, they made their temporary home in naval housing at Port Orchard, just across the river from where the ship was docked in Bremerton. The house was small—a kitchen, a bath, and a bedroom. A partition separated the bedroom from the kitchen, which was equipped with a wood-burning stove. Even though it was summer, nights were cold. The Navy furnished wood for the stove, but it also furnished an ax. Paul had to split the wood and carry it into their home.

The kitchen had no refrigerator, only an icebox. Ice was delivered daily, and Paul soon discovered how important emptying the tray beneath the icebox was. More than once when he forgot, he was reminded with very cold, wet feet as he walked to the bathroom.

The sailors who had returned from their leaves and reported back aboard ship rotated liberty—port side one day, starboard the next. The Navy ran a launch back and forth across the river to transport the sailors living in Port Orchard, many with new brides.

Paul managed to wrangle an extra liberty card—one from port side in addition to his starboard card. So instead of going home to his new bride every other night, he was there every night. When the boys came back after each liberty, they were supposed to place their liberty cards in the appropriate slot in the liberty box after they boarded ship. The box was rectangular, completely enclosed, and upright, the slots for the cards identified by divisions. Paul slid his starboard card into the Fifth Division slot, slapping his hand on the wood each time, but the yeoman who gave him the extra card warned him never to actually put that one back in the box. Paul pretended to slip it in the slot and slapped the wood with his hand. He never got caught, so he continued to take leave every day.

During the last couple weeks of leave, Paul became sick and ran a high fever, but he didn't go to sick bay for fear the pharmacist's mate would confine him to the ship. He just toughed it out until he felt better.

One day when he was out chopping wood, he glanced down the street and noticed several of his friends and neighbors walking toward the house in a big group. Without Paul's knowing, his new bride had arranged a party to celebrate his birthday. Paul and Jean were joined by four other newlywed couples and two of Paul's un-married buddies. Jean wore a white dress splattered with colorful bows as she played hostess to their guests.

Jean managed to create a real home in the small, crudely built house. She loved listening to the radio, and the couple soon had favorite songs to call their own, especially the one that mentioned the carousel in New York. But the time passed far too quickly. On their last day together as they lay in their bed holding onto each other, the radio played softly in the background. When "I'll Be See-ing You" began to play, Jean reached over to turn the radio up. The words, the melody, the new tender memories were more than Paul could handle. As he looked into Jean's soft green eyes, his own began to fill with tears.

"Turn it off," he whispered. "Please."

CHAPTER TWELVE

Typhoon

★★★★★★★★★★★★★★★

> *"It is easy to translate a distant sound into the shout of a man if one is intent and knows that the dark passing waters may hold a survivor or the still lingering spirits of the recent dead."*
>
> BB55 war diary entry, 22 December 1944

25 September 1944

The ship's overhaul was complete, and she left dry dock to begin trial runs and test out the repairs. When everything appeared to be in order, the crew spent several days loading supplies and ammunition before the ship started back down the West Coast. They had spent almost two months away from regular routine and gunnery practice, so for the first half of October, as the ship steamed down the coast to San Pedro and then Los Angeles, they participated in rigorous training exercises to fine-tune their skills firing the antiaircraft guns, launching and retrieving the Kingfishers, and

Bob Fennelly and his crew in the whaleboat (upper left) *executed the rescue of a pilot after his Kingfisher capsized.*
COURTESY OF BATTLESHIP *NORTH CAROLINA* COLLECTION

bombarding islands with the 16-inch and five-inch batteries. They practiced night and day, knowing that the Japanese tactics had begun to change. They needed to be ready for whatever was to come at whatever time the Japanese chose to attack. They knew the Japanese were good fighters, and their job was to always be better.

When the Kingfishers were launched and then recovered, a rescue-boat crew was always manned aboard ship in case of any problems. One day during trials, the deck crew had just finished a successful attempt at high-speed fueling, topping off the destroyer escorts while traveling at 12 to 15 knots rather than the usual five to eight, preparing for the anticipated acceleration in the war. Fifth Division put away the fueling lines and resumed normal cleaning duties.

When the time came to retrieve the Kingfishers, Paul Wieser stood ready at the crane as Bob Fennelly, his crew, a pharmacist's mate, and an engineer prepared to man the boat if it had to be dropped into the water. The maneuver would have to be accomplished with the ship in motion. As one of the planes came in to land, something went awry and it flipped over with its pontoons in the air. The boat crew hooked the lines to the whaleboat. Wieser swung the crane around, lifted the boat, and set it on the main deck next to the lines. The crew climbed in, and Wieser adjusted his controls, raised the boat above the lines, and swung it out over the ocean. The boat hook stood ready to release the clips as Wieser lowered the boat toward the water. The engineer prepared to start the engine at the exact moment the boat hit the water so it could pull away from the ship immediately. Starting the motor too early could damage the water-cooled engine, too late and the whaleboat could be sucked under the ship in its wake. As the boatswain's pipe gave the shrill commands, the synchronized maneuver sent the little boat zipping away from the ship the minute it touched water. Everything had worked fine to that point, but the water was choppy and Fennelly had to be precise, steering into the swells at an angle so the water neither crashed over the bow nor hit broadside and flipped the small boat.

By the time the boat reached the aircraft, both the pilot and his engineer were sitting on top of the pontoons, the only things still above water. The crew tossed a line with a monkey fist on the end toward the plane, but they weren't close enough for it to reach. Fennelly edged the boat closer to the aircraft, fighting to keep it from being swept against the plane by the swells. They tossed the line again, and the pilot caught it. He handed it over to his engineer, who slid into the water and was soon safely aboard the whaleboat. They repeated the procedure and brought in the pilot.

When Fennelly was prepared to turn the boat back toward the BB55, he heard a loud voice over the bullhorn.

"Tie a rope to her and pull her in," the command came.

Fennelly looked at the plane on one side, then at the proximity of the bow of the ship, now almost facing him and the wrecked aircraft. He felt sure that any attempt to tow the plane would send him, his crew, and the airmen he had just rescued under the ship and kill them all. Not wanting to disobey a direct order, however, he went through the initial motions to do what he was told. As he tossed the line, the plane sank, saving him from having to choose between certain death and disobeying an order. He turned his boat around and headed for the starboard side of the ship, where Wieser waited with the crane to bring them safely aboard.

They left the Southern California waters on October 15, headed for Pearl Harbor. For the first two days of the journey, the crew continued antiaircraft gunnery practice, launching the Kingfishers to pull targets, then retrieving them. But during the final four days, foul weather and rough seas prevented any training.

Almon Oliver and Eldon Means worked well together and had become a regular team on one of the planes. During their flying time in port, they had made a good enough impression, apparently, that their duties increased as the ship headed back to Pearl and inevitably back to the war. During down time, Means and Oliver had very little contact with each other due to the invisible but well-recognized line drawn between enlisted men and officers. That line became obvious inside the ship, the bulkheads painted green instead of white in the sections where the officers like Oliver lived and worked. The change in color alerted enlisted men to the area where officers' country began and their privileges ended.

But when they were at their duties, the very nature of their jobs demanded that Oliver and Means depend on each other, work together to achieve the same goal, and share a common bond of respect for each other's competence. Their lives depended on their ability to work as one unit, and they developed a close personal bond.

For several days after the ship arrived in Pearl Harbor on October 20, the crew participated in bombarding practice, using the west end of Kohoolawe Island. As the main and secondary batteries bombarded the island, the planes dipped in towing sleeves from time to time, so the entire crew at general quarters had to remain alert and be ready for anything. Bob Palomaris and Richard Fox on the bow 20s were ready, immediately opening fire as the towed sleeves appeared.

The *North Carolina* rejoined the fleet in Ulithi at the beginning of November but didn't stay long. The fleet's safe harbor had continued westward as the successful Allies gained control of islands and the surrounding waters from the Japanese. Ulithi lay between Guam and Yap islands in the Marianas, which the *North Carolina* had helped capture before her return to the States.

As the force steamed westward on November 6, the battleships fueled destroyers all morning, then received fuel from a tanker in the afternoon. A typhoon passing about 450 miles south of the fleet caused the seas to swell, tossing the destroyers in and out from the *North Carolina*, the rough waters rising and dropping out from under them. Wieser and Fennelly fought to regain control of the lines and stay upright on their feet, waves washing over the starboard bow and sweeping down the deck amidships, where the BB55 was attached to the fueling destroyers by lines and hoses. Sixty-mile-an-hour gales sent sea spray into the boys' faces and drenched their clothes. Their jeans hung heavy on their legs, soaked and sticking to their skin. Wind and waves and treacherous seas battered the fleet, washing away fueling lines and sweeping two crew members over the side of another vessel in the task force. The executive officer of the USS *Shealy*, a destroyer fueling alongside the *Washington*, was washed overboard and perished. Late in the afternoon as darkness fell, all fueling exercises were finished, but the typhoon was not.

The fleet steamed westward the next day while the storm continued to rage, crashing waves over the main deck, flooding a ventilator shaft, and knocking turbo-generators number three and number four and their switchboards out of commission. Running with the two remaining turbo-generators, the BB55 set her course to the northwest as the fleet slowed and headed away from the storm, attempting to reduce the pounding suffered by the smaller ships. By the third day, the winds decreased, and although the seas were still high, the skies began to clear and the daily routine got back to normal, the boys launching aircraft, holding gunnery practice, cleaning up, and repairing any damage done by the high winds and ravenous seas, including mopping up inside turret number one. One of the bloomers that covered the ends of its guns had been blown away by the winds, and the turret had flooded during the heavy squalls of rain.

By November 11, the skies were clear and the seas calm. Allied air strikes wiped out a Japanese convoy of four merchant ships and five destroyers and shot down 18 planes. Two snooper planes were also shot down nearing the task force. The fleet continued westward, heading for attacks on Luzon and Manila in the Philippine Islands. For several days, air attacks were launched with much success until dwindling supplies and worsening weather sent the force back to the harbor at Ulithi, where it arrived mid-month.

Ulithi was a huge atoll, the top of a sunken volcano. It was surrounded by a series of smaller islands, the arrangement creating a safe harbor for the fleet that was large enough for all the ships to anchor. The area was approximately five miles wide by 10 miles deep, and a torpedo net strung across the opening protected the ships harbored there.

When the ships were at Ulithi, the boys could go ashore on a little island called Mog Mog—nothing more than a flat expanse of sand—where they drank hot beer, played baseball, and returned to the ship with a bad case of sunburn. At night, they watched movies in the mess hall or on the fantail.

The planes from each ship rotated antisubmarine patrol duty while the fleet was anchored at Ulithi. One day as Oliver and Means were flying patrol, Oliver noticed what appeared to be a large life raft floating near the entrance to the atoll, close to the submarine net. He dropped altitude to about 50 feet and flew over to inspect the raft but saw nothing in it—no persons or supplies—so he continued on his patrol. But when he flew past the same area a little later, the raft had moved, not in the direction of the wind and the water current, but upwind instead. He flew close again and still saw nothing suspicious in the raft. He did report the sighting, but his report was received with skepticism.

Near dawn on November 20, before the crew manned general quarters for their regular dawn stand-to, a huge explosion was heard throughout the harbor. When the boys arrived at their battle stations, those with a view saw smoke barreling out of a tanker anchored across the entrance to the lagoon. Destroyers raced around inside the harbor dropping depth charges in response to a report of mini-subs that had sneaked past the torpedo net.

Both of the BB55 Kingfisher crews loaded depth charges and

Sailors crowded onto Mog Mog Island in anticipation of some beer and a little relaxation.
COURTESY OF BATTLESHIP *NORTH CAROLINA* COLLECTION

The Showboat's baseball team sported a winning record in games played against other ships' teams at places like Mog Mog. Bob Palomaris is standing fourth from the left.
COURTESY OF BOB PALOMARIS

flew off in search of the subs, Oliver piloting one of the planes. Throughout the morning and afternoon, suspect contacts were made. Inside the lagoon, where the ships had previously felt relatively safe, destroyers repeatedly dropped depth charges in one area in response to a swirling appearance on the water. Two Japanese sailors subsequently surfaced surrounded by debris that was apparently from their small sub, but the men drowned and disappeared before they could be taken captive. About a mile away, Oliver and the other Kingfisher pilot both spotted a mini-sub on the surface of the water, one crewman standing on the bow waving. The pilots each had two depth charges hanging from their pontoons and could have easily sunk the sub, but through communication, they decided the sub was unable to submerge, so they flew low circles in the vicinity to keep the craft in sight so the crew could be captured. But in swooped a group of three fighter planes, sinking the sub with a stream of fire from their .50 caliber machine guns. The plan to take prisoners exploded with the sub.

Fire burned fiercely on the stricken tanker for most of the morning until it sank at 1100 hours, 50 of her 350 crew members lost.

Two days later, the task force left Ulithi and headed westward again for more attacks in the Philippines—main target Luzon. The force steamed at 26 knots, and the weather steadily worsened, sending sheets of water over the bows, sloshing down the decks. But by dawn the next day, when the task force arrived within striking distance of its targets at Luzon, the bad weather had abated and the sky began to clear. The carriers launched planes to begin the air strikes. At noon, two explosions hit the water about 1,500 yards off the starboard beam of the *North Carolina*. The boys stayed at general quarters, waiting and watching, listening inside the gun mounts for a commence-fire order, fixated on the sky while manning the 20s and 40s, the heat and anticipation mounting.

About half an hour later, a flight of enemy planes closed in, and all the ships in the task force opened fire. Off the starboard side of the *North Carolina*, in a parallel course at about 3,700 yards, the *Essex* became the first target for the newest Japanese tactic—kamikazes. A single-engine enemy plane spiraled out of the sky straight down into guns on the port side of the carrier, sending a red-and-orange mushroom of flames exploding into the sky as the plane's gas tank erupted. Fire broiled underneath the *Essex*'s flight deck, but quick reaction from her damage-control crew had the flames extinguished in minutes, and she resumed launching aircraft.

A second plane came spiraling in toward the group at about 3,000 feet trailing white smoke, weaving and twisting to escape the barrage of antiaircraft fire rising from all the ships in the immediate vicinity. The plane crossed behind the *North Carolina* from starboard to port, then turned back in the direction of the BB55, only to change course again and streak between the *Essex* and the *Santa Fe* before nosediving into the ocean in a ball of fire and smoke.

At the end of the day, losses to the enemy far outweighed the damage to the American task force, although eight planes were lost and some carriers received extensive damage. Damages to the *Essex* were minor. Enemy losses included a heavy cruiser, which had been the main target of the Allied attack, one destroyer, many cargo ships and barges, and about 74 planes. But the willingness of Japanese pilots to fly suicide missions into the ships was almost incomprehensible and added a new sense of urgency to the gunners' accuracy. The enemy planes and the pilots flying them became weapons far more dangerous than the bombs, torpedoes, and machine guns they carried. Miss them and American sailors would surely die.

The task force steamed away for a fueling rendezvous as a three-quarter moon peeked through slight cloud cover. The antiaircraft gunners remained on alert in anticipation of retaliation for the damage they had inflicted on the enemy. Early the next morning as the task group joined the fueling group, colors were lowered to half-mast in honor of crew lost in the action the day before—14 on the *Essex*, 50 on the *Hancock*, 30 on the *Cabot*, and several on the *Intrepid*.

B-29s had begun their raids on Tokyo, and the Japanese losses in shipping were great. Surely, the enemy was becoming desperate. As the task force steamed peacefully for a couple of days about halfway between Ulithi and Luzon, a nervous anticipation of reprisal kept the officers and crew expectant. For the next few days, the ships conducted firing practices and waited for their next engagement. Signs of approaching bad weather began to manifest themselves in squalls and overcast skies on the last day of November. The force was ordered to return to Ulithi, where its ships joined a large gathering of combatant and noncombatant vessels, including an abundance of aircraft carriers.

The BB55 remained anchored at Ulithi for seven days, during which time landing craft were furnished to transport officers and enlisted men over to Mog Mog in three-hour recreation parties of about 350 men. Each enlisted man received three bottles of beer, retrieved from the brig, where it had been placed for protection.

10 December 1944

Fennelly finished his lunch, dumped his scraps, and stowed his tray. He walked up to Fifth Division quarters and pulled the latest Zane Grey book his father had sent him out of his locker. When the ship was in port as it was there in Ulithi, his only duty was to be on call for the captain's gig. So far, he had not received any gig assignments that day, and his boat was being repaired, so he planned to spend the entire afternoon lost in the tale of cowboys and Indians. He strolled out onto the fantail and slipped up under the catapult. That was his favorite place to read. It was as quiet, shady, and cool a spot as he could find in the South Pacific heat. He leaned back, opened his book, and began to read.

"Coxswain of the gig, go to the officer's deck." The words came blaring out of the loudspeaker almost as soon as he was situated.

Fennelly responded to the command and met the officer of the deck along with the lieutenant commander, who said he needed to be carried around the port to all the ships in the fleet.

"I'm sorry, sir," Fennelly replied. "My boat is in the skids getting a new gunnel."

"Well, take the one from Sixth Division," the OD told him.

When the BB55 was in port, the boats were moored in the water at all times, attached to a boat boom and accessed by crew via a swinging rope ladder with wooden rungs. Fennelly stuck his book into his waistband at the small of his back and walked over to the port side of the ship. If he had to wait long at any of the stops, the book would give him something to pass the time. He shinnied out onto the boom and grabbed the ladder. Fennelly found that going down the ladder by straddling the sides kept it from swinging as badly. When he was near the bottom, he let go to land on the engine of the Sixth Division gig. But when his feet made contact, he slid off, landing on his butt in the boat, his uniform streaked with diesel fuel. The boat was filthy, absolutely in no condition to be transporting officers, and Fennelly was shocked. He and his crew kept their own Fifth Division boat cleaned and shined at all times.

Fennelly regained his footing and climbed back up the ladder. He informed the officer of the deck of the condition of the boat, using his dirty uniform as proof. The OD called Sixth Division and commanded that the boat be cleaned and fueled immediately.

"You'll be called when the boat is ready," he told Fennelly, who went back to his quarters to change clothes and wait.

After what seemed like a long time, he received word that the boat was ready. He and his crew—a machinist's mate to run and take care of the engine and his boat hook to guide the bow—ran the gig up to the officers' accommodation ladder and helped the lieutenant commander board.

They began their journey from ship to ship in the fleet. Since the task force was set to sail soon, most of the accommodation ladders had been pulled aboard. When the whaleboat arrived at each ship, Fennelly used his bells to hail the officer of the deck. He became amused watching the same scene repeated over and over again. Crew could be seen scurrying around on the deck, lowering the accommodation ladder, and welcoming the officer aboard. After some time on each ship, the lieutenant commander would descend and climb back into the gig, and they would motor over to the next ship. Since the port was full of ships, none expecting a visitor, the excursion stretched through the afternoon and late into the night.

Finally, they had just one stop left before going back to the *North Carolina* for some shuteye. Motoring toward the final destination, the boat had traveled only about a hundred yards when the engine quit.

"What's wrong?" Fennelly asked his mechanic.

"Out of fuel," he replied.

"How can that be?" Fennelly shot back.

"Guess they didn't fill it up," the mechanic said.

Fennelly reached into his gear locker and brought out the flashlight. He was not good at signaling with a light, but his worries were relieved when the lieutenant commander reached out, took the flashlight from him, and signaled for help. They sat dead in the water waiting for about 30 minutes before a Higgins boat, the versatile landing craft the Marines used to storm the beaches, pulled up alongside. It towed them to the repair ship, and the exhausted entourage boarded.

The lieutenant commander approached the officer of the deck. "Get the boat cleaned up and fueled and make sure it is in good running condition. While we're waiting, take these men down to the mess hall and see that they have anything they want."

Fennelly looked questioningly at the lieutenant commander.

"Anything," the officer said. "You want steak and eggs, that's what you get."

The choice sounded good to Fennelly and his crew, so they sat in the mess hall of the repair ship and ate steak and eggs.

Motoring the boat back to the *North Carolina*, Fennelly heard reveille sound. He eased the boat up to the accommodation ladder. The officer mounted it and climbed up to the ship, then Fennelly motored back to the boat boom and tied the boat off. His tired but no longer hungry crew boarded. Fennelly went to the officer of the deck and explained what had happened. The OD instructed the boys to put a note on their bunks and sleep in.

That morning, the task force left Ulithi for another strike on Luzon, practicing as it traveled. The air strikes on targets in Luzon met surprisingly little resistance the next couple of days. Bad weather threatened and made flight operations difficult, then improved for a day before worsening again. During the three days of strikes, no enemy aircraft were spotted by the BB55.

With the weather continuing to deteriorate, the ships of the force left the area of immediate action to rendezvous for fueling. The larger ships could last awhile without refueling because they had large expanses of tanks, but the destroyers had to be fueled often. The destroyers would fare better in the monstrous waves and gale-force winds of the approaching storm if they had full tanks of oil, adding to their weight. Running out of fuel would be disastrous.

The BB55 and other battleships started fueling destroyers as quickly as they could, port and starboard. Wieser, Fennelly, and Palomaris were all working with the deck crew, first passing, then manning the lines for fueling. To fuel while under way, a destroyer would come alongside the battleship. The fueling crew first passed lines across the expanse of water, then the hoses to feed fuel into the smaller ship. Both ships traveled at the same speed and maintained the proper distance—too close and the destroyer could crash into the side of the ship, too far and the hoses would burst, sending fuel oil flying.

The North Carolina *fueled destroyers on both sides, trying to prepare them for the approaching typhoon. When the seas became too rough, fueling ceased.*
COURTESY OF BATTLESHIP NORTH CAROLINA COLLECTION

Even under favorable conditions, the process was dangerous as the deck crew unhooked the stanchion at the fueling location and laid the lifelines over. But with the winds picking up, squalls of rain pelting the boys, and waves slapping against the side of the ship, the decks became dangerously wet and slippery, and just standing up became difficult. Fueling operations on both sides of the ship at the same time left even less room for error.

The boys completed fueling one destroyer, then another as the storm continued to intensify. After about two and a half hours of fighting the elements, all fueling procedures were halted, and the remaining destroyers were on their own.

Upon instructions, Fennelly and Wieser on the starboard side started breaking down the fueling gear after the last destroyer was fed. Wieser came down from the crane to help stow the fueling lines. Fennelly had been working at the after-winch, which stabilized the line as it went over the side of the ship, so he was already on the main deck. The seas continually worsened, and the boys faced difficulty trying to keep their footing, the water splashing up the side of the ship and sending sprays of seawater into their faces. The waves continued to grow larger and rougher until one caught them all off guard. As the wall of water rushed over the side of the ship, the boys lost their footing and started washing down the deck. One sailor was thrown up against turret three. Fennelly feared he himself was going over the side but landed straddling one of the stanchions; he grabbed hold with both arms and prayed that he wouldn't go over. The water pushed Wieser down the deck, and he grabbed for the first thing he could find, catching himself by both hands on the edge of the splinter screen for one of the 20-millimeter guns; he felt his wedding band cut into his finger as he clenched the edge of the short metal wall with all the strength in his fingers, praying that he would see Jean again. Between sheets of water, the boys regained their footing and scrambled below decks before another wall of seawater could knock them down again.

Assigned to mess duty, Fox and three other crew members had been taking the tables and benches from the overhead racks where they were stored after each meal and getting things set up for lunch. They had just finished placing the last coffeepot and set of trays and cups on the tables when the ship was lifted by a large wave and slammed back down, sending the tables sliding across the floor and the pots of coffee and trays of cups flying through the air to crash onto the steel decks and shatter all about the room. No hot meals could be served. Lunch that day and meals throughout the rest of the storm consisted of a piece of bread and some Spam, something the boys could hold in their hands without the need of trays or utensils.

Palomaris completed his fueling detail and arrived down in his living compartment. He heard the captain come over the intercom and say, "All hands stand clear of the main deck." *No problem*, he thought. *I've seen enough of that today.* He changed into some dry clothes and sat on his bunk to play a game of pinochle with two of his buddies. The captain came over the intercom again: "All hands stand clear of the boat deck." That was one level above the main deck.

"The typhoon appears to be crossing our course," the captain wrote in the war diary, "but whether ahead, astern or where we are, has not been estimated with certainty." The commanding officers gambled about which direction to take the task force, and instead of steaming out of danger, they headed straight into the storm.

In the radio room, Chuck Paty listened to the messages coming across in clear English, no decoding needed. He heard carriers report waves washing over their flight decks. The destroyers were being tossed around like toy boats.

"All hands stand clear of all weather decks."

The last order meant that no safe place existed outside the confines of the ship. The boys wondered how high the waves were breaking. Fox and his buddies wanted to see what was happening, so they climbed up inside the superstructure as far as they could go, then all the way to the crow's nest using the outside ladders. They just wanted to see. But the winds howled and whipped their clothes and the sea spray and rain drenched them. The ship began to toss and roll with the waves; they had to hold on to keep from being thrown down onto the deck far below and washed out to sea. They stayed only about 15 minutes—they had seen enough.

Palomaris was winning his hand with a couple of dollars on the line when his division officer came into the compartment and said, "You, you, and you, come with me." He pointed out about 14 guys.

"Grab your life preservers," he said. "We're going topside."

Palomaris couldn't believe what he was hearing. But they were required to obey orders, so they grabbed their life preservers and followed the officer.

"You're going to tie down these fueling lines so they don't wash overboard," the officer said, and assigned each man to a specific location.

Most of the men were gathered near number-two turret, close to the front of the superstructure, but Palomaris and two others were sent to the tip of the bow on the port side. No sooner had they reached the bow than it began to rise, lifted by a huge wave at an amazing angle. Then the water dropped out from under it and the ship plunged into the trough between swells. At least five feet of water washed over Palomaris and the others, thousands of pounds slamming into them, knocking them off their feet, sending them sprawling. When they recovered their footing, they felt the ship's bow begin to rise again, and rise and rise.

Palomaris knew he was in big trouble. He looked for anything to grab onto and chose a cable for the 20-millimeter gun sights. When the ship plunged into the next trough, a 10-foot wall of water crashed over the bow. The cable Palomaris held tightly in his hands snapped and went with him as he tumbled and bumped into the anchor chain, then the ventilation shaft, the davit, and finally the spray shield that directed water off to the sides of the ship, away from the base and gears of the turret. All Palomaris could see as he washed toward the side were the lifelines. He reached both arms up as far as he could and grabbed. His body whipped in the wind like laundry on a line, but his grip held. A boy in his division named Roberts was battered, bruised, and broken but still hanging on outside the lifelines. Palomaris and another buddy pulled him in and carried him down to sick bay. All three of the boys were checked over thoroughly. Roberts's leg was broken. Palomaris was just badly bruised, but the doctor told him he probably would have broken his back had he not been wearing his life preserver. When they had all been cleared, the doctor gave them each a shot of brandy to warm them up and calm them down. That was when Palomaris learned there was legal liquor on the ship.

Fennelly worked his way up inside the superstructure to get a look at what was going on outside. Looking down on the fantail, he saw the waves wash away the supply of potatoes that had been stored just behind turret three and covered with netting latched down to padeyes on the deck. Nothing was left of the crates; nothing was left at all but a potato or two rolling around on the deck, then over the side. The ship began to roll to the side and back up, over and back up; Fennelly went down to the library to pass the time reading in a safer place.

The task force changed direction numerous times, trying desperately to find a course that would relieve some of the stress the storm was putting on the destroyers and other smaller ships.

The typhoon continued to intensify throughout that day and into the next. Paty ventured briefly from radio up through the superstructure to the bridge, four levels above the main deck. He saw

Seawater cascaded from the hawse pipes and scuppers of the USS North Carolina *as she surged upward out of a heavy swell in the aftermath of a typhoon in the Philippine Sea in mid-December 1944.*
COURTESY OF BATTLESHIP *NORTH CAROLINA* COLLECTION

Tons of water washed across the bow of the North Carolina, *where Bob Palomaris and others were ordered to secure fueling lines during the height of the storm.*
COURTESY OF BATTLESHIP *NORTH CAROLINA* COLLECTION

waves breaking as high as the bridge. The weather was so bad, the waves so high, the wind so strong, the rainsqualls so heavy that he could not see another ship anywhere. The ship rolled 10 degrees, sometimes 15 or 20; at least once, she rolled 30 degrees—at 35, she would not be able to right herself and would roll under the waves. *And what about a collision?* Paty wondered. He knew hundreds of other ships were out there, but they could not see each other. *How could the radar work, being twisted and battered like that?* But so far, it was working.

Back down in radio, as Paty listened, he heard destroyers call in and report their degree of list—25 degrees, 30 degrees, 40. Then silence. Carriers reported planes being washed off their decks. Some of the battleships lost their Kingfishers, torn right from their catapults. The destroyers that had been unable to fuel began to run out of oil; their engines shut down, and they were left helplessly bobbing like corks in the churning sea. Serious fires broke out on the

Cowpens, the *San Jacinto*, the *Monterey*, and the *Cape Esperance*. Not until midafternoon of the second day did the storm show signs of subsiding.

The ships began to assess damages when the storm finally abated on the third day. The *North Carolina*'s were minor. One 40-millimeter mount was temporarily out of commission; the sighting mechanisms for 15 of the 20-millimeter guns needed attention; and both Kingfisher aircraft had received minor damage. All damages could be repaired within 36 hours and were well within the capability of the ship's damage-control and other personnel. Although men were washed overboard on other ships, none of the close calls on the BB55 resulted in a man lost.

The task force fueled on the third day, then reversed its course to travel back through the area where the storm had hit in hopes of finding survivors. The ships from all three task groups of the force formed a continuous bowed line searching for sailors. The destroyers *Hull* and *Spence* were known to have sunk, and several other destroyers and their escorts were missing and feared lost. During the evening hours, shouts and whistles from survivors could be heard. The task force continued forward as destroyers began retrieving survivors. The commanding officer, four other officers, and 36 enlisted men from the *Hull* were rescued.

By day four, the seas showed little sign of the storm. Sharks had begun feasting on the bodies retrieved from the water that day. Boys standing watch on the *North Carolina* and other ships thought they heard cries for help as the stars cast streaks of light on the black water the fifth night, but no survivors and no bodies were found. Wieser thought about his childhood friend, the one who had joined the Navy after Wieser told him how great it was, the one who was assigned to the *Spence,* now lying somewhere beneath the black satiny swells.

The next time Palomaris saw the officer who had taken him and the other boys topside, he had a broken collarbone, arm, leg, and ribs. Palomaris heard he had also been broken down a rank or two for disobeying the captain's orders to stay below deck.

The task force returned to Ulithi not in the normal separate circular formations but in one continuous column five miles long.

The storm-battered fleet returned to the safety of Ulithi not in the normal separate circular formations, but in a single file that stretched for five miles.
COURTESY OF BATTLESHIP *NORTH CAROLINA* COLLECTION

Planes from the carriers towed target sleeves up one side and down the other to give the five-inch gun mounts firing practice. The ships zigzagged along, one big steel snake heading east.

On Christmas Eve, Ulithi Atoll held a massive expanse of ships five miles deep by 10 miles wide.

25 December 1944

A huge shipment of mail arrived aboard the *North Carolina,* and familiar Christmas carols streamed through the loudspeakers. Bright new signal flags aboard the *Washington* spelled "Merry Christmas" on her foremast. The task force remained anchored at Ulithi for the rest of the year, taking on supplies, receiving daily shipments of mail. The boys watched movies in the mess hall at night and played baseball games and drank beer on Mog Mog. Gunnery practice included simulated "Bonzai Joe" attacks, something the training plans

Ships of the Pacific Fleet gathered at Ulithi to regroup and pick up supplies before the next assignment.
COURTESY OF BATTLESHIP *NORTH CAROLINA* COLLECTION

had not included until that plane had come spiraling down vertically into the *Essex* at Luzon.

On New Year's Eve, Fleet Admiral Bull Halsey, commander of the task force, delivered a live message to the troops over TBS, the system for short-range communication among ships: "This is the Aztec himself. I wish you all a happy and prosperous New Year. All I can say is, 'Give the bastards hell.' "

CHAPTER THIRTEEN

Kamikazes

★★★★★★★★★★★★★★★★★★★

*"Marines on the ground, still engaged in combat, raised a
spontaneous yell when they saw the flag, screaming and
cheering so loud and prolonged that we could hear it quite
clearly on top of Suribachi."*

Radioman Raymond Jacobs, F Company,
Second Battalion, 28th Marines,
Fifth Marine Division, Iwo Jima

Plagued by almost continual bad weather, the new year began
with heavy strikes on the island of Formosa off the China coast,
taking the enemy by complete surprise. Six battleships and four
carriers participated in the operation, with destroyers spotting and
detonating rusty, weathered mines, some four feet across, that had
broken loose and were adrift. Despite the weather, the two-day attack destroyed 111 enemy planes and damaged or sank 40 medium
to small ships.

The Allied ships retired to the southeast during the night to
prepare for a full day of fueling. For a fleet that large, fueling was

time consuming. While the ships waited in line for the fuel tankers, a postman from a destroyer weaved in and out delivering mail to the ships. As a thank-you, the *North Carolina* loaded a big can of ice cream in the breeches buoy that brought the mail aboard, rather than returning it empty. When the BB55 took her turn attached to a tanker, her crew sent empty powder cans over to be refilled.

General Douglas MacArthur's land-based air strikes ran into difficulty neutralizing the enemy's airfields in Luzon, so assistance was requested from the Third Fleet. On January 7, Admiral Halsey spoke over the TBS radio, the first indication to the fleet that problems existed with the occupation in Luzon: "Luzon is now a bloody battleground. The enemy is now fighting to the death to stop our expeditionary forces and troops. Many of our ships have been hit hard in the past two days. Every undestroyed enemy plane is potential death to many of our comrades. This is the time of the great effort. Give the best and God bless you."

The carriers launched air strikes against Luzon that evening, and strikes continued on Formosa the next day. On January 12, the task force approached mainland China, the closest it had come to enemy homelands. Strikes began on Saigon and Camranh Bay with much success. One day blended into the next, rough weather continued, and air strikes progressed around intermittent days for refueling. Destroyers again reported damage from the pounding seas. When the ships refueled, spotter planes kept watch for the enemy. The task force stayed alert for submarines and enemy air attacks, but the resistance was unexpectedly light. That was the routine for the beginning of 1945, but it changed on January 21.

The weather calmed that afternoon. Little, if any, enemy opposition materialized even as Allied attacks sank several large ships in Tokyo Harbor. Just after lunch, the *North Carolina* began topping off two destroyers with fuel, one on each side. The destroyers snuggled into the wake, and crews heaved lines and attached hoses while the ships steamed along at 14 knots, executing the high-speed fueling they had practiced off the coast of California.

A group of fighters returned to the *Ticonderoga*, having completed their strikes. But unknown to anyone, two Japanese aircraft had tucked themselves into the group, hiding there in plain view as the planes began landing on the flight deck—yet another new tactic for the suicide pilots. One of the enemy aircraft crashed into the deck upon approach, bursting into flames and wrapping the *Ticonderoga* in a black veil of smoke. She turned away to operate independently from the group, fires raging on her hangar deck.

A few moments later, antiaircraft bullets split the dense smoke around the *Ticonderoga* and a second kamikaze spiraled down into her superstructure and exploded into red, yellow, and orange flames, black smoke billowing five times higher than her masthead. Prior to his demise, that pilot had also dropped a 120-pound bomb on the *Langley*. The Japanese pilots were willing to use their own lives as final weapons against the enemy.

The skies cleared for the first time that year as destroyers searched the waters and attempted to rescue any survivors blown overboard by the explosions on the *Ticonderoga*. One of her sailors, Earl Winthrop, was transferred to the *North Carolina* severely injured and badly burned, and the well-trained staff in the BB55's hospital fought valiantly to save him. But later that same day, Winthrop died; he was buried at sea off the starboard side of the Showboat.

The damaged ships formed a new, smaller task group with escorts and returned to Ulithi for repair, while the remaining ships launched new strikes against Formosa plus air and photo strikes against Okinawa, planning for future attacks there. That task completed, the group headed toward Ulithi, simulating battle scenarios and conducting gunnery practice all the way back to the atoll. When the *North Carolina* anchored in Ulithi on January 26, 1945, she had traveled 233,217 nautical miles since commissioning less than four years earlier. She had traversed 34,791 of those miles in just over a hundred days from the middle of October to her anchorage at Ulithi that January. She had also earned 12 battle stars.

The task group remained at Ulithi for overhaul, upkeep, and provisioning during the remainder of January and into the first part of February. For three full days—February 6 through February 9—crew unloaded the 2,700-pound armor-piercing shells for the 16-inch guns and replaced them with an abundant supply of 1,900-pound projectiles for upcoming bombardments.

Earl Winthrop was buried at sea after being transferred aboard the North Carolina *for treatment. The injuries he received when his ship, the* Ticonderoga, *was bombed were too severe, and he died in the sick bay of the BB55.*

COURTESY OF BATTLESHIP *NORTH CAROLINA* COLLECTION

The task group departed Ulithi on February 10 and rendezvoused with other groups of the force. Literally hundreds of ships—battleships, carriers, heavy cruisers, and destroyers—headed for the mainland of Japan, steaming between Iwo Jima and Okinawa on their way to launch strikes against air bases and industrial targets in Tokyo. In stark contrast to the debilitating heat the crew had endured for much of the war, the temperature at Tokyo dropped to 45 degrees, and crew working topside had to wear heavy-weather gear. They pulled their wool peacoats out of storage lockers and gratefully wore them when duty forced them topside. The gunners on the 20s and 40s, exposed to the elements, received full foul-weather gear—pants and jackets with fur-lined masks and hoods. The air raids struck Yokosuka Naval Base in the Japanese homeland and destroyed 400 enemy aircraft. The next day, task-force planes shot down 74 enemy aircraft and destroyed 32 on the ground.

★★★★★★★★★★★★★★

The island of Iwo Jima, located halfway between the Mariana Islands and mainland Japan, became even more strategically important as the American forces progressed. The Japanese launched kamikaze attacks from three airstrips there. If the Allies could take control of that island, Japanese attacks could come only from Okinawa or the mainland north. Control of Iwo Jima would complete the capture of all islands east of Japan and all landmasses to the south except Okinawa. Ten weeks of air raids preceded the massive bombardment planned in preparation for Marine landings on Iwo Jima.

19 February 1945

Reveille and breakfast came even earlier than normal on bombardment days, and the food was plentiful—steak and eggs and potatoes with lots of extras. The days promised to be long and arduous, so the protein and carbohydrates were even more important than usual. At 0530, the Showboat and others in her task group arrived in the vicinity of Iwo Jima and joined the forces already there to aid in the bombardment and subsequent Marine landings. A total of eight battleships, five heavy cruisers, three light cruisers, and 10 destroyers gathered for the onslaught, supported by aircraft from the carriers. Nearly 800 ships of every size, shape, and kind would participate in the Iwo Jima campaign. But occupation and capture would not be easy. Twenty-seven thousand Japanese troops prepared to defend the island, using artillery hidden in caves, 800 pillboxes, and three miles of tunnels on the eight-square-mile island.

Crew ate early and hearty when the day's plan included bombarding an island like Iwo Jima. The days were long, difficult, and dangerous. Meals after breakfast sometimes became just a bucketful of sandwiches delivered to battle stations.
COURTESY OF BATTLESHIP *NORTH CAROLINA* COLLECTION

General quarters sounded at 0545, and the boys scrambled to their battle stations. Richard Fox, Bob Palomaris, and the others on the antiaircraft guns would see action only in case of an air attack against the ships, but Paul Wieser, Bob Fennelly, and the boys manning the five-inch guns would be busy all day. More than 175 boys in each of the three 16-inch gun turrets would also be exhausted by day's end.

Almon Oliver and Eldon Means prepared their plane for take-off. The Kingfishers served an important purpose during shore bombardments—spotting for the gunners, sending messages back to the ships about the targets and the accuracy of the firing. Both of the BB55's planes would be in the air that day. Thorough preparation for the operation included a briefing on the command ship by the staff of the commanding Marine general. Pictures taken on earlier runs and detailed charts aided the communication between the spotter planes and the ships. A chart of the island was divided into numbered squares of about 100 yards each inside lettered squares approximately 500 yards each. Using the numbers and letters on the chart, the pilots could identify targets and record where shells hit so corrective information could be sent back to the ships if targets weren't being adequately struck.

Seventy thousand Marines waited to invade the island.

Their preflight checks complete, Oliver climbed into the pilot seat and Means, his radioman, into the backseat. They put on their helmets and headphones, strapped themselves in, and prepared for the blast of gunpowder that would send them rattling along the 60-foot metal catapult. Oliver slipped his hand into the securing handle and wrapped his fingers around the throttle, steadied his feet on the rudders, and gave the thumbs-up signal. At 0640, the blast hurtled them into the air.

Twenty minutes later, just before sunrise, the 16-inch guns began firing on assigned targets on the northern end of Iwo Jima from a distance of 10,000 yards offshore. With every rumbling roar of the 16-inch cannons, the ship shuddered, and no sailor aboard was spared the effects.

The ships made slow passes along the island, steaming one way, then the other. The guns did not fire in the rapid succession of antiaircraft artillery but in deliberate, targeted salvos, waiting for the spotter planes to report on accuracy so adjustments could be made, firing at predetermined targets, or responding to immediate requests from the ground. After each salvo, the spotter planes radioed results and corrections. Constant communication continued back and forth between the ship and the planes. Flying at a thousand feet or less, Oliver could see where the salvos landed and radioed back directions like "Up 100" or "Down 500" or "No change" after each salvo. He could see the constant firing from all the ships—the large shells from the main batteries of the battleships, the antiaircraft fire from the cruisers and the destroyers and the secondary batteries of the battleships. He was amazed at the sheer number of ships.

The plan called for the large ships to initially concentrate fire on the landing beach with the big guns, then lead up the beach with the smaller guns in front of the Marines as they landed. The five-inch guns opened fire at 0827, and the first wave of Marine landing craft, hundreds of them, sliced through the water toward landfall.

From the chart room on the communication bridge, three decks up from the main deck, Chuck Paty monitored the radio transmissions and had a good view of the action, but nothing compared to Oliver's as he flew overhead. He watched the wakes from hundreds of landing craft cut white circles in the water that became continuous streaks toward shore when the Marines began to land at 0859.

At first, Oliver saw no response from the Japanese, but as soon

Flying a scouting mission prior to the invasion of Iwo Jima, Almon Oliver saw ships circling in preparation while others steamed toward the island.

as a few of the craft had landed, the attack began from Mount Suribachi and a ridge line to the left, a barrage of fire that destroyed landing craft and killed Marines. Frantic calls for someone to locate the guns sent the 19-year-old Oliver down to 300 feet, flying low to try and see where the attacks originated. But the Japanese had prepared well, their mortars in caves on tracks so they could be rolled out and fired, then returned. The Japanese covered the muzzles with wet blankets to mask the locations.

Before noon, the spotter planes were running out of fuel. During other bombardments, the BB55 would leave the line of fire so her planes could land, be hoisted aboard, and be refueled and then relaunched, but at Iwo Jima, other arrangements had been made for rendezvousing with a destroyer on the windward side of the island and fueling while still in the water. Rough seas made landing difficult and takeoff from the water treacherous.

The bombardment continued throughout the day, and the crews of the 16s and the fives remained at general quarters. They could not leave to go to the mess hall for chow, so a member of each crew went down to retrieve lunch—a stainless-steel bucket full of sandwiches and a pot of hot coffee.

With so many ships participating in the bombardment, they sometimes got in each other's way. The *Salt Lake City* and the *Chester* were operating in the same sector as the *North Carolina* but closer to shore. On numerous occasions, shelling from the *North Carolina* was delayed as those two ships steamed back and forth within the Showboat's line of fire. Individual delays sometimes lasted minutes, and a full hour of delay was consumed by the end of the day. Efforts needed to be made to better coordinate the movements of ships so they did not diminish each other's performance, the BB55's captain later wrote. Lives depended on their accuracy and expediency.

More than 12 hours after the first salvo exploded on the beach, firing ceased. When the planes were recovered, Oliver and Means had been in the air for 14 hours except for brief refueling breaks. The ships retired northwest for the night, which placed them between Iwo Jima and the Japanese homeland. Regular watch resumed, and the thought of a good night's sleep was merely a dream. Some boys had the eight-to-midnight watch, others the midnight-to-four. And the Japanese did not let them rest. A half-hour after sunset, radar detected a bogie and air defense sounded. So, in addition to the gunners on the automatic weapons, the sailors who had spent their entire day inside the five-inch mounts rushed back to man their guns again. Only one of six reported raids manifested itself; ships within range opened fire. An hour later, the *Texas* started shooting and air defense sounded again, but the planes proved to be friendlies. The sailors stayed on high alert, knowing the Japanese were becoming desperate and wondering what other tactics the enemy had devised to fight back.

The ships returned to Iwo Jima for a second day of bombarding, then a third. When the port side was firing, the boys in the fives on the starboard side were allowed to climb outside their mounts. After several days of firing, even the thunderous booms from the 16-inch guns began to sound routine. Wieser wanted to see some of the action. He was gun captain inside the mount and had no view of anything outside, unlike Fennelly, who, as a spotter, could watch through the periscope. So Wieser and a few of the other boys decided to stand behind turret three and watch for a little while. They saw the huge projectiles soaring through the air and landing in explosive bursts on the island. They could see fires and smoke and explosions. But when they heard splashes in the water behind them—shells from another ship—they decided the main deck was not the safest place to be and returned to their mounts.

In the air on the third day, Oliver received a message from Marines on the ground asking for help. They were near the airfield and under attack; at a thousand feet, Oliver could see that the problem was serious. The only way he could help was to direct the artillery in front of the advancing Marines. Oliver contacted the Combat Information Center explaining the situation and received permission to proceed. Step by step, he relayed messages back to the ship, information the gunners needed to land a series of five-inch projectiles in the area. Then he took them closer and closer one salvo at a time until they were right on top of the Japanese. With the exact location established, the director was able to set the guns on automatic and fire a series of rounds close to the Marines but on top of the enemy.

Oliver received orders to fly into a small canyon and check out some Japanese vehicles reportedly hidden there. When he reached the canyon, he dropped altitude to 200 feet and swept through the base of the canyon. The ground beneath him erupted. Oliver looked overhead and saw a group of fighters—American planes—conducting an air raid above him. He was in their line of fire. Shots zinged past him from inside the cliff, redirecting his attention. Under attack from the enemy and obviously unseen by the friendlies, he deftly flew the plane out of the canyon to relative safety. Only later when he landed to fuel did he realize how close he had come to death. He discovered two holes in his plane's wings, whether from friendly shrapnel or enemy fire he did not know.

23 February 1945

From his vantage point on the bridge, and with the aid of the glasses there, Paty could actually see Japanese soldiers running around on the hills—not many, but an occasional sprinter going from bunker to bunker.

When the ship was so close to shore that only the five-inch guns could fire, one of the crew in turret one stuck his head out of the hatch on the bottom of the turret and yelled to Fox, who was on the bow in case air defense was called.

"Hey, Fox," he said. "Want to see something?"

"Sure," Fox replied.

"Come on in."

Fox climbed into the turret and looked through the periscope. He could see the Jeeps driving up Mount Suribachi, but he also saw some hit by enemy fire. He hated not being able to do more to protect fellow Marines being slaughtered on the island. His spirits were lifted a little later, however. When the first group of men raised the flag on top of the mountain, Fox witnessed it through that periscope. Fennelly watched the same amazing event through the periscope of mount three. But the scene was deceiving, as the fighting was far from over. For nearly a month after the American flag began flying atop Mount Suribachi, Marines continued to die on Iwo Jima. Fighting on the ground was intense, and the Marines suffered tremendous losses. When organized enemy resistance finally subsided on March 16, 1945, total American casualties included 6,821 killed, 19,217 wounded, and 2,648 with combat fatigue. Of the 28,686 total casualties, 23,573 were Marines. An estimated 20,000 Japanese were killed and 1,083 taken as prisoners of war.

After Fox and Fennelly had witnessed the raising of the flag on Mount Suribachi, Admiral Spruance ordered two battleships—the *North Carolina* and the *Washington*—to Tokyo in support of air strikes there. They left the Iwo Jima area that same day.

24 February 1945

Lieutenant John Burns—the BB55 pilot who had rescued 10 downed airmen in one momentous day—died when the F6F he was flying during training exercises at the United States Naval Auxiliary Air Station in Oceana near Norfolk, Virginia, crashed at the end of a service runway during an emergency landing. Burns was 26.

★★★★★★★★★★★★★★

During the next fueling rendezvous, the *North Carolina* fueled two destroyers before receiving fuel herself, but the first tanker did not have a sufficient supply to replenish the BB55. Her tanks reached a record low of 50 percent. So the fuel kings and deck crew worked twice as hard that day, retrieving the fueling lines from one tanker and rigging them to another to receive the remainder of the fuel needed before the ship set a course for Tokyo. The exhausting fueling duties continued the next day, as the BB55 topped off five destroyers. Heavy swells restricted the fueling activities to the starboard side only, instead of both port and starboard, so Wieser and Fennelly had to work twice as hard and the time needed for fueling more than doubled.

The change of weather became another enemy to battle. Tokyo

was covered with snow, and the fighter pilots wrestled their planes through snow and sleet squalls before the mission was called off and their energies were directed to another area for attack. When the weather finally lifted several days later, the BB55's task group headed back to Ulithi while other groups of the force continued to support the landings on Iwo Jima. The Showboat had expended so many projectiles during her participation in the bombardment that she was riding several feet higher in the water than normal and needed to resupply.

11 March 1945

Lights shone around the harbor and on the atoll. Blackouts weren't required there like they were out in the battle zone. Showing movies on the fantail allowed all the interested crew who weren't on watch to participate. The arrangement worked much better than down in the mess hall, where space was limited and the movie reels were rushed from one compartment to another until everyone had viewed each part of the movie. Fresh air, stars. Boys were lying on top of turret three, sitting on the five-inch mounts port and starboard with their legs dangling over the side, leaning up against the catapult bases, sitting on top of the air intakes—anywhere they could find a place to perch. The night was warm and pleasant, a relief from the icy days near Tokyo.

At 1945, night fighters were launched from land when island radar picked up bogies, but at four miles, the bogies disappeared off the screen. All ships were alerted at 2007. A few minutes later, an explosion sent flames barreling into the air as a kamikaze nosedived into the flight deck of the carrier *Randolph*. The BB55 crew rushed to general quarters, stunned by the surprise air attack in what was supposed to be their secure anchorage. First a submarine, now a kamikaze. No safe place existed.

Half an hour after the attack, BB55 radar picked up a bogie at 35 miles, but it faded a few minutes later. As the boys secured from general quarters, the loudspeaker crackled.

"Now hear this," the captain said. "You boys are manning your battle stations too damn slow!"

After the attack, full blackout was instituted from a half-hour after sunset until a half-hour before sunrise when the ships were anchored in Ulithi. Not even a cigarette could be lit topside. The *Randolph* lost 25 men in the attack, and another 106 were injured, but damage to the ship was repaired at Ulithi, and when the task force departed several days later, the *Randolph* was not left behind. The *North Carolina* once again rode low in the water with an ample supply of ammunition for the next phase of operations. Restocking had taken several days.

18 March 1945

Following the successful occupation of Iwo Jima, the Allied forces were ready to concentrate all their firepower on the Japanese homeland, which included the island of Okinawa, just south of the mainland. The fight for Okinawa began in earnest in the middle of March as the task force launched strikes against airfields in Kyushu. Left with little other defense against the advancing enemy, the Japanese relied heavily on kamikazes as their primary line of attack. The occasional bogie contacts the boys had grown accustomed to hearing became an almost constant staccato of bleeps for several days—detected then lost, detected then lost, detected then lost. BB55 crew in sky control could see enemy planes in the distance being shot down by ships in another task group. Nothing changed when the sun went down. Every few minutes, a bogie was detected, some within range of antiaircraft fire from ships in other task groups.

Task Group 58.3, which included the carrier *Enterprise* but not the *North Carolina*, garnered the most attention at first. The explosion from a 600-pound bomb dropped on the *Enterprise* could be heard aboard the Showboat. The detonation caused minor injuries and some casualties, but the ship continued operating with the force. In yet another task group, a foiled kamikaze attack landing close to, but not on, the *Intrepid* also caused damage and casualties, but not enough to affect operations.

By the time the carriers launched the first strikes on the Kobe-Osaka area of Okinawa just prior to sunrise on March 19, nearly 30 individual bogies or raid groups had been detected and followed, fired upon, or lost off the screen since midnight, and yet another group in the task force had come under attack by bombers. Air defense and general quarters sounded again and again on the Showboat.

Palomaris stood watch just under sky control at the uppermost part of the superstructure. The task group had turned into the wind for the carriers to begin launching aircraft for the morning strike. As his watch was about to end, Palomaris heard a report from air plot through his headphones.

"Bogie, 13 miles and closing."

Another one. Knowing air defense would surely sound again, Palomaris immediately began descending the ladders and staircases that would take him down the superstructure to the main deck so he could man his 20-millimeter on the starboard bow. As he neared the bottom, air defense sounded. He had a good head start, skipping most of the steps on the last ladder and sprinting up the bow to his gun. He yanked off the canvas cover, locked in a magazine, cocked the gun, and was ready to begin firing before anyone else manned his gun, but the plane was flying low, hedgehopping through the fleet, and the *Franklin* was just ahead of the BB55, off her port bow, blocking his shot, and the governor on his gun would not let him fire.

Palomaris watched in horror as the pilot dropped his load on the *Franklin*'s flight deck amidst the planes readying for takeoff, one bomb forward, one aft. Fire raged across the deck; the *Franklin* made a hard right turn; she was enveloped in clouds of black smoke from the burning fuel. Her planes began to catch fire and explode; crew members jumped or were blown overboard. The *North Carolina* made an emergency turn to avoid running over the injured men and colliding with the ball of fire that was their ship. Boys on the BB55 started tossing over life jackets and rafts and even shark repellent in an effort to aid the *Franklin*'s fallen. But the task force could not stop. Several destroyers remained behind with the *Franklin* as the rest of the ships continued westward toward Okinawa.

Constant reports of bogies throughout the day took on new immediacy for the crew, who didn't know when one of them would slip in like it did on the *Franklin* or when a whole group of enemy planes would attack in force. Amidst continuous threats, the task force carried out its mission for that day—air attacks against shipping in the Kobe area and strikes on aircraft and installations in the Osaka area.

Late in the night, the radar screens were silent, and dawn general quarters was uneventful the next day. By midmorning, radar began picking up bogies again, air defense sounded, and one enemy fighter ventured close enough to the group to be shot down.

Fueling destroyers was a constant necessity, so in spite of bogie reports, the *Monssen* came along the starboard side of the BB55 to fuel. An uneventful hour later, she cast off as fueling was completed. Wieser and Fennelly had just started securing the fuel lines and preparing for the next destroyer when air defense sounded, and they rushed to their mounts again. The carrier *Enterprise* and the cruiser *Astoria* opened fire with their five-inch guns. When that immediate threat had passed, the *Owen* came alongside starboard; Fennelly and Wieser secured from GQ and pulled out the lines. The fueling process began again. Fueling was only halfway complete when a bogie was picked up at 36 miles and closing, 17 miles and closing, 11 miles turning northwest and closing. A cruiser fueling a destroyer opened fire at a kamikaze diving on her; the plane crashed, but shrapnel or shells hit the stern of the destroyer being fueled, killing one man and injuring scores. The BB55 sounded air defense. Within seconds, the five-inch on the port side hit an enemy plane bearing in at four miles. The plane crashed vertically in a fiery ball over the water. Fueling complete, the *Owen* cast off, but the boys barely had time to store the hoses before more bogies were sighted. Every few minutes, a bogie was reported bearing down on the task force.

The starboard five-inch opened fire on one enemy plane bearing in at seven miles, then the port 20s and 40s picked it up as it got closer and crossed to the other side of the ship. The enemy under attack dropped a bomb intended for the *Enterprise*, but it missed, and the plane retreated at such a low altitude that the anti-aircraft guns had to cease firing for fear of hitting their own ships.

The barrage continued with sightings every few minutes, the starboard and then the port guns firing as the planes came in and crossed either in front of or behind the Showboat. Another bomb dropped near the *Enterprise* did not make a direct hit but still started a fire. As the day faded into dusk, then darkness, the enemy kept coming one after another, trying to drop a bomb or attempt a suicide dive.

Sometime amidst the mayhem, Fennelly dragged his mattress onto the main deck beside his gun mount—a few seconds saved if he ever had the chance to lie down on it again.

CHAPTER FOURTEEN
Okinawa
★★★★★★★★★★★★★★★★

> *"Fighting shoulder to shoulder with old and trusted comrades is a fine thing. Together we have watched our young and trusted comrades who did the actual fighting, and that too, is a fine and inspiring experience. I think all hands except the Nips can rejoice over the results produced by this team of 'old poops, young squirts, and Lieutenant Commanders.' "*
>
> *Admiral William F. "Bull" Halsey,*
> *commander, Third Fleet*

At the end of two seemingly interminable days off Okinawa, strikes and sweeps from the task force had destroyed 475 enemy aircraft in the air and on the ground and had damaged many more, sunk six small freighters, and damaged a couple of battleships, several aircraft carriers, two light aircraft carriers, two escort carriers, one heavy cruiser, one light cruiser, four destroyers, and one submarine. They also destroyed hangars, shops, arsenals, and storage facilities on the island.

Fire and smoke roared from the 16-inch cannons and five-inch guns on the Showboat as she bombarded Okinawa, softening the island for occupation forces.
COURTESY OF BATTLESHIP *NORTH CAROLINA* COLLECTION

The ships began a bombarding run on the southeastern end of Okinawa, diverting attention from the main landing forces farther north. When in position off the coast, the battleships *Washington*, *North Carolina*, and *South Dakota* formed a column, moving slowly in one direction, then the other, bombarding the island with 16-inch projectiles that exploded into predetermined targets. The ships took turns leaving the formation to refuel and relaunch their spotter planes. The enemy did not respond in any way throughout the day. The battleships were only three of more than 1,300 ships surrounding the entire island. Those ships continued to support the occupation and capture of Okinawa with air strikes throughout the remainder of March, passing through drifting mines and fighting off air attacks from enemy planes.

01 April 1945

Sixty thousand Marine and Army troops invaded Okinawa with little to no resistance. The ships of Task Force 58 continued to support the amphibious forces with air strikes. During the first few days of April, they battled bad weather while fighting off the occasional individual enemy aircraft that ventured within firing range. Japanese aircraft were given names—"Betty," "Judy," "Zeke," "Val," "Kate," "Frances"—by the Allied forces depending on what type of plane they were. When still just a distant blip on the radar screen, whether one plane or 20, it was a "bogie."

06 April 1945

Radar detected the first bogie of the day at 0232 hours at 42 miles. By sunrise, radar was tracking nine separate contacts and air defense had been sounded three times, although nothing came close enough to take under fire. The BB55 received warning at 0626 to expect raids throughout the day. By midmorning, the single bogie contact became groups of planes, first a group of two to three, then a group of three to five.

Just after noon, other ships in the task group began firing. The BB55 sighted a Judy diving at 4,400 yards, and the port antiaircraft guns commenced firing. Destroyers in the screen opened fire simultaneously, but firing ceased when the Judy splashed, its bomb just missing the *Cabot*. A bogie appeared at 30 miles, another at 39 miles; fighters shot down two at 26 miles. Simultaneous contacts were made at 42 and 41 miles, and one at 51. Another was closing in—19 miles, 14, 10. One at 43 miles, one at 32. One was shot down by destroyer gunfire, hitting another destroyer on its way down. Contacts at 43 miles, 14, 15, 12. Another at 12 miles, nine miles, nine miles and closing, five miles and closing.

With attacks seemingly inevitable, the ships increased speed to nearly their maximum and maneuvered radically, zigzagging to frustrate attackers. Carriers continued to launch and retrieve planes for making air strikes on Okinawa and intercepting bogies before they reached the force. At 1302 hours, the task group opened fire at an enemy plane at 9,000 yards. Bob Palomaris, Richard Fox, and the other gunners on the bow 20s opened fire along with other antiaircraft weaponry from the *North Carolina* and surrounding ships. Firing ceased when the bogie splashed at 3,000 feet.

Almost immediately, the zigzagging task group turned into the wind to aid the planes taking off for another air strike. Rough seas sent the 20-millimeter gunners into overdrive, unloading and covering their guns, then sprinting for higher decks before the waves washed over the bow as it dipped with the turn into the wind. Palomaris and his loader, Fred Pierce, headed for the boat deck, one above the main deck, but Fox and Ray Horn had to climb all the way up to the signal bridge, three levels up. The upper open decks were crowded with extra crew from the abandoned bow.

Standing on the boat deck, Palomaris saw another bogie coming in low, hedgehopping across a nearby cruiser. Instinct and training sent him running for his gun. He leapt down the steps to the main deck yelling, "Zeke, Zeke!" When he reached the spray shield in front of turret one, the plane came across the port bow of the Showboat. Palomaris saw the pilot—his flight jacket, helmet, goggles. If the pilot had turned his head toward Palomaris, their eyes could have met, but he stayed focused on his target—the carrier *Cabot*, just starboard of the Showboat. Water rushed across the bow again, preventing Palomaris from reaching his gun, but the ear-splitting cracks of fives and the rapid-fire pops of 20s and 40s came from ships all around the group. A loud bang blended into the other sounds. Hit and exploding, the Zeke crashed into the water before it reached the carrier.

Inside mount three, Bob Fennelly and the other boys heard a hell of an explosion and saw a bright flash through the small hotcase door on the side of the mount, but they could not stop to find out what caused it. Inside mount seven, Paul Wieser was oblivious to what was happening outside. He knew only that the kamikazes were coming in and the crew had to shoot them down. Inside the mount, the boys could see nothing, but seven levels up in Batt II, Chuck Paty could see. Batt II was the secondary steering position for the ship. In case the bridge was knocked out, the group of officers and enlisted men in Batt II would take over. The small area was manned by about 15 people, so some of them actually stayed outside on the deck. Paty's job was to man the radio, and he had to wear headphones. The short cords did not let him venture out on the deck very far. The little radio spouted information: "Enemy bombers on the port side. Dive bombers on us now."

All the ships in the group had been firing for several minutes when Paty heard an extremely large boom more like the 16s than the fives, 20s, and 40s that fired during an air attack, followed by a sound like someone had thrown a handful of mega marbles against the bulkhead. Still sitting, he glanced toward the porthole; the entire tower was briefly blanketed in smoke, and then he saw someone fall. Paty jumped up and ran to the door. Everyone was looking down over the rail, and he was afraid the ship had been bombed. He saw men lying everywhere on the signal bridge four levels down and around the 40-millimeter mount and the director one level higher. Blood flowed across the deck. Then he saw the damage—a huge hole in the side of the director, made by a five-inch American shell. A pharmacist's mate was lying on the deck. He had been hit by shrapnel—the marbles Paty had heard—but was not seriously injured. Paty saw dozens of pieces of jagged metal lying all over the floor and bent to pick one up. It was unbearably hot, blistering his hand at the touch. How more people crowded inside the small space were not injured, he did not know.

Fox was the last person to reach the signal bridge. The 20-millimeter firing on the bridge and the 40s just above his head were deafening, so much so that he didn't really hear the explosion. Almost immediately, he felt something hit him in the back of the leg and thought someone had kicked him. He looked down and saw his pant leg smoking, men lying everywhere, bleeding and screaming. Fox saw one sailor—the gunner from the signal bridge 20-millimeter—who was severely injured. Fox was not sure he was alive but focused his attention on that boy. He had obviously been hit from behind, his groin area torn to shreds, parts of his insides lying on the deck beside him.

"Saffron, help me!" Fox screamed above the noise. "We've got to get him to sick bay."

Fox and George L. Saffron carefully laid the trailing parts of the boy's anatomy on his stomach and picked him up. One grabbed him under his shoulders, while the other slipped between his legs and lifted them into his arms. They carried him gingerly and started down the many levels toward sick bay. Scaling the first few levels of the superstructure was difficult, maneuvering the critically injured boy through the crowd of panicked and stricken sailors and down several flights of stairs, his feet bumping against the metal handrail on each side regardless of how careful his rescuers were. But as they entered the main deck hatch to go below, the stairways narrowed and steepened. Scaling them alone and healthy had taken training. Carrying an injured shipmate down them seemed almost impossible, but they conquered the odds. They had no choice.

They were some of the first to reach sick bay, and the sailor they carried was obviously the most critically injured, so a large group of pharmacist's mates rushed to their aid with a stretcher, retrieved the boy, and carried him straight to the operating room.

"You're injured," a corpsman said to Fox.

"I'm okay," Fox said. "Will he live?"

"I don't know," the corpsman said. "Now, let me see that leg."

While the corpsmen dug shrapnel from his leg, Fox wondered about the boy, where he was from, if he had a wife, a girlfriend, family somewhere back home waiting and worrying about him. Fox didn't see how he could possibly survive his injuries. He didn't even know the boy's name.

★★★★★★★★★★★★★★

In addition to their spotting duties, the Kingfisher OS2Us flew rescue missions. Their ability to land and take off from water made them especially suitable for the task. A fighter pilot shot down near the small island of Ie Shima awaited rescue, and the BB55 boys in both planes were called to action.

Almon Oliver and Eldon Means manned their plane and readied for takeoff. They had flown many missions together by that time in the war and had come to depend on each other during flights. Oliver knew he could rely on Means, respected his competence, and liked him as a person. The respect and admiration were mutual. The explosion of gunpowder shot their plane rattling down the catapult and into the air off the port side, followed within a minute by the other Kingfisher off starboard.

The pilots gained altitude, then leveled out for the flight. Oliver could see ships in all directions, several vast task groups making up the force, spreading out for miles. Their flight in search of the missing pilot was uneventful—no bogie sightings or warnings from ship's radio that danger lurked. About halfway to their destination, the planes were recalled. The Japanese had captured the pilot.

After each mission, when the planes approached their mother ship, they landed in the water and were lifted back aboard by a crane. Swells posed few threats to the Kingfishers, but choppy, rough water could be dangerous. To minimize the threat, the ship turned sharply in the water, creating a slick for a plane to use as a landing ramp.

One Kingfisher landed, was lifted aboard on the port side and safely placed in its cradle on the catapult. The ship and the pilot communicated through blinker, code, semaphore, or signal flags. As Oliver prepared for landing, he saw the "Charley" flag at half-mast on the starboard yardarm. That meant the ship would be preparing a slick for him on the starboard side. As the BB55 changed course to cruise out of the wind, Oliver dropped to 500 feet, flying a course parallel to the ship. When he reached a distance of a quarter-mile ahead of the ship, the Charley flag was two-blocked—raised to full height—which meant it was time to execute the landing. In moves as choreographed as a ballet, Oliver began circling a 360-degree approach and the ship made a radical turn of 90 degrees, creating the slick when its stern shifted in the water. From the fantail of the BB55, a crewman threw a smoke flare so Oliver could align his approach, landing into the wind as close as he could to the ship when she had finished her turn.

Upon touchdown, Oliver revved the engine to taxi the plane onto a sled hanging from a boom extending off the side of the ship. The sled, about 10 by 20 feet, was made of heavy rope knotted to form one-foot squares. When Oliver taxied onto it, a spring-loaded hook on the bottom of his center float caught in the sled. The ship was actually towing the plane as the crane swung overhead to pick it up.

Means climbed out of his rear seat carrying the sling from the front cockpit of the plane up onto the starboard wing. When the crane swung into position over the towed aircraft, Means hooked the sling onto the crane and stood on the wing holding onto the cable while the plane was lifted onto the ship, the pilot still in the cockpit. Oliver and Means had been together almost a year and had flown so many missions for the *North Carolina* that the complicated maneuvers had become routine.

Rising slowly up the side of the ship, the plane had been hoisted only about 10 feet into the air when it suddenly dropped back into the sea, missed the sled, and flipped tail over cockpit. The cockpit immediately filled with water, and Oliver struggled to escape under 10 feet of ocean in the wake of the ship, still strapped in his seat and wearing an inflatable life vest and a parachute. The water stung his eyes and his chest felt heavy as he wrenched the straps loose, pushed the cockpit door open, and fought his way to the surface, gulping deep breaths of fresh air. He grabbed onto the one float that was still intact. The ocean was choppy, and he searched frantically for any sign of Means. He saw him about 15 feet away and tried desperately to get his attention.

"Inflate your vest!" he yelled to Means, but his radioman did not respond.

"Means!" he yelled louder. "Means, swim over here, Means!"

Oliver gulped huge mouthfuls of salt water as he called again and again.

"Inflate your vest! Inflate it!"

Oliver knew that Means was an excellent swimmer, and although the radioman had given no indication that he heard the calls, Oliver was still hopeful even when Means disappeared in the shallow of a huge swell. Oliver continued to call over and over as he clung to the float, rising and falling with the swells, waiting to be rescued, watching his ship steam off with the task force.

★★★★★★★★★★★★★★

Shards of shrapnel and shell fragments had killed three boys working on the 40-millimeter gun mount and its director just below where the projectile had ripped into the port director for the five-inch guns. On that level and the signal bridge below, 44 boys were injured, some critically, others like Fox not severely. An auxiliary sick bay was set up in the wardroom officers' mess on the main deck. Palomaris and many of the other boys, some slightly wounded themselves, helped carry the injured for treatment.

The dead—Edward Elmer Brenn of Brooklyn, Connecticut; John Malcolm Watson of Dunnellon, Florida; and Carl Emil Karam, Jr., of Memphis, Tennessee—were prepared in sick bay for burial. They were sewn inside canvas bags along with two five-inch projectiles and laid on individual stretchers, then each covered with an American flag.

Fox showered and started getting ready. He was assigned to serve as part of the honor guard for the burial at sea. He had heard that three boys were being buried and wondered if one of them was the sailor he carried down to sick bay. He pulled on his khaki pants, careful not to knock the bandage off his leg and cause it to bleed, then checked to be sure the creases were properly pressed. He was sure the boy had died, didn't know how he could have survived losing all that blood. Fox stuck his arms in his khaki shirt, buttoned the cuffs, and started buttoning the front. He closed his eyes mo-

John Malcolm Watson and Edward Elmer Brenn enjoyed a night on the town, their smiles innocent of the tragedy that would claim their vibrant young lives on April 6, 1945.
COURTESY OF BATTLESHIP NORTH CAROLINA COLLECTION

mentarily, hoping he could make the horrifying images disappear. He tucked his shirttail into his pants, fastened them, and buckled his belt. Somebody had said all the ones who died were on the other deck. He sat on the side of his bunk and put on his black socks and shoes. So many injured sailors had been lying everywhere he had to step over them and into their blood just to get off the signal bridge. He stood and walked to his locker, took his black tie off the hook, and pulled it under his collar and around his neck, letting it hang while he fumbled to push those tiny, aggravating collar buttons through the holes. So many people had said so many different things, some he knew were wrong. He looped the tie over, over, around, and through, tying a perfect knot and pulling it tight. He just didn't know. Maybe he'd never know, maybe he didn't really want to know. He placed his cap on his head, grabbed his rifle, and mounted the steps to the main deck.

The three coffins lining the bow rail of the North Carolina *contained the bodies of the sailors who died when a five-inch shell pierced a director of the BB55. The flying shrapnel also wounded 44. This was the first time that a burial at sea aboard the ship involved more than one victim.*
COURTESY OF BATTLESHIP NORTH CAROLINA COLLECTION

The boys had seen burials at sea before, and they never were easy to watch. Some of the crew chose not to go at all, and some couldn't go because they were on watch. They had never buried more than one at a time—on the island they had, but not at sea. Every deck and the top of every gun mount with a view to starboard aft of mount seven was full when the three flag-draped bodies were carried to the lowered lifelines that evening.

But the boys all kept a watchful eye toward the sky, even when taps cried.

★★★★★★★★★★★★★★★

The destroyer on rescue duty did not reach Oliver for what felt like hours, and he continued to call for Means although his hope was dwindling. He watched for any signs of sharks; at least he was not bleeding. When he finally saw the USS *English* approaching at a steady clip, his joy was overshadowed by fear that her crew did not see him bobbing up and down in the huge swells, rising and then falling out of sight. The ship was coming in fast, way too fast to stop anywhere near Oliver, and his heart rose in his chest. He did not want to die that way, not under the bow of a ship sent to rescue him. The *English* finally slowed, but not soon enough or close enough to attempt a rescue. Oliver realized the crew had seen him when the ship circled and came alongside him about 50 feet away. A boatswain attempted to throw a monkey fist to him but could never toss it quite far enough to reach, and Oliver hesitated to let go of the float and try to swim to the line. Others tried as well, and when that plan failed, they used the line gun to shoot the line across. Oliver grabbed hold of the line, reluctantly releasing the float that had kept him alive. The rescuers pulled him in toward the destroyer, the rough seas making it difficult. The ship pitched and rolled so violently that sometimes the deck was almost underwater and Oliver was washed away, then it would rise 10 feet in the air, bringing him so close to the hull that he feared being slammed into it. The rescue took several frustrating attempts before it was successful.

When he was safely aboard, Oliver headed directly to the bridge to talk to the officer of the deck.

"I had a crewman with me. Can you please search for him?" Oliver pleaded.

A crane on the fantail of the ship was used to hoist the Kingfisher planes back aboard after landing. Eldon Means died when something went wrong during the retrieval and his plane fell back into the water while he was standing on the wing.
COURTESY OF BATTLESHIP *NORTH CAROLINA* COLLECTION

The destroyer searched the area until ordered to abandon the effort, but the crew did not find Means or any sign that he had ever been there.

"The tail slammed down hard when we capsized," Oliver said to no one in particular as he stood on the bridge and the search gave up no clues. "It must have hit him in the head and knocked him unconscious. He was a good swimmer; he could have made it to the float. He was a fine young man, an outstanding sailor."

★★★★★★★★★★★★★★★★

At 1845, carriers in the task force completed recovery of their fighters participating in strikes and sweeps in support of the Okinawa operation. Half an hour later, the Showboat secured from air defense. Within an hour, a bogie was picked up at 75 miles; kamikazes remained a never-ending threat.

That night, sitting in his bunk, Gerald Kass of F Division began his diary:

April 6, 1945—At sea today I am starting this log on events happening in the Southwest Pacific. The main reason I am writing this log is because three men in my division got killed today. . . . And I knew them all well. . . . I was on the signal bridge when it all happened. . . . I could hear the shrapnel hit against the steel on the side of me.

Brenn, Chief Firecontrolman, 21 years old, was killed from the shrapnel of the shell. It went through his left side and left leg. He was on X director six, right below Sky II. The best guy you ever want to meet.

Watson, fire controlman 1/c, was killed—his right leg was blown completely off. A large piece of shrapnel went all the way through his head. He was all shot up from his hip down. He was also hit in the heart. He must of died instantly. He was just telling us that he never wanted to take out any life insurance because it was like betting the government he was going to get killed. Watson was with Brenn when he got it.

Karam, seaman 1/c, must have been killed instantly. The shrapnel went through his helmet and head and shot the lower part of his body all to hell. His face was bloody and his eyes seemed to be in back of his head, his face was all blue. And I was just telling him at chow this morning after they passed the word over the speaker for all hands to be alert that this might be his last show. I guess I was right. He lived in Tennessee and was 18 years old. He had a beautiful girl and he was a 4.0 guy.

The main reason why the destroyer fired and hit us was due to the fact that a Jap suicide plane flew over our bow low to the water even with our superstructure between us and the destroyer. Our whole port battery opened up on him, they identified him as a Judy. We shot him down and he crashed on the starboard side of the carrier. It was too late—the destroyer had already missed the plane and hit us. I hope I never see a day like today again.

I went to where the bodies lay below decks after it was all over and knelt down and prayed for them, beside them. 44 others were wounded and one radioman lost too.

★★★★★★★★★★★★★★★

Means's death had a deep personal effect on Oliver. He mourned the young man while he spent the next few days confined to a stateroom on the destroyer before being returned to duty on his own ship.

But war did not offer the boys on board the BB55 time to mourn their comrades lost to friendly fire. Before sunrise the next day, the carriers began launching aircraft to search for a Japanese fleet that had been reported. The search planes made contact at 0825 hours, and all task groups received orders to strike with every available plane. The carriers started launching aircraft at 1000 hours, and the bogies began again—48 miles, 42, 30 and closing. Air defense sent the antiaircraft gunners running. At seven miles, the ships were firing. Fighters splashed two Vals. A kamikaze spiraled into the carrier *Hancock*, causing her flight deck to burst into flames, burning

Richard Fox received a Purple Heart from Captain Oswald S. Colclough for injuries he received during the friendly-fire incident aboard the North Carolina *on April 6, 1945.*
COURTESY OF BATTLESHIP *NORTH CAROLINA* COLLECTION

15 planes, blowing men overboard, and blinding her crew with smoke. Bogies at 13 miles, 37, 58. Fighter pilots splashed a Judy. A bogie first detected at 24 miles closed to 16, then 13, then disappeared. Another picked up at 43 miles closed to 33, then 26, then back out to 27, 28, and 31 before it was lost. Detected at 38 miles, a bogie was identified as three planes when they closed to 25 miles. Fighters shot down three bandits at 25 miles, a Judy at 15, a Kate at 14, then two more Judys. Bogies at 36 miles, one at 35, another at 30. Fighters splashed one bandit. A bogie detected at 20 miles was identified as a Judy at 17 miles. Fighters splashed one Judy at 10.

Detected at 14 miles, a bogie closed to 12 miles, 10 miles, nine miles, seven miles, 7,000 yards, and then the starboard antiaircraft battery opened fire on the enemy plane diving on the carrier *Essex* at 6,000 yards. The plane crashed at 3,000 yards, and the boys ceased firing. Fighters shot down a Betty, but then a diving attack started on Task Group 58.1. The ships shot down one Frances, then another. A bogie was spotted at 15 miles. Air defense sounded.

By 1856 hours, the carriers had recovered their aircraft involved in the strike on the Japanese fleet. They had lost seven planes in the strike but had sunk the Japanese battleship *Yamato* and all the other ships in the enemy force except three destroyers.

For the remaining days of April, the *North Carolina* continued guarding the carriers that launched the aircraft flying strikes on Okinawa. She also bombarded the island while ground troops fought to capture the strongly defended territory. What had begun as a lightly contested landing on April 1 turned into the deadliest battle of the Pacific campaign—indeed, perhaps the costliest battle ever fought by American troops under such hellish conditions. One day blended into the next for the boys of the BB55, who practically lived at general quarters, the threat of kamikazes always present, the thought of that bloody April 6 never far from their minds but haunting them especially each time the ships opened fire on a bogie bearing down on the force.

The damage inflicted on the *North Carolina* by friendly fire on April 6 was more than could be repaired at sea or even at Ulithi, so as soon as the Okinawa campaign was complete at the end of April, the ship returned to Pearl Harbor for repairs, arriving May 9 and heading back to action on June 28.

06 June 1945

During an awards ceremony at Pearl Harbor, Oliver received the Navy's Air Medal. His citation read, "For meritorious achievement in aerial flight as pilot of an observation plane based on board the USS *North Carolina* during operations against enemy Japanese forces on Iwo Jima and Okinawa Shima from February 21 to April 19, 1945. Completing several spotting missions over strongly defended enemy defenses during this period, Lieutenant, Junior Grade Almon P. Oliver skillfully performed his assigned duties despite heavy enemy aircraft fire and assisted his ship in bringing accurate gunfire to bear on hostile positions. His courage and devotion to duty were in keeping with the highest traditions of the United States Naval Service."

10 July 1945

Only one target remained—the Japanese homeland. Just before midnight on July 9, a large group of friendlies was contacted at 88 miles and determined to be B-29s flying toward dawn raids on Tokyo. The night was black and overcast, hundreds of ships steaming together with no lights to guide their way or to alert each other to their locations. They relied on their radar, which was still primitive at best, and radio communication, which was kept to a minimum, to avoid running into each other. Seven scouting submarines preceded the task groups to locate enemy picket lines. In the leading task group, the number of destroyer pickets was doubled.

General quarters sounded at 0325—exceptionally early by the clock, though the sun would rise one hour later. The weather was threatening, the ships encountering moderate rain showers as they passed through a cold front. At 0400 hours, the task force was 180 miles from Tokyo and 130 miles from the Honshu coast—the designated position for the strikes to begin. The force turned into the wind; the carriers launched fighters to join the land-based B-29s already in the air. The attackers achieved complete surprise. That day's raids, mainly on airfields, were successful, and the task force made a quick getaway to the west at 26 knots.

The next day was dedicated to fueling destroyers, dodging and exploding mines, and conforming to the movements of the carriers as they launched routine patrols. The ships rendezvoused with a fueling group early on July 12 and then proceeded toward the designated location for air strikes on the Hokkaido-northern Honshu area on July 13. The weather had deteriorated so much by that day that the scheduled attacks were postponed 24 hours. The *North Carolina* fueled seven destroyers.

For the next few days, the carriers launched air strikes against Japan. The BB55 Kingfishers were launched each day for rescue duty, scouting for any downed pilots. On July 16, her Kingfishers were launched and transferred to two other ships for safekeeping during the next day's bombardment of Honshu. Throughout the day on July 17, the BB55 covered the carriers as they continued to launch planes for strikes on the Tokyo area. Two hours before sunset, she left the formation to join another task group for the bombardment to begin.

The weather had improved, but light rain and overcast skies limited visibility to about a mile. At 2035, radar picked up land thought to be the high mountains along the east coast of Honshu, 57 miles away. The task force steamed toward them. As the force closed in on the Japanese homeland, precautionary general quarters sounded at 2057.

Bombardment began almost three hours later. Since Palomaris's battle station was on one of the 20-millimeters and they were not manned during bombardments, he and his buddy Pierce decided to watch the action. They climbed up one flight to the boat deck and were surprised to find that about eight other boys had the same idea. They soon began to wish they had stayed below but were simultaneously awestruck by the view.

The 16-inch guns began firing on their first target, the Hitachi Refinery. They fired four minutes without stopping—two rounds per gun per minute, 18 deafening *ka-booms*. The ship lurched with every shot, and the boys had to hold onto something to keep from losing their balance. Fragments of powder bags flew through the air, but what fascinated the boys most was their ability to actually see the huge 1,900-pound projectiles arching toward their targets and see them hit in explosive fiery contact. Mesmerized, they watched the *North Carolina* strike the Hitachi Refinery, two locations of the Hitachi Engineering Works, and the Hitachi Steel Works. When the crew secured from general quarters following the bombardment, the first few minutes of the next day had already begun. Not one bogie had been detected during the raid.

Her bombardment duties complete, the Showboat continued to support and protect the carriers as they launched their fighter pilots for attacks on the Japanese homeland, rendezvousing at sea periodically with tankers, ammunition ships, and supply ships, as the force had no time or place to return to safe harbor. The BB55 Kingfishers took turns with OS2Us from other ships serving rescue duty for downed pilots. For several days during the last part of July and into the first part of August, the force kept track of a dangerous typhoon to the southwest of their point of operations. By August 4, the storm moved toward Korea and no longer posed a threat to the ships.

09 August 1945

When the first atomic bomb was dropped August 6 on Hiroshima in the southwestern part of Japan, the *North Carolina* and other ships in the task force were fueling and steaming northeast to execute strikes on air installations in Honshu and Hokkaido. Russia declared war on Japan two days later. When the United States dropped the second atomic bomb August 9 at Nagasaki, the BB55 was providing support for air strikes on strategic targets in northern Japan, including military installations on Ominato at the northernmost tip of Honshu.

The Showboat's seaplanes were on rescue duty that day. Pilots Ralph Jacobs and Almon Oliver remained on alert, prepared to launch within 10 minutes if called upon to effect a rescue. No calls came until late in the day. Ten pilots were thought to have survived being shot down. At least one Corsair pilot from the carrier *Essex* had been spotted in a life raft about five miles off the coast of Hokkaido. The force was still about 300 miles out to sea and the day was waning, so no rescue attempts would be made until morning.

★★★★★★★★★★★★★★★

Essex pilot Vernon Coumbre thought about his family back in Lombard, Illinois, as his life raft bounced and bobbed, tilted and turned in the rough water. He had survived being shot down by the Japanese. The 24-year-old pilot hoped he would have the chance to relive those moments through tales told to children and maybe even grandchildren someday after this hellacious war was over and he was safely back at home. He had been in the water since midmorning, and the strong winds and high seas prevented any control over the direction his raft took. Coumbre saw land coming closer and closer. He realized he was invading the homeland of Japan alone in a life raft. When he landed, he pulled his raft up into a clump of trees, barely cover at all, and hid in a bamboo thicket hoping the right people found him first. As darkness fell, it overshadowed his hope but did not extinguish his will.

★★★★★★★★★★★★★★★

Into the evening, conversations began among the commanding officers of the *North Carolina* and the fleet's flagship as to the feasibility of attempting the rescue with OS2Us. Approached for his opinion, Jacobs discussed with the navigator where the ship would be if the planes were launched at dawn and how much closer she would be when the rescue was completed five or six hours after takeoff. Having enough fuel was a monumental concern.

Information and knowledge in hand, Jacobs and Oliver discussed the rescue.

"What do you think?" Jacobs asked Oliver. "Can we do it?"

"It will be close," Oliver said, "but I think we should have enough fuel."

"As long as everything is perfect and nothing slows us up," Jacobs responded, "but how often does that happen?"

"Do we have a choice?" Oliver asked.

"Of course not," Jacobs agreed, then went to talk to Captain Hanlon.

"Sir, Lieutenant Oliver and I have agreed that we will be able to make the rescue," Jacobs explained, "provided there are no unexpected delays in flight that will use up the small margin of safety we have allowed in the planes' fuel consumption."

Several hours later that evening, the BB55 pilots were informed that since the attempt would not be made until early the next morning and rescue duties would rotate to another ship, their services would not be required. So Oliver went to bed and slept soundly.

★★★★★★★★★★★★★★★

Coumbre was not sleeping. Trying to become invisible, he heard the Japanese searching in the vicinity where he was hiding. He tried not to breathe for fear they would hear him. He hoped and prayed that he had not been forgotten or given up for dead.

★★★★★★★★★★★★★★★

"Get up," Oliver heard early the next morning from an orderly standing over him and shaking him. "Get your flight suit on."

"But I don't have flight duty today," Oliver said.

"You're going to Ominato."

★★★★★★★★★★★★★★★

Just before dawn, Coumbre heard the low drum of airplane engines. As the sound grew into a roar and he became certain the aircraft were friendly, he rushed from his hiding place pulling his raft. He sent up a signal and began trying to paddle out into the bay, but the rough water and strong winds made his efforts fruitless, slamming his little craft back up against the shore. He reluctantly retreated to his hiding place and waited.

★★★★★★★★★★★★★★★

Without breakfast, pre-briefing, navigation data, or anyone in his backseat, Oliver soon found himself catapulted into a rainy, foggy, overcast sky. He picked up course behind Jacobs, who was heading the rescue mission and did have the navigation data. Jacobs's backseat was empty as well, saved for the pilot they were hoping to pluck from the bay at Ominato.

As they flew, shots suddenly came from below. They had accidentally flown over the rescue submarine, which had surfaced and would act as an emergency station between the rescue site and the BB55. Jacobs and Oliver immediately used voice radio to identify themselves as friendly, and the firing ceased. They headed toward Ominato Bay, joined by escorts—four F6F Hellcats and four F4U Corsairs—that would be their overhead cover during the rescue attempt and fight off enemy aircraft that could come at the slower, smaller Kingfishers from any direction. The area of rescue was between a Japanese Army base to the south and a combination airfield and Navy base to the north. Oliver forced himself to think about anything but the odds of returning safely themselves, much less the slim chance that the pilot had not been captured and that a rescue could even be made with the weather churning the sea into foam.

Coumbre saw the Kingfishers about noon, escorted by aircraft from his own ship. He ran out onto the sand waving his arms in big, bold gestures to get their attention. As Oliver and Jacobs neared the coastline, it erupted in antiaircraft fire. But when Oliver saw Coumbre waving furiously ashore, he focused on their mission while shots flew around him.

Coumbre watched helplessly from below as the lead pilot of the escort group, who was also his best friend and shipmate, flew his Corsair in low to drop a rescue pack and never pulled out of his descent. His plane crashed and disappeared in the tumultuous seas.

"I'm going in," Jacobs radioed to Oliver. "Stay airborne and circle close by."

From 1,500 feet above, Oliver could see five-inch shells from the shore battery splashing around Jacobs as he skillfully landed the small floatplane within 50 feet of the shore. But the seas were treacherous, and the winds twisted the plane in the water, its tail pointing toward land.

As Coumbre struggled through the breakers toward his rescuer, Jacobs realized the downed pilot would never be able to reach the plane on his own, so he grabbed a line with a cork float on the end that had been stowed in his backseat. Standing up with one foot in his seat and the other outside on the wing to balance himself, he slung the rope round and round like a cowboy ready to lasso a calf and gave it a hearty heave toward Coumbre, who was reaching deep water and having extreme difficulty fighting his way through the pounding surf. Oliver watched from above as five-inch shells hit near Jacobs's plane, sending plumes of water shooting into the air. Under fire again himself, Oliver had his attention briefly taken away from the rescue below while he dodged incoming fire.

When he looked back down, he saw the Kingfisher taxiing away from land and was amazed at how quickly Jacobs had completed the rescue. The plane zipped along in the choppy water, and Oliver mentally applauded the rescue's imminent success. But as he continued to watch, the plane didn't take off as quickly as it should. The choppy water could impede takeoff, but as the moments passed, Oliver began to worry that something was terribly wrong. He descended on the taxiing plane and flew alongside. The cockpit was totally empty.

Shells exploding around him, Jacobs had lost his balance when he tossed the line to Coumbre. His foot had accidentally made contact with the throttle, sending the plane in one direction and him in the other. He bounced on the wing and slid into the storm-tossed and bullet-riddled water with Coumbre.

Fire came in off the beach and exploded all around them. Coumbre and Jacobs thought they would be safer floating on the water if a shell exploded underneath them, so they floated awhile and stood up awhile, then floated awhile and stood up awhile. The fire diminished when it was redirected toward their escaping plane.

Oliver saw them in the water being washed ashore and knew the only way the rescue would be successful was to take the plane to them. Amidst continued five-inch fire from the shore batteries, Oliver landed in the chop. He maneuvered his plane so as to let the raging wind and heavy surf aid him as he literally backed the craft onto the beach.

The moment the main float made landfall, Jacobs and Coumbre scrambled toward the two-man plane.

"Get him in and I'll send someone back for you!" Oliver yelled to Jacobs over the roar of the wind and surf and the drone of the airplane's engine.

"Hell no!" Jacobs retorted.

He shoved Coumbre into the backseat, then climbed in with him, straddling him nose to nose to fit into the small compartment. Oliver then had two very large, very wet pilots in his backseat. He revved the engine and started taxiing away from shore. Geysers of water from a continued onslaught of shore fire spouted up around him as he prepared to lift the overloaded craft out of the tumultuous sea. To his minor surprise and great relief, the Kingfisher lifted off without acknowledging that it was being asked for far more than it was designed to do. As they flew out of Ominato Bay, Oliver saw United States Navy fighters strafing the runaway plane so it would sink and not come into the possession of the enemy.

Oliver crossed his fingers as he stared at the waning fuel gauge. When he neared the location of the emergency submarine, he decided to continue toward home, since he was unsure how the overloaded plane would land in the choppy seas. Oliver had been flying continuously for seven hours when he began to set up for landing behind the *North Carolina*. He saw the Charley flag at half-mast on the starboard side and began his parallel run alongside the ship, pulling ahead. When the Charley flag was two-blocked, he started his 360-degree approach and looked at his gas gauge lying on empty. The ship executed its turn, repeating the movements of hundreds of landings, but as Oliver began his descent, he noticed turbulence. For the first time in his more than 15 months of combat flying, the landing slick was not sufficient. He pulled out of the landing and circled away. Oliver looked at his fuel gauge again, knowing it couldn't drop any lower. On the second try, the slick was smooth and the landing flawless.

When they were successfully hoisted aboard, Oliver learned that he had less than a cupful of gas in the Kingfisher's tank. And his own tank was on empty as well.

"You look like you could use a drink," one of the doctors told him, and gave him a full bottle of brandy.

Oliver took it to his cabin, where he savored every drop. Safe in his bunk with the brandy's warmth washing over his body, the 21-year-old hero fell into a deep, sound, and dreamless sleep. He did not hear the eruption of cheers and the general chaos below decks when at 2100 hours the news that the Japanese government had made an offer to surrender was broadcast triumphantly over the ship's loudspeakers.

CHAPTER FIFTEEN

Victory

★★★★★★★★★★★★★★★★

"*Any enemy planes approaching the task force are to be shot down, not vindictively, but in a friendly fashion.*"

Fleet Admiral William F. "Bull" Halsey,
15 August 1945

While the terms of the Japanese surrender were being worked out, air strikes continued against Tokyo air facilities, rail and shipping facilities, and factories. On August 15, the carriers launched predawn strikes against Tokyo, but upon receipt of the Japanese acceptance of the Allied terms for surrender, the strikes were called back.

The force remained vigilantly aware of possible threats, and rightfully so. Before noon that same day, five obviously uninformed Japanese planes were shot down as they aggressively approached the task force. And for days afterward, the errant bogie here or there posed a real and dangerous threat to the fleet. The task force operated about 200 miles southeast of Tokyo Bay awaiting word on developments of the surrender and what part it would play in the historical event. The *North Carolina* had earned 15 battle stars—more, her boys thought, than any other battleship in the fleet. They felt she deserved to be part of the official surrender.

18 August 1945

At 1300 hours, officers and crew gathered topside as Captain B. Hall Hanlon presented Distinguished Flying Cross medals to Lieutenant R. J. Jacobs and Lieutenant Junior Grade Almon P. Oliver. Oliver's citation read,

> For heroism and extraordinary achievement in aerial flight as pilot of a Navy seaplane, attached to the USS *North Carolina*, during an air-sea rescue mission in connection with carrier-based air strikes against enemy Japanese forces on Northern Honshu and Hokkaido Islands, August 10, 1945. Braving intense antiaircraft fire from enemy shore installations to rescue several fighter pilots who had been shot down in the area, Lieutenant, Junior Grade Oliver landed his plane within a few yards of the shore in a small bay at a Japanese naval base. Skillfully maneuvering his plane through the dangerous surf while under hostile fire, he succeeded in rescuing from the hands of the enemy a fighter pilot and the pilot of an accompanying seaplane which had been downed during the same rescue mission. His courage and expert airmanship were in keeping with the highest traditions of the United States Naval Service.

20 August 1945

Richard Fox waited on the fantail of the ship with his comrades

Pilots Ralph Jacobs and Almon Oliver received Flying Cross medals from Captain B. Hall Hanlon for their participation in rescuing a downed pilot from the Japanese homeland.
<small>COURTESY OF BATTLESHIP *NORTH CAROLINA* COLLECTION</small>

from the BB55 Marine detachment who would be transferring from the *North Carolina* for occupation of Tokyo—one officer, 74 Marines, and five Navy personnel. The USS *Garrard* transport took station ahead of the BB55, and the Showboat maneuvered into position with the transport alongside to starboard. Paul Wieser had the crane ready to secure the lines that would support the breeches buoy for transfer. It was a chair of sorts, dangling from lines that ran from one ship to the other while the ships were still in motion, steaming at eight to 10 knots.

First, their gear was transported across the divide between the moving ships using cargo nets. Then it was time for personnel. The sailors, who had a mostly friendly competition going with the Marines, taunted them with promises to dunk them in the ocean midway between ships. Fox watched as first one, then another Marine took his trip across the lines. No one was dunked. Knowing his turn was coming, Fox didn't care if they did dunk him. The war

Sailors were transferred in a breeches buoy attached to a highline connecting two ships across the expanse of rolling ocean.
COURTESY OF BATTLESHIP *NORTH CAROLINA* COLLECTION

was over, and he would soon be going home to see his mother and father and his 11 brothers and sisters. He was the next-to-youngest, and his older sisters wrote him often, keeping him informed of things going on at home. But mail had been slow in coming the last few months that the ship had been in constant motion, so he had received no contact from them at all, and the thought of seeing them soon made him miss them even more.

Simultaneously, the USS *Runels* came alongside to port to receive three detachments of sailors who had volunteered to be part of the occupation forces. They were divided up into three crews that each included two officers and 33 enlisted men. Bob Fennelly and Chuck Paty were part of Prize Crew #1. They each received a field pack with canteen, rifle, ammunition, belt, and helmet. But the sailors had not handled rifles or handguns since boot camp, so they had strict orders not to load them.

As he waited for his turn to be transported across the water, Paty thought about his discussions with many of his shipmates during the preceding weeks. Throughout the war, the BB55 had helped soften up the beaches for occupation by the amphibious forces and had helped support the invasions as they took place. Iwo Jima and Okinawa had been especially bad, so many boys dead, but everyone knew taking the Japanese homeland would be worse. And the boys knew it was coming. They had spoken in worried tones about how bad it might be. But then they heard about the atomic bombs; the surrender came, and the invasion wasn't required. Paty was sure thousands of American lives had been spared. Now, he, Charles Malvern Paty, Jr., of Charlotte, North Carolina, was going to be part of an occupying force in Tokyo. The thought made him proud and anxious at the same time. *What if it were a trick?*

When his time came to crawl into the little breeches buoy and hold on for the ride, he was very nervous. The seat was canvas, and he worried that it might fall out from under him. The lines dipped and swayed back and forth. Paty held tight to the ropes securing the buoy to the pulleys being hand-operated on each ship. He tried not to look down at the water moving between the two vessels. If he fell in, he knew the ships would not stop for him. They couldn't. He would just have to hope he didn't get sucked under either one of them, then wait to be picked up by a destroyer somewhere in the vicinity. He tried not to think about it. When the chair arrived with a thud on the deck of the *Runels*, he was relieved.

While Fennelly waited on the fantail, he reread the letter that each member of the occupation forces had received from the commander of the landing forces. The final paragraph began with a warning: "In theory we are entering surrendered territory that has been evacuated by enemy armed forces. In fact that may not be wholly true. We go prepared to take over this Naval Base in a formal, dignified manner. We hope that no misguided fanatics will make it necessary for us to use arms. But we must keep in mind that our enemies have previously been treacherous. Their codes are different than ours. We may have a little difficulty. However, we do not anticipate trouble and we do not seek it."

Fennelly's turn to cross arrived. Being part of the deck crew, he had operated the pulleys and lines and breeches buoy and cargo nets for years, but he had never been transported across by them.

He knew a little too well what could go wrong. He had made a conscious effort during the war to avoid thinking of the things that might scare him or make him nervous or sad, so he didn't look down and avoided thinking about what could happen if he fell. Instead, he thought of all the times the crew had made successful transfers, especially the bags of mail and that Purple Heart cake and ice cream they sent over to the *Kidd* after they accidentally fired star shells into her side. In no time at all, his dangling feet were on solid deck again.

The *Garrard* had moved on, filled with Marine detachments from many different ships—battleships, cruisers, and carriers—and the boys spent the time in transit sharing stories about the things they had done and heard and seen during the war. Their banter created a lighthearted atmosphere, although they could not be sure what awaited them ashore on the Japanese homeland.

Aboard the *Runels*, everything was crowded. She was a destroyer converted into a transport ship and was not designed to hold as many as had boarded her. The living compartments were packed with boys everywhere, but at least the ship had good food. Two hundred miles lay between where they transferred and the shores of Tokyo. On the first day, Paty was assigned to the radio shack for watch duty—the 12-to-4 shift. The radio compartment was small, and it seemed strange to Paty since the BB55 was all he had ever known. But he enjoyed learning how the small ship worked.

The trip took seven days. One of the first things the boys had to endure, in addition to the overcrowded accommodations, was shots. Not since boot camp had they faced those needles. And even the ones at camp were nothing compared to the typhus shots given the second day aboard the *Runels*. Paty's whole arm stung like someone had pumped acid into his veins, and it was so sore for the next 24 hours he could hardly lift it. He developed a fever and became sick on his stomach, fighting his way through the crowded sleeping compartments to the head over and over again.

On the seventh day, land appeared on the horizon, and as the day waned and the transports entered Tokyo Bay, Paty was awed by Mount Fuji silhouetted in the sunset. In direct contrast to that beauty, the Japanese battleship *Nagato*, bombed and burned out, sat in the harbor. The *Runels* passed slowly by it. Paty couldn't help worrying that it might be a trap, that Japanese gunners could be waiting there, ready to open fire on the unsuspecting American troops. The *Runels* continued to Sagami Wan, where white flags flew from large buildings and small houses and embankments that resembled earthen forts. Along the shore, two men, naked and running up and down the water's edge, tried to get someone's attention. One of the other ships sent a motor launch in to pick them up. The boys later learned that the men were prisoners of war who had been released from a prison camp on the island.

30 August 1945

The *Garrard* carried her troops to the Atsugi Air Base, where concrete runways ran straight into the ocean, so seaplanes could float in and then engage their wheels and taxi to the hangar. The Fourth Marine Raiders landed first to make sure the location was secure for the rest of the Marines to come ashore. The Raiders carried in the supplies and hand grenades and rations and dumped them in a pile for the other boys to gather up on their way in. When the area was secured, Fox and his shipmates would transfer to a Higgins boat for transport to shore.

They had received mail that day, and while Fox waited for transfer, he took out one of the many letters that had finally arrived from home. A very long lull between mail calls had caused the letters to back up. He eagerly anticipated reading each word of every letter in the fat little bundle, but words in the first one he opened caught him off guard.

"Things have been so different at home since Daddy died."

Fox did not know. He had not heard. His father was dead.

"All clear. Prepare to transfer."

Fox slung his bag of bad news over his shoulder and stood in line. As the boys waited to scale the net hanging over the side of the transport into the Higgins boat that would take them ashore,

Fox's buddy noticed the dejected look on his face.

"The war's over. This will be the easy part," he said to Fox. "Cheer up!"

Fox did not respond.

"Hey, Fox, why all the gloom and doom? In case you forgot, the war is over."

"I got a letter," Fox said. "From my sister."

"Yeah, well, that usually makes you happy."

"She said our dad died. I don't know when or where or how. Just he's dead."

Fox climbed over the side of the transport, tucked his toes into the holes in the net, grabbed hold, and started descending the knotted squares. The ride to shore was short, and when the boys departed the landing craft, they gathered to await instructions.

"We're going in. We'll pick up our rations and eat first," his sergeant said. "Fox, stay here and watch the gear."

His detachment marched off, leaving Fox there alone on enemy soil. He saw his buddy glance back over his shoulder as the boys disappeared over the slight rise. Fox knew why the sergeant had picked him. He never had liked Fox and always gave him the dirty duty. *Fine. I don't care.* But the longer he sat there alone, the heavier the news weighed on his heart. He pulled his mail back out and began to read the other letters. His father had died in July, and the Red Cross had sent him a telegram, his sister said. The telegram never reached him.

He soon saw the sergeant walking back down the hill toward him and stuffed his letters into his bag, then wiped his sleeve across his face.

"I heard about your father," the sergeant said. "I'm sorry I picked you."

Fox said nothing.

"I'll go back and get someone to relieve you so you don't have to stay here by yourself," his sergeant continued.

Fox looked at him and said, "No, sir, that's not necessary. I'm fine."

★★★★★★★★★★★★★★

Paty had heard that the prize crews were going to take Japanese ships back to the States. He saw that as a fast track home, and it was the main reason he had volunteered for the duty. But as the landing craft beached itself near the Yokosuka Naval Base, Paty was beginning to second-guess his decision. His mind raced. *Okay, so no guns fired on us from that battleship, but there are buildings and hills and caves everywhere. What if the Japs are lying in wait there? They never have given up easily, the kamikazes were proof of that. How can anybody be sure they really surrendered?*

Paty could see what resembled a drill field in front of a row of brick buildings, maybe barracks. The field wasn't large, perhaps a hundred feet long, but it stretched down to the beach. The boys disembarked from the craft.

"Keep your rifles at the ready," their officer told them.

A lot of good that does, Paty thought. *They're not even loaded.*

As the boys from the BB55 landed, troops from other ships simultaneously occupied enemy territory, slowly sweeping the beaches until they were certain no surprise attack was imminent.

"We're going to march over to the first building there."

Paty and Fennelly looked in the direction the officer pointed. The building was taller than many, about three stories. They could see bicycles in a rack outside the building when they were closer, and a guard standing at the large double metal doors—a Japanese guard in uniform. Fennelly didn't see a gun, but he knew that didn't mean it wasn't there. Paty's worries intensified. *What if the whole building is full of troops waiting to open fire on us as soon as we get up the steps?* Fennelly looked at the guard and realized he was as nervous as they were. He wondered what the Japanese soldiers had been told about the evil Americans.

The boys walked right past the guard into the building through the front door. It was not a barracks but an office building. The entrance opened into many different offices with high-quality furniture. Paty presumed officers once staffed them. But they looked as if the occupants had just gotten up and walked out the door thinking they'd be right back. Pictures and framed certificates hung on the walls. Papers and pens lay on the desks right where they had last been used. Many of the boys started to plunder the offices, looking in cabinets and pulling out drawers. They found samurai swords and pistols and other souvenirs. Paty discovered a cute little pair of powerful binoculars. The boys couldn't take much because they did not know where they were going from there, so Paty stuck just the binoculars in his pocket.

While some of the boys continued looking through the rooms on the first floor, Paty and Fennelly and a few others decided to go upstairs. From a door at the top of the stairs, they heard talking. They walked tentatively toward the door and saw that it opened into a huge room maybe a hundred feet long with rows and rows of telephone switchboards, the type operated by lines with plugs that could be pulled from one socket and stuck into another. Two young Japanese sailors sat at the first two switchboards wearing headsets, obviously engrossed in interesting conversation with someone on the other end of the line. When they looked up and saw a group of American sailors staring at them, they were startled. Fennelly could see the fear in their eyes. But one of them pulled up his mouth-piece and tried to communicate with the boys, offering them a chance, in very broken English, to talk to a girl.

One of the sailors accepted the offer, took the headset, sat down at the switchboard, and started talking. He talked and laughed for a few minutes, then got up and handed the headset back to the Japanese sailor.

"Couldn't understand a damn thing she said," he admitted to the group as they went back down the stairs. "But she had a fine, sweet voice." He laughed again like he had with the girl.

They went from building to building, finding much the same thing in each one—abandoned offices waiting for someone to return to work. Behind the buildings, the group walked over to a sharp little hill at the edge of the naval yard. In the side of the hill, several large tunnels were filled with stacks of every kind of ammunition Paty could imagine. *What if they're in there and decide to blow up the whole hill and take us all with them?* Paty worried. But nothing happened.

The officers who had been leading the boys around all afternoon took them to their living quarters, a two-story wooden barracks on the opposite side of the yard. Even though the rooms were surprisingly clean, the boys were ordered to start cleaning thoroughly—every corner, every wall, everything in the room, and every inch of the floor. They toted in buckets of water and soap and brushes and started scrubbing. Paty, Fennelly, and the rest of their crew were bunking upstairs, so the chore was even more difficult, as they had to lug the water buckets up the stairs. While the boys had been touring the yard, their supplies from the ship had been delivered for them. They covered the mattresses on the single-stacked bunks with their mattress covers.

They had just finished their cleaning and were unpacking their gear when a shot rang out. *I knew it*, Paty thought. *So this is it. They're going to kill us in our beds.* But the bullet came through the floor, into the room, and out the roof. They soon found out that one of the boys in the barracks below had been fiddling with his rifle, loading it against regulations, and it had fired.

The Japanese bathrooms were puzzling. The building was beautifully tiled and clean. But the bathrooms contained no toilets—nothing to sit on, just holes in the floor. Fennelly later learned that Japanese military personnel had their own personal stools that they carried to the bathroom with him. But the Americans did not have stools and had to do the best they could without them. Fennelly could hear the water running below and wondered if a creek was washing everything away. *No wonder we were told not to drink the water,* he thought. As coxswain, Fennelly was in charge of a group of 12 sailors. They formed a working party to retrieve fresh water for the boys to drink. New auxiliary fuel tanks filled with fresh water from the ship were delivered to shore, and the boys had to transport them to the barracks.

Some of the boys didn't do much for the rest of the occupation but scrub the floors in the barracks and walk the grounds. Paty never heard another word about taking Japanese ships back to the States and presumed that must have been just a rumor. He was disappointed, as he had looked forward to trying to work their radios. As the days passed, he remained both amazed and apprehensive about the number of enemy sailors, both enlisted men and officers. He didn't understand why they were free to walk around like that. They were the enemy. He had spent the last four years of his life fighting them. As the days progressed, more Allied officers appeared, occupying some of the offices in the first buildings the boys had seen, but the enemy still roamed at will, or at least that's the way it seemed to Paty.

Many of those Japanese were actually part of working parties. Fennelly used them to help transport water and to help with other chores assigned to his group of men. When one of them balked, a Marine would threaten to shoot him, and he would fall right in line. The gun barrel eliminated all communication barriers.

Fox and the other Marines toured the island the first few days, especially the steep hills directly behind the Navy base. They were honeycombed with machine shops, areas dug out so that everything was hidden. The Marines picked up souvenirs including Japanese guns and ammunition. During the next few days, Fox stood watch duty along the shoreline. In preparation for the inevitable invasion, the Japanese had built barricades with stacks of lumber eight feet high. The stacks were full of rats so numerous and so big that when they started running in droves, some of the guys mistook them for Japanese attacking and fired at them. The Marines had been allowed to load their guns.

From inside a cave atop one of the hills, a lone Japanese holdout threw hand grenades down at the troops, but he remained far enough away to pose no immediate threat.

★★★★★★★★★★★★★★★★

When Fennelly finally found some leisure time and tried to check out more caves, Marines guarded the entrances. But he and several of the boys from his crew wandered around anyway to see what else they could find. The rain threatened every day but didn't fall hard enough to deter their search, and they eventually found the mouth to one cave not guarded. Fennelly reasoned with himself that since that cave was unguarded, it must not be off limits like they had been told, but he knew he was just making excuses. He really wanted to find some saki.

The cave opened into a tunnel that led into a small room. It looked as though someone had been living there—a mattress was on the dirt floor, and a row of long-necked brown bottles was lined up against the wall.

"Saki!" one of the boys shouted.

While that sailor struggled with the cork in his bottle, Fennelly kept searching. In one corner, he found a small box about eight inches wide, 12 inches long, and four inches deep. The wood was reddish brown, perhaps mahogany, and it closed with two stainless-steel latches. Fennelly carefully opened the box and peered inside. Empty. But taped in the lid, a small picture of a Japanese sailor looked back at him. Papers with writing that Fennelly could not read were also attached to the lid.

"This mess tastes like vinegar!" one of the boys shouted, breaking Fennelly's reverie.

"Bring it with you if you want it," Fennelly said, closing the box and tucking it under his arm.

They followed another corridor into a large room. Fennelly was amazed to find all types of printing equipment abandoned there—presses and inks and plates. The boys rifled through the equipment, and Fennelly chose two small plates about four inches square to carry with him. He wrapped them in paper, then carefully opened his treasure box and laid the plates inside.

"Which way?" one of the boys asked, realizing that four corridors led out of the room and they had no idea which way they had entered.

"I don't know."

"Me either."

"Let's try this one," Fennelly said, pointing off to his left.

He was their boss, so they followed him. The corridor wound around several curves with numerous openings, and they began to worry that they would not find their way out. The small flashlights they carried with them did not shine brightly.

"Mine's out," one of the boys said, shaking the flashlight and trying to make it come back on.

Fennelly pointed his light down the corridor, and they saw nothing but black wall. Still, they continued walking. The tunnel took an abrupt turn to the right, and the boys saw light. They also saw the back of a Marine.

"Back up," Fennelly whispered.

The boys backed around the curve so they could no longer see the opening or the guard.

"Okay," Fennelly said, considering all their options. "I don't want to go back the way we came because I don't know which way to go. But we don't want this guy to shoot us either. We'd better make a lot of noise so he knows we're coming."

"American noise," one of the others said.

So the boys started whistling and talking loudly to each other as they turned the corner and headed toward the opening. The Marine was startled but knew they were friendlies, so he did not shoot.

"How did you get in here?" he demanded of the sailors.

"Through an opening on the other side," Fennelly answered. "Sir."

"Get out and don't come back in," the guard said, and the boys went on their way.

02 September 1945

Fennelly's crew transported officials back and forth to the USS *Missouri* in preparation for the impending ceremony. The official surrender was signed aboard the *Missouri* in Tokyo Bay while the BB55 boys were ashore on the base. Paty didn't even know it happened, and the *North Carolina* played no special role in the event.

★★★★★★★★★★★★★★★

Not long before the boys returned to the BB55, which had anchored in Tokyo Bay with many more Allied ships, they were given an opportunity to choose a souvenir. Fennelly and Paty stood in front of a heap of rifles, a pile of pistols, and a stack of swords that had been gathered up for the boys. They were told to choose anything they wanted, but they could pick only one. They both chose rifles with bayonets on the end. The Marines marched to the armory and faced similar options. They could choose a rifle and a bayonet, but that was all. If they were caught with anything else, they would be in a lot of trouble. Fox didn't want to be in any

The official surrender was signed September 2, 1945, aboard the USS Missouri, *anchored in Tokyo Bay.*

trouble at all, so he just opted for one rifle. But the boys had already stockpiled bandoliers of ammunition that they had found in the caves. Rather than get caught and risk impeding a quick return home, they threw all the ammo into a large barrel outside their barracks. The night before they left, a big celebration commenced. Someone started a fire in the barrel. The party scattered as the rounds began to explode, creating an unexpected and dangerous fireworks display.

The sailors returned to the BB55 on September 5 and the Marines on September 6, but they all had the same surprise waiting for them when they walked up the gangplank. The occupation forces, rather than being welcomed back as conquering heroes, were herded

Sailors and Marines returning to the ship after the occupation of Japan were welcomed with a thorough dousing to kill fleas and other pests they might have picked up ashore.
COURTESY OF BATTLESHIP NORTH CAROLINA COLLECTION

onto the fantail and told to strip, one piece of clothing at a time. Fennelly took off his hat and held it out. A sailor with a pump sprayer doused it with fumigating powder. "Drop it." He took off his shirt and held it out. Sprayed and dropped. "One shoe." Sprayed and dropped. "That sock." Sprayed and dropped. "The other shoe." Sprayed and dropped. The process continued with each person until they were all standing on the fantail completely naked.

"Hold your nose with one hand and cover your eyes with the other. Elbows up."

The sailors with the spray guns turned their attention to the boys, spraying them from top to bottom with the same powder. Fennelly had been fighting fleas all week, and even squeezing them between his fingernails didn't kill them. The Navy had found a better way, and the boys were thoroughly fumigated.

Some thanks, Paty thought. *We could have been killed, and this is the reception we get?*

The Showboat departed Tokyo Bay and headed for Okinawa, arriving three days later. That day was spent fueling, provisioning, and picking up 650 extra passengers for the long-awaited trip home. The ship was en route to Pearl Harbor the next day and arrived on September 20, having crossed the International Date Line and repeated a day along the way.

Those going to the West Coast disembarked at Pearl Harbor to board another ship, which made the sailors going home to the East very happy. They could travel straight from Pearl through the Panama Canal and up the East Coast without detouring up the West Coast first. But the trip home would still be a long one, and most of their duties continued with the exception of firing practice, which had consumed so much of their time during the war. The ship remained in Pearl Harbor five days—which was five days longer than most of the boys would have liked.

Paul Wieser (center) *and his friends Ernie Zietsman* (left) *and James Collins* (right) *walked along King Street in Honolulu with invigorated purpose in 1945. The war was over and the ship was heading home after the brief stop in Hawaii.*
COURTESY OF BATTLESHIP NORTH CAROLINA COLLECTION

Fueling remained a difficult and dangerous task that had to be done frequently. On the next leg of their journey home, the boys had one particularly frustrating day of fueling. The only good thing about that day was not having to worry about bogies. The BB55 was steaming toward the Panama Canal Zone, which would take the boys to their final leg of the trip home. One destroyer steamed along starboard to fuel at 0736 hours, and three minutes later another destroyer snuggled into the port side. After two hours, the first two were successfully fueled, and the ship took another destroyer along each side and fueled both without incident.

But when the destroyer *Grayson* came along starboard for fuel at 1305, everything started going wrong. The weather began to deteriorate. Twenty minutes into fueling, both fuel lines parted, spraying fuel oil everywhere. The *Grayson* moved to the port side to finish fueling, but both hoses separated on that side, too. The seas were getting rougher and rougher. The *Grayson* pulled along starboard to try again, but she ran into the *North Carolina*, crumpled one of the destroyer's 40-millimeter gun shields, and cast off without receiving any fuel at all. All fueling attempts were canceled for the remainder of the day. The following morning was no more promising, but finally about midafternoon, the *Grayson* successfully fueled along the port side of the BB55.

★★★★★★★★★★★★★★★

Once the war was over, the boys allowed themselves to talk about the future and what they were going to do when they got home. Bob Palomaris's time in the Navy wouldn't be over until early 1946, but he knew he wanted to go back to baseball. He had written to several teams asking for the chance to try out. He wanted to pick up where he had left off when he had to turn down an offer to play professional ball that had come just days after he joined the service. New York Giants manager Mel Ott responded to his letters mailed from the ship, telling Palomaris to contact his scout Micky Shadder when he got home.

Wieser just wanted to see Jean again so they could really start their life together. They had enjoyed only those few shorts days back in the summer of 1944. Every time he heard "I'll Be Seeing You" on the radio, he thought about their last night together in that little Navy house in Port Orchard.

Paty was ambivalent about what he needed to do when he got home. He had asked Marian to marry him, and she had accepted, but now he worried that the decision had been made in haste. Those days in Seattle had been enchanting, but less than three weeks wasn't much time, and he had seen her only every other day when he had liberty. Their romance had really been born not in Seattle but in the letters that followed during the height of the war. She lived on the West Coast and wouldn't want to leave, he was quite sure. And he certainly didn't want to leave the East Coast. The distance between their lives would be difficult to overcome. Someone would have to make great sacrifices. But he had made a vow, a promise to her, so when he got home, the first thing he was going to do was buy a ring and travel to Seattle to see Marian.

Fennelly just wanted to get home. He didn't talk on a serious level about much of anything anymore. He had already begun bottling things up inside. But he laughed at the guys in his division who joked about opening a bar and a brothel. Based on what they had seen during the war, they were sure they could make some real money.

The ship finally reached the Panama Canal Zone on October 8, nearly a month after she had left Tokyo Bay. For the boys so anxious to get home, the trip seemed interminable. Once again, however, as the ship entered the fresh water of Gatun Lake, the boys gave her a good scrubbing with lots of soap and an abundance of water running through the hoses. They enjoyed it as much as they had the first time, spraying each other more than they did the ship, but they were not the same naïve, inexperienced boys who had passed through in the other direction in the summer of 1942. And they never would be.

Their first grand entrance into a home port would not be New York, as the crew expected. Their captain was from Boston, so the first Americans who would have the opportunity to welcome home the Showboat would be Bostonians.

Richard Fox (third from left) *and his friends celebrated victory at a bar in Panama on their way home.*

The boys took liberty in Panama City, many drinking and carousing despite the warnings of venereal disease that had been pounded into their heads for years. For 25 cents, Palomaris bought a bunch of the biggest bananas he had ever seen. Fennelly had gotten into some big trouble fighting on liberty when the ship was at Pearl Harbor. He was lucky that the captain hadn't thrown him in the brig. He was instead restricted to the ship, so he did not go ashore in Panama at all. Fox had his picture taken in a honky-tonk drinking beer with three of his buddies. Many of the boys picked up souvenirs to carry home. They hoped they would not see Panama again anytime soon.

Paty sent a telegram home to his parents. For the first time since he had joined the Navy right after the Pearl Harbor attack, he was allowed to tell them where he was and where he was going:

1945 OCT 9 AM 7 54

ARRIVED CANAL ZONE TODAY WILL AR-
RIVE BOSTON 18TH LIBERTY IN PANAMA
CITY THIS AFTERNOON

LOVE MARVERN JR.

His name was misspelled, but the message was clear.

The ship started through the canal on October 11, cheering civilians lining both sides. The BB55 was only inches narrower than the passage she traveled; people could have literally reached out and touched a sailor. Some did. A spirit of jubilation surrounded the ship. People ashore threw fruit to the sailors, and they in turn tossed their white Dixie Cup caps to the throng of admirers.

When safely across, the ship moored in Cristobal Harbor. Once again, the boys took liberty. Upon their return to the ship, some of them tried to bring beer and liquor with them. Waiting in line to board, Fox saw the guards confiscate hidden bottles from the boys in front of him. They tossed the bottles in nearby trash cans, and the glass shattered. Fox laughed as he realized many more seamen must have tried and failed. A steady stream of alcohol flowed from the bottoms of the barrels.

The next morning when Palomaris opened his eyes, he saw two small, dark, beady ones staring right at him, surrounded by a scaly little face. He had dreamed about screeches and squawks and other weird sounds all night, so, thinking maybe he had drunk way too much, he closed his eyes again. When he opened them the second time, the dark ones were even closer, and he saw teeth.

"What the hell!" he yelled, and the boys in his quarters started howling.

One of his buddies held a baby alligator over Palomaris, the

Safely through the Panama Canal and back in the Atlantic Ocean for the first time since the summer of 1942, the North Carolina *steamed toward home.*
COURTESY OF BATTLESHIP NORTH CAROLINA COLLECTION

reptile's small tail flipping back and forth and his jaws opening.

"Where'd you get that damn thing?" Palomaris asked.

"We bought them over in the city," his buddy answered. "To take home."

"Them?" Palomaris queried.

"Yeah, lots of stuff, but I'm the only one that got an alligator."

Some of the boys had brought exotic animals like parrots and monkeys aboard as souvenirs to carry home.

"Now hear this," a familiar voice came over the loudspeaker. "We will be departing at approximately 0800 hours. I know you have been away from home for a long time, but when we arrive in Boston Harbor, you will all be quarantined with those bastardly little creatures you smuggled aboard until an all-clear is issued."

None of the exotics remained passengers for very long.

★★★★★★★★★★★★★★★★

Wieser did not go ashore at all—he didn't drink, wasn't interested in the women, and certainly didn't want a monkey or a parrot. But he received something in Panama that made the last leg of the journey home miserable—a new division officer who came from money and chose Wieser as his pet project for the rest of the trip. He watched over Wieser incessantly, second-guessing everything he had done successfully for years at sea under conditions much more treacherous than the East Coast of the United States during peacetime. Every time a destroyer came alongside to fuel, the new officer told Wieser what to do, explaining techniques that the young officer had only learned from books. Wieser ignored the unwelcome advice and proceeded with the tried-and-true methods that had taken the ship safely through the war.

When citations were awarded for those boys who had spent countless hours performing fueling duties—a vital and perilous task during the war—Wieser's name was omitted.

17 October 1945

Navy Day. The Showboat steamed toward Boston Harbor, her navigators sighting the Nantucket Shoals Light through the darkness at 0134 hours. Many ships of the fleet had already departed at other locations—Charleston, South Carolina; Norfolk, Virginia; New York—so the remaining group was small, just five ships. When the ships neared the harbor, the destroyers entered first. Then the *North Carolina* waited for the *New Mexico* to enter. Late in the afternoon, the crew lined the rails of their Showboat as she made her grand entrance into the harbor amidst a throng of cheering civilians lining the shores. Fireboats sprayed victorious streams of water into the air, a tunnel of watery swords under which the BB55 passed. She was greeted by a bevy of Navy tugs that snuggled in close to escort the battle-weary, highly decorated lady into safe harbor at home.

Decorated tugs in Boston Harbor welcomed the war-weary ships and triumphant crews back to the States.
Courtesy of Battleship *North Carolina* Collection

CHAPTER SIXTEEN

Shipmates Forever

★★★★★★★★★★★★★★★★★

"I've always heard that a seagull is a spirit of a seaman that is no longer with us. . . . If I ever get to the point that I can't walk to this ship, and you see a big seagull upon battle two on the splinter screen, don't chase it away. Throw him a fish and call him Joe."

Rear Admiral Joseph Stryker,
former BB55 officer

07 April 1999

Richard Fox stands on the signal bridge of the *North Carolina* with his wife, two daughters, a son-in-law, and two teenage grand-daughters. He has visited the ship a few times since she was res-cued from the scrap heap back in the 1960s, to be preserved as a World War II memorial on the Cape Fear River in Wilmington, North Carolina. His wife accompanied him to those crew reunions, held annually aboard ship. But this year, his whole family has decided to come. He is getting older, and he guessed his children wanted to see where he had spent those historically important years of his life.

Fox has arranged for Marine guides to escort his family through the ship and describe the parts that are open to the public for tour. Even though he served on the ship several years, there are many parts of the floating city he has never seen, and he certainly doesn't know how they operated. He is glad that his family seems to be enjoying the narrated tour, walking across the fantail to see the Kingfisher, hearing about the daring rescues at sea. They climb inside one of the turrets of the big guns, the 16-inch cannons. The girls take turns looking through the telescope focused on downtown Wilmington. Someone has left it aimed right at the steeple of a church.

They follow the tour below decks to the mess halls and galley and sleeping quarters. Their voices echo and their footsteps clank against the metal decks. They peek inside the showers and the heads with their rolls of light brown, rough toilet paper. "Yuck," comes the teenage response. They visit the post office, the soda fountain, and the gedunk. The girls are amazed that the ship made its own ice cream.

"We watched movies over there," their grandfather tells them, pointing to the screen rolled up and hanging overhead against a bulkhead in one of the mess halls.

They visit the sick bay and the Marine quarters, officers' country, the carpenter shop, the print shop, the engine rooms, the radio room. The girls sometimes look glassy-eyed—as teenagers often do—when the military jargon becomes boring, too detailed to hold their attention. Their grandfather worries that they are losing interest. He wants them to enjoy their vacation.

When they reemerge on the main deck, they walk forward up the bow and stand next to Fox's 20-millimeter gun. His son-in-law tries to get him to acknowledge the fact that he was credited with shooting down at least one enemy plane.

"A lot of us were firing" is all he will admit.

They walk back down the bow, past the huge anchor chains

and two 16-inch gun turrets, then climb up the stairs two levels to the signal bridge. They linger. Fox grows quiet, then begins to relate the horrifying hours of April 6, 1945. Even after 54 years, the sounds of exploding guns and spiraling planes and screaming shipmates still ring in his ears as he allows himself to be transported back to that character-defining moment in time.

"My gun was up there on the bow," he tells his family. "Where I showed you. When the ships turned into the wind so the carriers could launch their planes, big waves splashed over the front of the bow, and we had to run up here to keep from being washed overboard."

"It came all the way up there?" one granddaughter asks.

"Yep, that high, so I had to run up here. This was my assigned position."

"That's a long run," one of his daughters says.

"It is, and most of the time I was one of the last ones to get here, since I had to go so far. There was one time, it was in April of '45, we had kamikazes coming in everywhere; the sky was just full of them, and all the ships started shooting. Those suicide bombers dipped down between the ships like this, and some of the gunners just followed them. I had just gotten up here, and it was really crowded. There was this great big bang, and I felt something hit my leg. I thought somebody kicked me, but when I looked back, my pants were smoking."

Fox turns and points to the deck one flight up. He has a hard time determining just where the shell penetrated, so he asks one of the sailors standing nearby if he knows where it hit.

"Right there." The sailor points up to the left to the tall oval structure. "That's where that five-inch shell knocked a big hole in the director. If you look real close, you can see the seam where they patched it, and underneath that you can see dents where the shrapnel flew around and hit everything."

"Yeah, that was it," Fox agrees. "There were people screaming and blood running down the decks. My pants were smoking, and my leg hurt, but not too bad. When I turned around to see who kicked me, I saw this guy lying right over there."

He points, and his family looks in that direction to the empty deck. A small group of tourists begins to gather as he continues his story.

"There was one guy, he was hurt bad, real bad. I thought he was dead, but he wasn't, not yet, so I grabbed my buddy and told him to help me take him down to sick bay. I just knew he was going to die before we got him there, but he didn't. We picked him up; he was hurt real bad, shot in the groin. We carried him down those steps and then those over there and then through that hatch all the way down to sick bay."

Fox's family and the growing gathering of tourists and shipmates are so engrossed in his story that a silence envelops them as he talks, remembering details as if the incident had just happened, as if it were still happening.

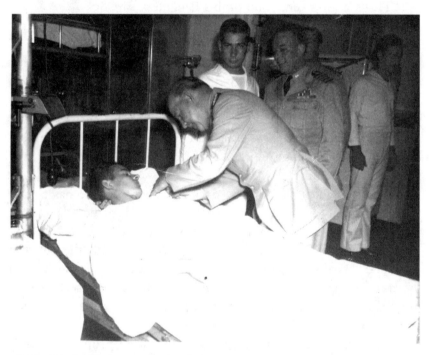

Richard Reed, seriously injured by friendly fire on April 6, 1945, received a Purple Heart from Rear Admiral Edward W. Hanson while Captain Oswald S. Colclough stood close by.
COURTESY OF BATTLESHIP *NORTH CAROLINA* COLLECTION

"We had a time keeping his legs from getting caught; those ladders are so small, and he was bleeding bad." He pauses. "I never knew what happened to him, if he lived or died. I didn't even know his name."

When Fox stops talking, the silence lingers for a moment, broken only by the squawk of a sea gull hovering overhead. His granddaughters each take hold of his hands, and he looks down at them. The admiration beaming up from their beautiful young faces humbles him. Then someone taps him on his shoulder. Fox turns and looks into the watery eyes of a man about his own age.

"I'm the one," he says. "I'm that boy. My name is Richard Reed, and you saved my life. Thank you."

During the crew's 1999 reunion, Richard Reed (left) meets Richard Fox, the shipmate who helped save his life. Until that day, Fox did not know who Reed was or if he had survived.

Whitey's Restaurant and motel on Market Street in Wilmington would not be the obvious choice for tourists flocking to the coastal community. But as the boys of the BB55 return each year, the nearly antiquated one-story motel comes to life. The restaurant's marquee is annually prepared with "Welcome Former Crewmembers of the Battleship *North Carolina*." The boys tape posters in the windows of their rooms, which open onto a long, covered sidewalk facing a burgeoning traffic flow. The posters identify them as former crew members. They write their names on the posters as well, so they can visit back and forth between rooms and avoid knocking on the wrong door.

Ever since the motel's owner became instrumental in helping bring the ship to town and offered property for her final resting place at Eagle Island, he has become almost a saint to the former crew members. Being able to return to their ship and walk her decks

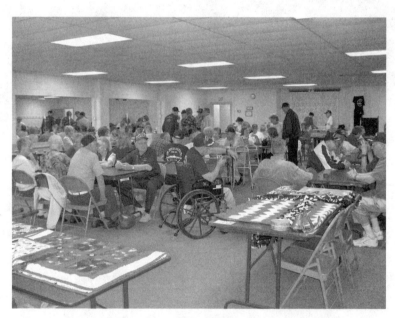

Crew members and their families and friends gather at Whitey's meeting room during the 2005 crew reunion to reminisce with former shipmates and old friends.
PHOTO BY THE AUTHOR

means more to them than they can express. As the men aged and many could no longer negotiate the ship, Whitey's evolved from just a place to sleep and eat to the central location for their business meetings and celebratory parties.

The men may have lived long, full lives, witnessed monumental changes, and become elderly citizens who humbly accept the mantra of the "greatest generation," but when they return for their reunion each year, they change back into proud, high-spirited, patriotic boys on a mission. As they register in the motel conference room for the four-day reunion, many wander, push their walkers, click their canes, or roll their wheelchairs over to a table full of photo albums, log sheets, copies of the ship's souvenir photo album, called *Showboat*, and a copy of crew member Chuck Paty's compilation, called *BB55 Day by Day*.

Paty spent years doing research at the National Archives, reading the ship's logs and war diary, and studying historical accounts of the war. From what he learned and entries in his own diaries, he constructed a four-part day-by-day accounting of where the ship was located and what was happening to her from the date the keel was laid to the date she entered her mooring in the Cape Fear River. The first part includes a chronological listing with brief tidbits of information for each day. Days when the BB55 was attacked or otherwise directly involved in firing her weapons at the enemy are highlighted in yellow. The second section includes dated maps on which Paty has tracked the ship's movements each day using the dead-reckoning method of navigation. The third section includes excerpts from his diary embellished with facts that he didn't know when he was writing the entries but subsequently learned. And the last section is a collection of photos. The book is a magnet for the boys turned men, who truly appreciate their former shipmate's labor of love.

While doing his research, Paty also created an alphabetical listing of the names of all crew members each time they appeared in the ship's logs and made a log of his own that briefly told each crew member's history. The sailors flock around that log, looking up their own names and names of boys they remember, marking errors and omissions. Paty found the ship's logs to sometimes be incomplete.

But *BB55 Day by Day* is the only representation of Paty at the 2005 reunion. For the first time since the association formed in 1962 and the reunions began, health problems for him and his wife, Sue, have prevented his attendance. But he is present in spirit and speaks through his work.

Paty did not marry Marian. Immediately after discharge, he traveled by train to Seattle to see her and took the ring he had promised. Her family welcomed him in their home and fed him well, but not long after he arrived back east on the train, he received a package in the mail with the ring and a note from Marian that said marriage was just not the right thing to do. He could not have been more relieved.

Also on the memories table, a scrapbook full of pictures belonging to former crew member Gordon Knapp becomes a topic of conversation. Knapp obviously took pictures with his own camera on ship and in port following the war. He was a postwar crew member.

"Hey, Gordon," crew member Daniel Schroll asks, sitting at the table with his wife, "how did you get those pictures? We weren't allowed to have cameras on the ship."

"I had two cameras," Knapp answers, "one for black-and-white and one for color. The exec knew I had them, too. You just didn't stick them up in the officer's face."

Knapp relishes reliving the time he just knew he was going to the brig because he got caught taking pictures of crew loading 16-inch ammo. But being buddies with the right people kept him free, he tells his shipmates. "All the exec did was say, 'Let's just don't have any more.' "

Scott Pfeiffer, son of a deceased crew member, sits browsing through memorabilia and eavesdropping on the sea stories being swapped at the table.

"Do any of you remember when the ship hit a whale?" Scott asks. "My dad said the bow cut it right in two and the ocean filled up with blood."

Daniel Schroll

"There's no question we hit a whale," Knapp responds. "But I don't know any of those details."

"Paul Wieser was on the ship the whole time," offers Schroll. "Anything you need to know, just ask him."

Then Schroll continues with a sea story of his own.

"The scaredest I ever was with all the battles we were in and everything was when we got torpedoed. You can't believe how it shook that ship, as big as it was. If you ever stood in the end of a rowboat and know how it shakes, that's how it shook that ship."

"Did you know that one of these *Showboat* books is selling on eBay for $339," Knapp states more than asks. It is a yearbook of sorts, a photo album from the war that each one of the sailors received when the conflict was over. The spine of the one at the reunion is broken and the pages falling out.

"It could be $3,000 and I wouldn't part with mine," Scott responds.

"I remember going through the chow lines, and when you hold your tray up they give you one spoonful of stuff," Schroll says, beginning another memory. "This one guy was arguing because he wanted more, so the cook took the big wooden spoon out of the coffee urn and whopped him on the head with it. Knocked him out! You could go up and get more, but you had to wait. They didn't want you wasting it. We could eat all we wanted, but we had to eat all we took."

"I think for the guys who spent time on this ship," Mrs. Schroll says to no one in particular, "that it was such an important time in their lives they will always talk about it. It was the biggest thing in their lives, actually."

Her husband has found a rapt audience in Scott, who wants to soak up every detail he can.

"I assume you've seen the potato peeler," Schroll says to Scott.

"Actually, I haven't been on the ship yet."

"Well, the cook, he told me what to do. I put the potatoes in, and he didn't tell me how long it took to peel them, so I went out in the mess hall talking to some of the guys, and when I came back my potatoes were about that big around." Schroll curves his forefinger into his thumb until the hole they create is about the size of a dime.

Scott laughs.

"Boy, he got mad. He said, 'Damn you, Schroll, I gotta have them.' I told him I'd hurry up and put in some more, and he said, 'You better.' I never will forget that."

"My dad told me that one time his tour was to go around the ship and check all the compasses and the clocks," Scott begins. "He would take a timepiece with him and would go to each clock and set it. The way for him to have a couple of drinks was he'd go down there and put a crack in the compass on purpose. Then he could go to the storage area to get alcohol to go in the compass." Liquid compasses are used in many ships; alcohol is an ideal fluid because it freezes at a very low temperature.

"There was this one guy," Schroll remembers, "who had his locker right by mine. Ours were near where the incinerator was. Anyhow, he had his door open and he was drinking this Listerine. It was about 80 percent alcohol."

"I heard they put alcohol in their coffee," Scott says. "They could get coffee anytime of day or night. They lived off coffee."

"They warned us not to buy the coconut juice off the natives when they put us off on an island to give us a rest period," Schroll says, pulling up from the recesses of his mind yet another aging memory. "When we were in Noumea, New Caledonia, the natives were so big, and they had their hair all curled up, and they carried these great big knives. They were scary, those guys were, but we could buy homemade wine or whatever it was. They had it in bottles with real long necks."

Scott listens attentively as Schroll continues with other sea stories.

"There's so many things you know that sometimes you forget about them," Schroll says. "But when you get together, you start thinking about them. I've only missed one reunion since '64."

"My dad had his blue wool uniform downsized to fit me when I was about nine," Scott says, recalling a cherished memory of his own. "I don't know where it is now."

A cake with a picture from a previous reunion proclaims that former crew members of the battleship North Carolina *will be "Shipmates Forever"—a sentiment with which they all concur.*
PHOTO BY THE AUTHOR

Sea stories abound as crew members and their families register for the reunion and mingle in the conference room, excited to see each other one more time.

★★★★★★★★★★★★★★★

That night, after those who were physically able had made a trip to visit the ship, they gather back in the conference room for the ship's 64th birthday party. Two cakes are decorated with edible pictures. One has the words "Shipmates Forever" and an early reunion group photo under number-three turret, where they continue to pose each year for photos. The other bears a photo of the commissioning crew and the greeting, "Happy 64th Birthday, Showboat, 1941-2005."

During the birthday party, Ron Johnson, who served aboard the ship as Ron Frascona, entertains a table of partiers with his tale about the night he found out that maybe he wasn't such hot stuff after all. Frascona had come aboard when he was only 14, when a nun from the orphanage in California where he grew up helped him join the Navy. He boxed on the Showboat and later continued boxing for the Navy.

Ron Johnson
PHOTO BY THE AUTHOR

"We were at a Golden Gloves tournament in San Francisco. We went into a bar where the longshoremen go to drink," Johnson begins. "We were bragging and all this stuff because I thought I was hot stuff. At that time, I had won 75 fights, and I thought my stuff didn't stink. They had this little lady bartender, and I started giving her a hard time."

With his boisterous storyteller style, Johnson has the undivided attention of everyone at his table and some standing within hearing distance, in spite of the noisy atmosphere in the conference room.

"And she said to me, 'If you don't sit down and be quiet, I'm going to put your ass on top of that jukebox.' I asked her if she knew who I was, and she said, 'No, and I don't give a shit. You pop off one more time and you're gonna go up there.' I did. I popped off one more time, and she came around the bar and came towards me."

Johnson's audience begins to lean in toward him so they won't miss a word in the din of '40s music and conversations around them.

"At that time, I only weighed 134 pounds, and she was about half as wide as this table is long, but short. As soon as she came up to me, I knew she was gonna do me bodily harm. I threw a punch, and she ducked under that punch, and she threw a punch and hit me right on the jaw, and *bam*! I went to the floor."

His audience gasps. Their response spurs him on.

"I was out like a light. Then she picks me up by the rear end by the strap on the back of my sailor suit and sat my butt on the jukebox and said, 'Now, you little bastard, you stay there until I tell you to get down,' and I did. I stayed right there."

"Did you ever go back to that tavern again?" asks 92-year-old shipmate Angelo Grippo.

"No," Johnson replies. "Never went there again." Everyone laughs. "Ain't gonna get hit twice."

Grippo begins flipping through his original notebook from electrical school, which is full of diagrams and writing he did while studying for his work aboard ship.

"I don't understand much of it anymore, even if I did do it," he admits to his comrades at the table. "I brought it and this yearbook

Angelo Grippo, 2005
COURTESY OF DREWIMAGE

to show a guy who was an electrician on the ship with me. Thought he might get a kick out of seeing it. But he's not here. I don't know where he is." Grippo joined the Showboat crew near the end of the war.

"I boxed on the ship for a while," Bob Fennelly says to Johnson. Fennelly is wearing a yellow Hawaiian print shirt with palm trees splashed across it, blue jeans, and tennis shoes—and his BB55 former crew member cap. "I was 130 pounds."

"I was 135," Johnson says. "We may have boxed each other. I was Frascona then."

"Might have," Fennelly responds. "I think I remember you. But I didn't box very long. I had this one fight where the guy was hurt bad and they kept yelling at me to hit him again, hit him again. If I had hit him again, it might have killed him. I didn't box anymore after that."

Buses pull into the Whitey's parking lot early, and the crew members and their guests load up for an hour-long trip to the Center for Naval Aviation Technical Training at the Marine Corps Air Station New River, a base so technologically advanced that it has become the prototype for the entire Marine Corps. The reunion agenda took the group south to the Dixie Stampede dinner show in Myrtle Beach, South Carolina, the night before, but the late hours and fast pace appear to have weighed more heavily on the younger crowd than on the boys.

Upon their arrival, Lieutenant Colonel Steve Choate of the United States Marine Corps welcomes the group.

"It is an honor to have World War II vets," Choate says. "I was a big fan before it became the popular thing to do."

The respect he voices is obvious in the faces and actions of all the Marines on base as they meet and salute their predecessors in service to their country. The elderly boys greet the young ones with handshakes and thanks as they tour the base. The BB55 boys are enthralled as they learn about the unbelievable technology being used here. As the World War II sailors sit in front of the small desktop computers used for training and troubleshooting, they remember the computers aboard their ship—big as a room—that were amazing, state-of-the-art technology when the Showboat was built. Before they leave the base, many of the boys climb into V-22 Osprey helicopter simulators and take a "flight" around the air base.

The day wanes, and the sailors are exhausted as they board the bus for the trip back to Whitey's and another party. Inside the bus, heads bob as opened-mouthed sleepers miss the exchange taking place toward the front of the bus—shipmates compiling a list of nicknames for things on the ship.

Leo Bostwick begins a list that continues to grow for the rest of the reunion.

"What did we call our bunks?"

"A fartsack."

"What name did we give the captain?"

"Old man."

"What did we call the hospital corpsmen?"

"Pecker checker."

Boys all around the bus who are not sleeping chime in.

"I've got one. What did we call chipped beef?"

"Foreskin on a raft."

"I thought it was shit on a shingle."

"No, that was a hamburger."

"How about that room in sick bay for venereal disease?"

"You mean the clap shack?"

"Yeah, that's right. Clap shack."

"Who was the sin bosun?"

"The chaplain."

"Ice cream?"

"Gedunk."

Multiple sailors chime in on most questions. Before they realize it, the bus is pulling into the motel, and they must prepare for a big dinner to celebrate the anniversary of V-J Day, which isn't actually until September, but there is no harm in getting an early start. They never know how many of them will be left in September.

30 April 2005

A large entourage gathers on the fantail of the ship, a brilliant blue sky, warm Southern sunshine, and soft spring breezes inviting them aboard for the annual memorial service.

Paul Wieser, in full white dress uniform with his boatswain pipe hanging around his neck, leads the living-history crew of sideboys across the fantail to take their positions, much as they would have done to carry a shipmate for burial at sea. They are followed by the presentation of colors by living-history crew depicting the Marine honor guard.

Speaking to the large crowd gathered that morning, association president Gordon Knapp begins the service with a stirring tribute to those who have passed on, the numbers growing exponentially each year:

★ Sixty-four years ago, these decks filled with a new crew who worked to bring this ship alive for four glorious years. Many have passed on to that station where we hope all of us will be shipmates again. Shipmates again at that final anchorage in the harbor still unknown to mortal men. We don't know the waters there, but we know the course to steer.

We believe that our shipmates set their course by the beacons given to us and have reached that harbor safely and now are on the muster roll of our supreme commander. Some gave their lives in battle that they might leave behind a land still free. Some spent years building a strong defense on the shores of this country for which our forefathers shed their lives' blood in making the United States of America.

As the years roll on, one by one we end our days, the anchor is dropped to rise from the waters no more. Though our heads are bowed in memory for the loss of our shipmates, there is pride in our hearts for the many things they did to keep the record of our country untarnished. We will remain awaiting our orders, still inspired then to do our utmost to live to the ideals set by them and to leave behind a free country and the Stars and Stripes still the standard of liberty.

Former crew member Gordon Knapp delivers the 2005 memorial-service address while living-history crew and former crew members act as sideboys to commit the memorial wreath to the waters surrounding the ship.
COURTESY OF BATTLESHIP NORTH CAROLINA COLLECTION

Former crew member Lou Popovich walks to the ship's bell in preparation for the farewell to shipmates. The list is long—91 shipmates who have died in recent years but have not yet been memorialized. Most have died since the previous reunion one year earlier. Popovich reads, "The toll of the ship's bell reminds us of the reverence we owe to our departed shipmates and to those who guard our country upon the sea, under the sea, in the air and upon foreign soil. Let it forever be a reminder of the faith they confide in us and in silence breathe a prayer for our absent shipmates."

He rings two tolls of the brass bell. As each name of a departed shipmate is voiced in clear and reverent tones, a single bell toll pays tribute to him. The sound does not cease from one toll to the next; throughout the reading of 91 names, it reverberates constantly across the waters of the Cape Fear until the final name is read and the peal reluctantly drifts off into the distance.

Living-history crew chaplain Sion Harrington gives the benediction: "We pause with reverence and love to pay final tribute to honored and departed comrades. . . . May the memories of these our brothers departed ever bring a smile to our lips and warmth to our hearts."

Wieser leads the sideboys to man the lines, and the gathering of shipmates, friends, and relatives sings "Amazing Grace." Wieser tosses the memorial wreath of red, white, and blue silk flowers over the lifelines into the waters surrounding the ship. A 21-gun salute echoes across the river, followed by the mournful melody of taps. As the colors are retired, a sea gull present during the service lets out a cry, lifts off its perch on the boat crane, and flies across the crowd.

One service is over, but another is just beginning. The sideboys, the living-history honor guard, and other crew members form a wide column to lead Scott Pfeiffer to the bow of the ship with a small black box clutched tightly under his arm. Robert George Pfeiffer, who served in the navigation department on the *North Carolina* from May 20, 1944, to October 18, 1945, died February 11, 2003. More than two years later, his son has come all the way from Michigan, bringing his father's ashes to rest in the waters surrounding the ship he loved.

Former crew members of the North Carolina *form a line of sideboys to lead Scott Pfeiffer to the bow of the ship for his father's memorial service and the disposition of his ashes.*
PHOTO BY THE AUTHOR

When the gathering has made its way to the bow of the ship, the Marines from the air station take their positions fore and aft, and Scott walks toward the lifelines, passing between the columns of sideboys in dress whites. Scott wears black—his slacks, his shirt, his tie—and he holds in front of him the black box that contains his father's ashes.

"What a great day to be alive!" Scott shouts above the brisk wind blowing across the bow. "I am the son of Robert George Pfeiffer and his loving wife of 60 years, Gloria. Today, I would like

Robert G. Pfeiffer
COURTESY OF SCOTT PHEIFFER

to think I represent the sons and the daughters of America's 'greatest generation.' You are my heroes, and I love you. I owe you. You are not forgotten. Thank you."

Scott turns and faces the rail, then steps up on the edge and tilts the box over the side. Again, the sea gull cries out. As Scott watches his father's ashes lift into the breeze and drift down to the waters off the starboard bow, he says, "See ya, Pops."

A soft spring breeze carries the ashes of Robert George Pfeiffer to the water surrounding the ship he loved.

Photo by the author

Acknowledgments

History is like a treasure hunt—one small tidbit of information offers clues to the next, which leads to another discovery that answers some questions while eliciting others. When the event is as important as World War II and the specific subject as beloved as the USS *North Carolina,* found treasures can become overwhelming, and the writer's job evolves from finding facts to following feelings. That's the path I traveled while writing this book—a story not as much about the ship as about the boys who brought her to life. The former crew members of the battleship *North Carolina* are an amazing group of Americans, and I am proud to know so many of them and to call them my friends.

Words are insufficient to express my appreciation to the USS *North Carolina* Battleship Memorial museum staff, especially museum services director Kim Robinson Sincox, curator Mary Ames Sheret, and former curator Angela McCleaf. They took me into their fold and always made me feel welcome aboard ship and in the ship's archives. Kim has been amazing from the very first day we met—willing to help in any way she could, sharing and often boosting my enthusiasm, offering advice garnered from years of experience, finding and providing contact information, always smiling. I would not have known where to begin without Kim.

In fact, my treasure hunt started with a different project in the archives of the ship. While working on my Master of Fine Arts in creative writing at the University of North Carolina Wilmington, I answered a request from Kim for a "ghost writer" to work on a project based on supernatural encounters by the ship's staff. Believing that ghosts are only as interesting as the once-living persons who might be lingering, I began reading the deck logs in search of information on crew members who died while serving on the ship. Kim invited me to visit the National Archives with museum staff in the fall of 2000, and I discovered new information there that helped my research and added to the museum's collection as well.

In April 2001, I spent six days aboard ship during the crew reunion helping with the oral-history project headed by the ship's webmaster, Randy Drew, and his brother Steve Drew. I conducted interviews while they made video recordings and snapped still photographs. By the time the ghost-book project took a different path and neither the battleship commission nor I was involved, I was so hooked that I could not imagine abandoning my research. I envisioned a new project, one that eventually became what you are holding in your hands—*Boys of the Battleship North Carolina*. The journey to its completion has been amazing and has changed my life forever.

Kim allowed me to write an article about my vision for the book in *The Annunciator*, a newsletter sponsored by the Friends of the Battleship *North Carolina*, mailed several times a year to former crew members and supporters of the ship. From that letter, I began to receive phone calls, letters, and e-mails from scores of former crew members all across the country offering their recollections. A brother of one of the crew members who died while serving on the ship sent me a box from California full of pictures and every original document his parents had received from the Navy that pertained to his brother's service, death, and burial. He asked me in return if I could find out just where and how his brother had died. Gilbert Skelton found welcome relief in learning that his brother William was not in the shower when the torpedo struck and took his life. Gilbert died a couple of years after I returned a box filled with his original documents, all the information I had discovered about his brother, and photos of the ship he always wanted to visit but never had.

The deeper I dove into the project, the more I understood that it would be without doubt the hardest thing I had ever attempted to do. In fact, the task became so daunting that I ran away from it for almost three years. But the guys never gave up on me, and I can only hope that the result fulfills their expectations.

A handful of "the boys" have been especially supportive, and I would be remiss not to mention them by name. Bob Fennelly and his wife, Juanita, from Welaka, Florida; Paul Wieser and his wife, Millie, from Culpeper, Virginia; and Chuck Paty and his wife, Sue, from Charlotte, North Carolina, welcomed me into their homes and made me feel like a member of the family. Bob, Paul, and Chuck are three of the sailors who were aboard the ship from beginning to end and are therefore the main characters in this book.

Lincoln Hector and his wife, Virginia, of Alberton, Montana, followed me through the ups and downs of the project and always made me feel special, even though we have met only through e-mail, letters, and photographs. Lincoln's e-mails evolved from "How's the book coming? I'm 83 and won't be around forever, you know" to advising me to "stop and smell the roses." Thank you, Lincoln, for all your love and support, including the *Rocky Mountain Rider* subscription, a special gift to remind me—through my love of horses—to slow down and enjoy life. Lincoln celebrated his 87th birthday in October 2006.

Others who became super special to me through phone conversations, e-mail, letters, or visits include Joe Smits of Idaho, Walter Ashe of North Carolina, Bob Palomaris of Utah, and Herb Weyrauch of Minnesota. They always answered my questions—sometimes e-mailed at two in the morning—promptly and with enthusiasm, and they continued to help throughout the editing process.

I offer a very special thanks to each former crew member who participated in the ship's oral-history project, those who agreed to personal interviews with me, and all who converse on the BB55 chat line managed by Darrell Adams, editor of the ship's newsletter, the *Tarheel*. Thank you, Darrell, for all you have done for me and continue to do for the guys. Although I could not incorporate everyone into the book, I hope that all of you understand that everything you shared with me shaped the book in some way. Although your name may not appear in the text, you are a vital part of the story, and I treasure the thoughtfulness of your participation.

My treasure hunt unearthed so much information and offered so many directions to search for new clues that I found myself unsure which way to turn. I was reminded of the time when my daughter was two years old and received several puzzles for Christmas. When they no longer challenged her after a few days, she began dumping all the pieces from all the puzzles into one pile, then choosing just the right pieces to complete one project at a time. My zest for learning everything I could about the ship and her crew unwittingly created a pile of pieces that could have resulted in numerous projects, and only by choosing each piece carefully could I create the one I envisioned. So I began picking out the ones with the shape, color, and texture that would fit together in my mind and on the page. The book began to breathe, but my choices left holes that only specifically directed research could fill.

One method of searching in the ship's archives is through subject files. In the "Launching" file, I found an August 2000 e-mail from Herbert B. Turkington to Angela McCleaf, who was curator at the time. They had obviously been corresponding about several ships, but in that particular e-mail, Turkington recalled a vivid memory of attending the launching of the USS *North Carolina* when he was only eight years old. I was able to contact him by e-mail, and he confirmed his memories, then added that his father had lifted him onto his shoulders, a small detail with a visual impact. Using his descriptions, technical information from the Navy, newspaper reports, photos, and other information in the "Launching" file, I was almost able to re-create the day the ship was launched and the story began. But I also needed information about the Brooklyn Navy Yard to truly understand the sights, sounds, and significance of that event.

Although his name never appears in the text, Dr. Leonard C. Silvern helped me understand the Brooklyn Navy Yard and how a capital ship was constructed. He served as a supervisor there when the *North Carolina* was built and for many years following her launch. He always answered my e-mailed questions promptly with much detail. Thank you, Dr. Silvern.

Ten men officially died in action on the *North Carolina*, but I found that many more succumbed to accidents or natural causes while they were serving aboard the ship. I wanted to bring them all back to life on the pages of the book, and with the help of their shipmates, I have been able to do that for some of them. For others, I was forced to settle with mentioning them by name and stating the facts about their lives and deaths that I discovered in official documents.

Tommy Thompson, the ship's first casualty, became something of a legend—a newlywed decapitated by the loading tongs, or so people said. Most associated with the ship knew some version of his story. While I could never confirm the existence of a wife, the possibility—probability, even—certainly exists. Official Navy documents and the ship's logs confirmed the facts of his death and disproved decapitation, but only through Joe "Smitty" Smits, a shipmate who worked with Thompson in the engine room, did I learn about who he was as a person—his physical appearance, temperament, likes, and dislikes. Only through Smitty, who went up the trunk line just ahead of Tommy, could I understand Thompson's thoughts.

Likewise, only through shipmate Lester Tucker did I learn so much about George Conlon, the ship's first sailor killed in action. National Archives documents gave me his wife's name and mother's name, but Lester told me about Conlon's relationship with fellow shipmates and the joshing they continually gave him about the girl he loved, married, and left behind.

Mike Marko's account of the moments just before the torpedo attack placed Leonard Pone in the shower—that and a memory from Pone's friend Mario Sivilli, whose name doesn't appear in the text but who remembered in great detail seeing Pone heading for the shower; Sivilli is very thankful that he changed his mind at the last minute about taking a shower himself. With the help of documents sent to me by William Skelton's brother, information in the National Archives, technical information in the ship's archives, living-history recollections, and details recalled by shipmates including Mike Marko, I was able to re-create the moments leading up to and following the torpedo attack, including the moment Albert Geary was washed overboard, vividly remembered by shipmates who saw him vanish.

Robert Alexander Nelson's death was a bit more difficult to re-create. While many remembered the incident, no one knew Nelson's name or anything else about him. I found the facts in the National Archives, then learned the details of how it could have happened and why it should not have happened from pilot Almon Oliver, who wasn't on the ship at the time but explained the technical aspects of how the machine gun fired and what steps a pilot was required to take after flight to prevent such an accident.

Oliver was also my source for many details about the people involved in the daring rescues at sea. He worked closely with Eldon Means and furnished what I know about Means and his death. In one of his e-mails, Oliver included text from an August 12, 1945, Task Force 38 press release that detailed the events of the Honshu rescue and included quotes from Coumbre, Oliver, and Jacobs. In files at the ship's archives, I also discovered the event as told by Jacobs, so I could re-create the rescue from the viewpoints of all three participants.

The rescue by John Burns of so many downed pilots was a well-reported event in newspaper articles, magazine articles, and museum displays on the ship. Burns's file in the ship's archives is bulging with information. But only through shipmate Lester Tucker and a letter written by Burns to a friend—a fairly recent addition to the burgeoning file—was I able to understand who Burns was as a human being and what a tragedy his untimely accidental death was.

Subject files in the ship's archives include excerpts from living-history interviews conducted many years ago at East Carolina University, plus diary excerpts, more recent interview excerpts, log pages, and news clippings. No file is fatter than the one about the torpedo attack, so information for that event was not scarce. Through the efforts of Captain Ben Blee, whose theory on how one submarine did so much damage has become an accepted account of the incident, some of the Japanese submariners involved in the attack visited the United States during a BB55 crew reunion in 1986. Blee's account of the events of that visit provided fodder for my re-creation of the deadliest day in the Showboat's history.

Individual crew files, officer files, subject files, the war diary, deck logs, action reports—all collected within the archives of the ship—provided most of the information that I needed, but the compilation and retelling would have been dry and lifeless without the crew members who relived events for me through eyes filled with tears or lit by laughter, voices strong and proud or broken by sad memories. And I was fortunate to be able to explore the ship, measure spaces, and close my eyes and travel across time, then call upon all my senses to envision everything that I had been told. Never a history buff before, I was entranced by the boys and tried hard to tell their story. But I needed help and training to do them justice.

My professors at the University of North Carolina Wilmington filled that need and have been wonderful inspirations to me. They championed my efforts during my undergraduate and graduate studies, and I feel blessed to have had the opportunity to learn from each of them. My three-man thesis committee—David Gessner, Phil Furia, and Philip Gerard—offered gracious praise and excellent ideas for editing. Phil Furia was exceptionally supportive in my publication efforts both locally and on a national level, and I am uplifted by his faith in the book's future. But I must offer a very special thanks to Philip Gerard, my thesis director, who has embraced this endeavor from the first day I entered his office and asked him if he thought it could be done. His faith in my ability to write this book never wavered, even when the project overwhelmed me and scared me wordless. His positive response to the finished product—his references to *when*, not *if*, it would be published, his recommendation to the person who would become my editor, and his advice to me on how to pursue publication—has been humbling and gratifying. Thank you, Philip, for that faith, encouragement, and support.

Through the help of Philip's recommendation, my first book found a home at a publishing company willing to take a chance on an untested author. My editor there, Steve Kirk, gave me words of encouragement and suggestions for tweaking the text to make it stronger. Thank you, Steve. And thank you, Carolyn Sakowski, president of John F. Blair, Publisher, and your staff for giving me this opportunity to launch what I hope will be a long and productive writing career, even if I am beginning later in life. I find it fitting that I am about the same age that John F. Blair was when he launched a new career himself—a book-publishing company that has become well known and highly respected. I am proud for my work to be part of its book list.

The book would never have come to fruition without some very valuable time dedicated solely to writing. As owner, editor, and publisher of a weekly community newspaper while working on the book, I found my creative-writing time in short supply. I was very fortunate, however, to have a staff that most business owners can only dream about. They took up the slack and gave me the time I needed to make the book a reality. I thank each one of them, but especially Ann Beach, Anna Jordan, and Katie Cromartie, who handled day-to-day duties expertly without supervision. Writer and assistant editor Susan Whitley moved to town and asked for a job, coming to work at the paper just when I needed her most, allowing me to take a few crucial weeks completely away from my responsibilities. Then, just a few months later, she was gone, moved away. I think she was a product of divine intervention—my creative-writing angel.

I owe gratitude to my family, especially my husband, Steve, who shouldered the brunt of the emotional turmoil I experienced struggling to write a book worthy of the boys it portrays. Steve learned when to offer support, when to whisk me away from the stress, and when to just leave me alone and let me work. He has sacrificed much, and I am eternally grateful. My beautiful, intelligent adult children—Joy, Kim, and Brad—are a constant source of support, encouraging me, believing in me, loving me. I am proud to be their mother. And I'm proud to be the daughter of a remarkable woman, Eusely Malpass Horrell Blackburn, who is age 84 at this writing and is a source of inspiration to everyone she meets. She has joined me on this journey, attending crew reunions with me, traveling to Florida with me to visit the Fennellys, and always believing that I can achieve anything I set my mind to do. Thanks, Mom.

Although he is not here in body, my daddy is always with me in spirit, and I thank him for the foundation of a Christian home and faith in God, with whom all things are possible.

Select Bibliography

I list here only the writings that I used as references or from which I lifted quotes in the making of this book. This bibliography is by no means a record of all the works and sources I consulted or the interviews in person, by e-mail, or by phone that I conducted. Much of the narrative was derived from information contained in personal interviews spanning more than five years and including scores of former crew members and other persons directly involved with the ship.

The Battleship *North Carolina* Collection, located in the ship's archives in Wilmington, North Carolina, is the principal source for historical material related to the battleship.

"Action Report, 10–27 November 1943." *USS Enterprise CV-6: The Most Decorated Ship of the Second World War.* 1998–2003. http://www.cv6.org/ship/logs/action194311.htm.

Ashe, Walter. Interview with author, October 16, 2005.

———. Personal diary. December 1941–September 1942.

———. Telephone conversations and correspondence with author, 2001–6.

"Attack on Pearl Harbor." *Wikipedia.* http://en.wikipedia.org/wike/Attack_on_Pearl_ Harbor (August 14, 2005).

Battleship North Carolina. 1999-2006. www.battleshipnc.com.

Belford, Jackson. Oral-history interview, April 8, 1991, for East Carolina Manuscript Collection. Battleship *North Carolina* Collection, Wilmington, N.C.

Blee, Ben W. *Battleship North Carolina (BB-55).* Wilmington, N.C.: USS *North Carolina* Battleship Commission, 1982.

————. Papers. Battleship *North Carolina* Collection, Wilmington, N.C.

Burke, Julian T. *Battleship North Carolina Oral Histories.* http://www.battleshipnc.com/teach_reso/oral_history/battle/first_battle.php (June 19, 2004).

Connors, H. F. "Launching of USS *North Carolina.*" *Anchors Aweigh* (June 18, 1940). "Launching" file in Battleship *North Carolina* Collection, Wilmington, N.C.

"European Timeline." *WWII 60th Anniversary Committee to Honor Those Who Served.* http://www.60wwii.mil/Presentation/Timeline/euro_timeline.cfm (February 24, 2006).

Fennelly, Robert. Interview with author, November 26–27, 2001.

————. Interview with author, October 4, 2005.

————. Oral-history interview, April 6, 2001. Battleship *North Carolina* Collection, Wilmington, N.C.

————. Telephone conversations and correspondence with author, 2001–6.

Fox, Richard. Telephone conversation and correspondence with author, 2005–6.

Halsey, William F. Dispatch. Battleship *North Carolina* Collection, Wilmington, N.C.

Hector, Lincoln. Telephone conversations and correspondence with author, 2001–6.

Jacobs, Raymond. "Heroes: The Marine Corps." *World War II Stories in Their Own Words.* 2001–6. http://carol_fus.tripod.com/marines_hero_ray_jacobs1.html (January 5, 2006).

Kaplan, Leonard. "The Launching of the *North Carolina.*" *Journal of the American Society of Naval Engineers* 52 (1940): 449–73. This article may be found in the Battleship *North Carolina* Collection, Wilmington, N.C.

Kass, Gerald. Diary. Battleship *North Carolina* Collection, Wilmington, N.C.

Marko, Mike. Personal diary, December 8, 1941–September 14, 1942.

Marko, Paul. Telephone conversations and correspondence with author on behalf of his father, Mike Marko, 2005–6.

Oliver, Almon P. E-mail and other correspondence with author, 2001–6.

"Pacific Timeline." *WWII 60th Anniversary Committee to Honor Those Who Served.* http://www.60wwii.mil/Presentation/Timeline/pac_timeline.cfm (December 17, 2005).

Palomaris, Robert. E-mail and other correspondence with author, 2005–6.

Paty, Charles M., Jr. *BB55 Crew.* Rev. ed. Vol. 1. Charlotte, N.C.: 2002.

———. *BB55 Day by Day.* Rev. ed. Charlotte, N.C.: 2004.

———. Interview with author, October 25, 2005.

———. Telephone conversations and correspondence with author, 2000–2006.

Rosell, Charlie. Oral-history interview, October 5, 1992, for East Carolina Manuscript Collection. Battleship *North Carolina* Collection, Wilmington, N.C.

———. Telephone conversations and correspondence with author, 2005–6.

Services for the Burial of the Dead at Sea. Bureau of Naval Personnel Information Bulletin, January 1944. Battleship *North Carolina* Collection, Wilmington, N.C.

Silvern, Leonard C. E-mail correspondence with author, 2005–6.

Smits, Joseph. E-mail and other correspondence with author, 2001–6.

Stryker, Joe W. Journal. Battleship *North Carolina* Collection, Wilmington, N.C.

Taylor, William R. Diary. Battleship *North Carolina* Collection, Wilmington, N.C.

Tucker, Lester. Correspondence with author, 2001–5.

USS *North Carolina* Action Reports, August 24, 1942–August 10,

1945. Battleship *North Carolina* Collection, Wilmington, N.C.

USS *North Carolina* Casualty Reports, November 14, 2000. United States National Archives and Records Administration, College Park, Maryland.

USS *North Carolina* Deck Log, April 9, 1941–September 2, 1945. Battleship *North Carolina* Collection, Wilmington, N.C.

USS *North Carolina* War Diary, December 7, 1941–September 2, 1945. Battleship *North Carolina* Collection, Wilmington, N.C.

Weyrauch, Herbert. Oral-history interview, April 7, 2001. Battleship *North Carolina* Collection, Wilmington, N.C.

————. Telephone conversations and correspondence with author, 2001–6.

————. Weyrauch family tapes, April 6–9, 2001.

Wieser, Paul Anthony. Interview with author, October 19–21, 2005.

————. Telephone conversations and correspondence with author, 2005–6.

INDEX

Russia. *See* Soviet Union

Saffron, George L., 283-84
Sagami Wan, 309
Saigon, 263
Saipan, 200, 215
Salt Lake City. See USS *Salt Lake City*
San Diego, Calif., 21, 167
San Diego Naval Training Station, 47, 220
San Francisco, Calif., 106, 206
San Jacinto. See USS *San Jacinto*
San Pedro, Calif., 17, 106, 168, 241
San Pedro Harbor, 105
Santa Fe. See USS *Santa Fe*
Saratoga. See USS *Saratoga*
Schroeder, Henry, 111
Schroll, Daniel, 334-37, *335*
Schroll, Mrs. Daniel (Shirley), 336
Scout Observation Unit (SOSU), 213
Seattle. See USS *Seattle*
Seattle, Wash., 218, 223, 236, 321, 334
Second Marine Division, 183
Shadder, Micky, 320
Shanghai, 20, 25
Shangri La. See USS *Shangri La*
Shangri La Island, 164
Shealy. See USS *Shealy*
Shepard, Seth A., 25
Shibasaki, Keigi, 184
Show Boat (musical), 64
Showboat. *See* USS *North Carolina*
Sinatra, Frank, 91, 238
Singapore, 113
Skelton, William, 139-40, *140*, 143, 146, 149-50
Smits, Joseph "Smitty": aboard ship, 13, 27, 40, 91-93, 104, 121; going home, 205-6; joins Navy, 17-18; on liberty, 66-67, 101-3, 161; youth, 16-17, *16*
Sohl, 95
Solomon Islands, 113, 116, 118, 120, 127, 194
South Dakota. See USS *South Dakota*
South Pacific, 113, 133, 150, 171, 182, 195, 198, 199, 203, 219
Soviet Union, 50, 296

Spence. See USS *Spence*
Springfield rifle, 100
Spruance, Raymond A., 193, 273
SS *Lurline*, 167
Standard Oil, 41
Stansbury. See USS *Stansbury*
Stephenson, 95
Stone, 122
Stone, Oscar, 139, 143, 146, 149
Stringer, Louie, 133
Stryker, Joseph, 327
Stubblefield, 121, 123
Sturgeon, Bob, 133
Sullivan, Jerome, 208
Sunday Mirror, 36
Svenningsen, 95

Tang. See USS *Tang*
Tarawa, 183-84, 186
Tarheel, 59-60, 77
Task Force 16, 113-14, 120-21
Task Force 17, 78
Task Force, 37, 193
Task Force 38, 193
Task Force 58, 193, 199, 201, 205, 281
Task Force 61, 120
Task Group 58.1, 293
Task Group 58.3, 275
Taylor, Mr., 19
Taylor, Mrs., 19, 23-24
Taylor, William R., 62
TBS, 261, 263
Temple, Shirley, 208, 218, 230-31, *231*
Texas. See USS *Texas*
Thomas, Frank P., 174, 188
Thompson, Thurman "Tommy," 92-93
Ticonderoga. See USS *Ticonderoga*
Tinian, 200, 215
Tirpitz, 87, 95, 104
Tokyo, 249, 265, 273, 274, 294-95, 303, 305, 307, 308
Tokyo Bay, 304, 308, 316, 317, 319, 321
Tokyo Harbor, 263
Tokyo Rose, 222
Tongatabu, 116, 148, 150, 155
Torpedo Junction, 133